Experiences of Mental Health In-patient Care

D0147556

This book offers an insight into the experience of psychiatric in-patient care, from both a professional and a user perspective. The editors highlight the problems in creating therapeutic environments within settings which are often poorly resourced, crisis-driven and risk-aversive.

The contributors argue that for change to occur there needs first of all to be a genuine appreciation of the experiences of those involved in the unpredictable, anxiety-arousing and sometimes threatening environment of the psychiatric ward. Each chapter comprises a personal account of in-patient care by those in the front line: people who have been admitted to a psychiatric ward; their relatives; or those that provide the care. These accounts are followed by two commentaries written from different perspectives, suggesting lessons that can be learnt to improve the quality of care.

Experiences of Mental Health In-patient Care will be useful for all mental health professionals, including mental health nurses, psychiatrists, clinical psychologists, occupational therapists, arts therapists, social workers and trainees, as well as service users and carers organisations.

Mark Hardcastle is a consultant nurse with Sussex Partnership (NHS) Trust and a Visiting Fellow at the University of Brighton.

David Kennard is a clinical psychologist and group analyst, formerly Head of Psychology at The Retreat, York, and is Chair of ISPS UK.

Sheila Grandison is the Head of Arts Therapies at East London and The City Mental Health NHS Trust.

Leonard Fagin retired in 2006 as an NHS consultant psychiatrist and Clinical Director at North East London Mental Health NHS Trust and is an Honorary Senior Lecturer at University College London.

Experiences of Mental Health In-patient Care

Narratives from service users, carers and professionals

Edited by Mark Hardcastle, David Kennard, Sheila Grandison and Leonard Fagin

Routledge
Taylor & Francis Group

LONDON AND NEW YORK

First published 2007 by Routledge
27 Church Road, Hove, East Sussex BN3 2FA

Simultaneously published in the USA and Canada
by Routledge
711 Third Avenue, New York, NY 10017

*Routledge is an imprint of the Taylor & Francis Group,
an Informa business*

© 2007 Mark Hardcastle, David Kennard, Sheila Grandison &
Leonard Fagin

Typeset in Times by RefineCatch Limited, Bungay, Suffolk

Paperback cover design by Hybert Design

British Library Cataloguing in Publication Data
A catalogue record for this book is available from the British Library

Library of Congress Cataloging-in-Publication Data
Experiences of mental health in-patient care : narratives from
   service users, carers, and professionals/edited by Mark Hardcastle
   . . . [et al.].
      p.; cm.
   Includes bibliographical references and index.
   ISBN–13: 978–0–415–41081–6 (hardback)
   ISBN–10: 0–415–41081–9 (hardback)
   ISBN–13: 978–0–415–41082–3 (pbk.)
   ISBN–10: 0–415–41082–7 (pbk.)
   1. Mentally ill–Rehabilitation. 2. Mental health services.
I. Hardcastle, Mark, 1961–   .
   [DNLM: 1. Psychotic Disorders–psychology–Case
   Reports. 2. Psychotic Disorders–psychology–Personal
   Narratives. 3. Hospitalization–Case Reports. 4. Hospitalization–
   Personal Narratives. 5. Mentally Ill Persons–psychology–Case
   Reports. 6. Mentally Ill Persons–psychology–Personal
   Narratives. 7. Patient Care–psychology–Case Reports. 8. Patient
   Care–psychology–Personal Narratives. WM 40 E96 2007]
   RA790.5.E974 2007
362.2–dc22   2006030204

ISBN: 978–0–415–41081–6 (hbk)
ISBN: 978–0–415–41082–3 (pbk)

The ISPS book series

The ISPS (the International Society for the Psychological Treatments of the Schizophrenias and other Psychoses) has a history stretching back some fifty years during which it has witnessed the relentless pursuit of biological explanations for psychosis. The tide is now turning again. There is a welcome international resurgence in interest in a range of psychological factors in psychosis that have considerable explanatory power and also distinct therapeutic possibilities. Governments, professional groups, users and carers are increasingly expecting interventions that involve talking and listening as well as skilled practitioners in the main psychotherapeutic modalities as important components of the care of the seriously mentally ill.

The ISPS is a global society. It is composed of an increasing number of groups of professionals organised at national, regional and more local levels around the world. The society has started a range of activities intended to support professionals, users and carers. Such persons recognise the potential humanitarian and therapeutic potential of skilled psychological understanding and therapy in the field of psychosis. Our members cover a wide spectrum of interests from psychodynamic, systemic, cognitive, and arts therapies to the need-adaptive approaches and to therapeutic institutions. We are most interested in establishing meaningful dialogue with those practitioners and researchers who are more familiar with biological-based approaches. Our activities include regular international and national conferences, newsletters and email discussion groups in many countries across the world.

One of these activities is to facilitate the publication of quality books that cover the wide terrain which interests ISPS members and a large number of other mental health professionals, as well as policy makers and implementers. We are delighted that Routledge Mental Health have seen the importance and potential of such an endeavour and have agreed to publish an ISPS series of books.

We anticipate that some of the books will be controversial and will challenge certain aspects of current practice in some countries. Other books will promote ideas and authors well known in some countries but not familiar to others. Our overall aim is to encourage the dissemination of existing knowledge and ideas, promote healthy debate, and encourage more research in a most important field whose secrets almost certainly do not all reside in the neurosciences.

For more information about the ISPS, email *isps@isps.org* or visit our website *www.isps.org*

Brian Martindale
ISPS series editor

International Society for the Psychological Treatments of the Schizophrenias and Other Psychoses Book Series
Series Editor: Brian Martindale

Contents

Illustrations

Each section of the book opens with an illustration. Interspersed throughout the text, these illustrations represent the personal account—visual rather than written—of an art psychotherapist and were made in response to her experience of some of the rhythms and movements of acute care settings. These linear drawings, with their skeins of overlapping lines, have taken the hand as a motif of identity and human contact. So many lines: in metaphorical pursuit of the lines of enquiry, of searching, of hoping, of gaining and losing contact, of the possibilities and constraints, the uncertainties and anxieties within mental health in-patient care as spoken about in the narratives of the text. On the one hand, on the other hand; many hands drawn together. Repetitive, feint, heavy, changing lines with disappearing, emerging, transforming hand-overs. Along the lines, out of line, cross the line, down the corridor; end of line, fine line, on the line, take the line. Somewhere along the line, tree-lined; read between the lines . . .

Sheila Grandison

Acknowledgements

The editors would like to thank all our contributors for their generosity, enthusiasm and openness that have made this book possible.

Excerpts from I NEVER PROMISED YOU A ROSE GARDEN by Joanne Greenberg (Copyright © 1964 by Hannah Green; Copyright Renewed © 1992 by Joanne Greenberg) used by kind permission of the Wallace Literary Agency, Inc. as agents for the author, and Henry Holt and Company, LLC, publishers.

All drawings by Sheila Grandison from the series *'along the lines of', 2005–2006, mixed media on paper* and reproduced by permission of the artist. Photography: Barts Medical Illustration.

Contributors

Catherine Allen, Consultant Clinical Psychologist, Bolton, Salford and Trafford Mental Health NHS Trust, Psychology Services, Bury New Road, Prestwich, Manchester, M25 3BL.

Cris Allen, Deputy Director of Nursing, Sussex Partnership NHS Trust, Downsmere, Princess Royal Hospital, Haywards Heath, West Sussex, RH15 4EX.

Janey Antoniou, Freelance trainer and writer on mental health issues. Correspondence c/o David Kennard, Editor.

Trish Barry, Social Worker (senior practitioner) Deliberate Self-Harm/Psychiatric Lead and Psychotherapist, Accident and Emergency Department, Royal Hampshire County Hospital and Adolescent Department, Tavistock Centre, Winchester and Eastleigh NHS Trust, Romsey Road, Winchester, Hampshire, SO23 5DG.

Anne Margaret Beales, Director of Service User Involvement, Together (Working for Well-being), First Floor 82a Wick Street, Littlehampton, West Sussex, BN17 7JS.

Kamaldeep Bhui, Professor of Cultural Psychiatry and Epidemiology and Hon. Consultant Psychiatrist, St Bartholomew and The London Medical School and East London and The City Mental Health NHS Trust, Centre for Psychiatry, Joseph Rotblat Building, Charterhouse Square, London, EC1M 6BQ.

Anne Christine Borthwick, Resident Friend (Quaker Chaplain), The Retreat Hospital, Heslington Road, York, YO10 5BN.

Professor Len Bowers, Professor of Psychiatric Nursing, St Bartholomew School of Nursing and Midwifery, City University, Philpot Street, London, E1 2EA.

Geoff Brennan, Nurse Consultant for Psychosocial Interventions, Berkshire Healthcare NHS Trust, Prospect Park Hospital, Honey End Lane, Tilehurst, Berkshire, RG30 4EJ.

Maria Cañete, Consultant Adult Psychotherapist, East London and The City Mental Health NHS Trust, Psychology Dept of Royal London Hospital (St Clement's), 2a Bow Road, London, E3 4LL.

Anna Chickwama, Acute Ward Nurse, Correspondence c/o Mark Hardcastle, Editor.

Rachel Christian-Edwards, Therapies Manager/Head Occupational Therapist, Dorset Healthcare, St Anns Hospital, Canford Cliffs, 69 Haven Road, Poole, Dorset, BH13 7LN.

Keith Coupland, Nurse Consultant, working with psychosis, Gloucestershire Partnership NHS Trust, Brownhill, Swindon Road, Cheltenham, GL51 9EZ.

Dr Richard Duggins, Specialist Registrar in Psychotherapy, Northumberland, Tyne and Wear NHS Trust, Regional Department of Psychotherapy, Claremont House, Off Framlington Place, Newcastle upon Tyne, NE2 4AA.

Dr Arturo Ezquerro, Consultant Psychiatrist in Psychotherapy and Clinical Governance Lead, Central and North West London Mental Health NHS Trust, Psychology and Psychotherapy Service of Brent Mental Health, Willesden Hospital, Harlesden Road, London NW10 3RY.

Gráinne Fadden, Consultant Clinical Psychologist/Meriden Family Programme, Birmingham and Solihull Mental Health NHS Trust, Tall Trees, Uffculme Centre, Queensbridge Road, Moseley, Birmingham, B13 8QV.

Dee Fagin, Senior Clinical Nurse and Psychotherapist, Correspondence c/o Mark Hardcastle, Editor.

Dr Leonard Fagin, Consultant Psychiatrist (retired) and Honorary Senior Lecturer, University College, London. Correspondence c/o Mark Hardcastle, Editor.

'Gina', Service User, Correspondence c/o Mark Hardcastle, Editor.

Sarah Goodfellow, Ward Manager, Sussex Partnership NHS Trust, The Sussex Centre for Children and Young People, Princess Royal Hospital, Haywards Heath, West Sussex, RH15 4EX.

Professor Kevin Gournay CBE, Professorial Fellow, Institute of Psychiatry (London), Kings College, De Crespigny Park, Denmark Hill, London, SE5 8AF.

Sheila Grandison, Head of Arts Therapies, East London and The City Mental Health NHS Trust, Newham Centre for Mental Health, Glen Road, Plaistow, London, E13 8SP.

Mark Hardcastle, Consultant Nurse, Sussex Partnership NHS Trust, The Sussex Centre for Children and Young People, Princess Royal Hospital, Haywards Heath, West Sussex, RH15 4EX.

Kate Hughes, Senior Occupational Therapist, Correspondence c/o David Kennard, Editor.

Jan Olav Johannessen, Chief Psychiatrist, Division of Psychiatry, Stavanger University Hospital, Postboks 1163 Hillevaag, 4095 Stavanger, Norway.

'Joe', Service User, Correspondence c/o Mark Hardcastle, Editor.

Lis Jones, Co-Director of Nursing/Director MHCOP Services, Camden and Islington Mental Health and Social Care Trust, Executive Office 2nd Floor East Wing, 4 St. Pancras Way, London, NW1 0PE.

David Kennard, Consultant Clinical Psychologist/Group Analyst, formerly at The Retreat, York, freelance since retirement. Correspondence to The Retreat, 107 Heslington Road, York, YO10 5BN.

Jen Kilyon, Carer, Correspondence c/o David Kennard, Editor.

Daniel Kirk, Carer, Correspondence c/o David Kennard, Editor.

Jo Kirk, Carer, Correspondence c/o David Kennard, Editor.

'Louisa', Hotel Services Assistant, Correspondence c/o David Kennard, Editor.

Simon Lawton-Smith, Senior Fellow, Mental Health, The King's Fund, 11–13 Cavendish Square, London, W1G 0AN.

Jenny McAleese, Chief Executive, The Retreat, Heslington Road, York, North Yorkshire, YO10 5BN.

Bill McGowan, Senior Lecturer (Mental Health), Institute of Nursing and Midwifery, Faculty of Health, University of Brighton, Robert Dodd Building, 49 Darley Road, Eastbourne, East Sussex, BN20 7UR.

Dr Susan F. Mitchell, Consultant Psychiatrist, The Retreat, 107 Heslington Road, York, YO10 5BN.

Professor Richard Keith Morriss, Professor of Psychiatry and Community Mental Health, University of Nottingham and Nottinghamshire Healthcare NHS Trust. University of Nottingham Division of Psychiatry, A Floor, South Block, Queen's Medical Centre, Nottingham, NG7 2UH.

Kevin Norwood, Service User, Correspondence c/o Mark Hardcastle, Editor.

Claire Ockwell, Operations Co-ordinator, CAPITAL, The Hub, 73 Queensway, Bognor Regis, PO21 1QL.

Rachel Perkins, Director of Quality Assurance and User/Carer Experience, South West London and St George's Mental Health NHS Trust.

Cliff Prior, Chief Executive, Rethink, Royal London House, 22–25 Finsbury Square, London, EC2A 1DX.

Rev. Mike Pritchard, Chaplaincy Team Leader North, North East London Mental Health NHS Trust and Whipps Cross University NHS Trust, Tantallon House, Goodmayes, Barley Lane, Ilford, Essex, IG3 8XJ.

Malcom Rae, OBE FRCN, Joint Lead, Acute Care Programme, National Institute of Mental Health in England (NIMHE).

Glenn Roberts MD, Consultant in Rehabilitation and Recovery, Wonford House Hospital, Dryden Road, Exeter, Devon, EX2 5AF.

Thom Rudegair, Clinical Director, Te Whetu Tawera (Auckland Acute Mental Health Unit), Auckland Hospital, Grafton, Auckland, New Zealand.

Paul Scally, Nursing Assistant, Forward House, Slade Road, Birmingham, B23 7JA.

David Shiers, Carer and Joint Lead NIMHE/Rethink Early Intervention Programme, NIMHE, West Midlands, Osprey House, Albert Street, Redditch, Worcester, B97 4DE.

Mike Shooter, Consultant Psychiatrist, Ty Boda, Upper Llanover, Near Abergavenny, Monmouthshire, NP7 9EP.

Nigel Short, Service User and Cognitive Behavioural Psychotherapist, Sussex Partnership NHS Trust, Eversfield Centre, West Hill Road, St Leonards on Sea, TN38 0NG.

Dr William J. E. Travers, Consultant Psychiatrist, North East London Mental Health Trust, South Forest Centre, 21 Thorne Close, Leytonstone, London, E11 4HU.

Bill Turner, Mental Health Advocate, Mind, Horsham Hospital, Hurst Road, Horsham, West Sussex RH10 6AS.

Trevor Turner, Consultant Psychiatrist and Clinical Director, The City and Hackney Centre for Mental Health, Homerton University Hospital, Homerton Row, London E9 6SR.

Dr Judith Varley, Carer, Correspondence c/o David Kennard, Editor.

Judy Wilson, Chief Executive, North East London Mental Health Trust, Trust Head Office, Goodmayes Hospital, Barley Lane, Ilford, IG3 8XJ.

Forewords

Rachel Perkins

Director of Quality Assurance and User/Carer Experience, South West London and St George's Mental Health NHS Trust

Most people can expect to go into a general hospital at some time in their lives, if not as a patient, then as a visitor. They are the subject of repeated television drama series and hold no mystery. The same cannot be said of psychiatric hospitals. Popular images are based not on experience but on myth. On the one hand there are the Bedlam style images of caged 'raving lunatics'. Places where 'they' – the insane – are contained either for their own safety or the safety of the rest of 'us'. On the other hand, there is the *One Flew Over the Cuckoo's Nest* image of places where those who are falsely deemed insane are incarcerated and subjected to demeaning and degrading 'treatments'. Is it any wonder, then, that they hold such fear for many who do enter their doors?

Most people will never experience the reality of entering a psychiatric in-patient ward. But what is reality? The extraordinary collection of accounts contained in the pages of this book demonstrate that psychiatric in-patient wards look very different depending on your position in relation to them. The experience of someone occupying the role of patient is quite different from that of the person whose status is that of a visiting relative, friend or carer. The roles of patient and carer share the fact that they are not elective – the incumbents did not aspire to, or apply for, their relative positions like the staff who work there. Albeit from different perspectives, the users and carers share the experience of being thrust reluctantly into an alien and often frightening world that was not of their choosing.

On every page of the book I found in the accounts of users, carers and professionals gems that encapsulated so much of my own differing encounters with psychiatric in-patient care.

My first foray into the mysterious world of the mental hospital was in 1970 when, as a teenager, I did voluntary work visiting elderly long-stay patients in the forgotten back wards of an old asylum. With considerable trepidation I entered the gates, walked through the extensive grounds and in through the rather grand main entrance of the administrative building – so far so good. It was not until I reached the wards that the real nature of the world I had entered became apparent. The smell of urine was overwhelming. The dormitory with its rows of beds each separated from the next by a locker with its Gideon's Bible. The people who inhabited this foreign land sat silent on chairs lined up against the walls of the day room, clad in ill-fitting clothes with resigned expressions on their faces, some of whom made strange movements with their mouths. I poured tea that came out of the pot ready milked and sugared and wracked my brains about what to say to these strange creatures who had spent decades – most of their adult lives – in this place. Over the months I felt a certain pleasure when some seemed to welcome my visits but my overwhelming feelings were of inadequacy and anger: inadequacy because I could do so very, very little to improve their lot, anger at the discovery that I lived in a society that could consign so many people to these appalling conditions. This experience undoubtedly fuelled the radical political activism that was to characterise the next decade of my life, but not once did I imagine that such places would occupy such a prominent position in my future life.

My second encounter with the psychiatric in-patient world began a decade later when, on completing my PhD in experimental psychology, I decided against an academic career in favour of a clinical psychology path. I went back to the psychiatric in-patient world as an assistant psychologist . . . and rose eventually to the lofty position of 'Consultant Clinical Psychologist' and 'Clinical Director'. The in-patient world looked very different from this professional gaze. I had a range of therapeutic skills to offer. I experienced the satisfaction of seeing people regain control of their lives and move on. I could exert some influence over the way services worked and help to close some of those dreadful old back wards . . . But in over a quarter of a century working in mental health services I also know too well the numbing and exhausting impact of the distress, anger, despair of those whom I have had the privilege to serve; the agonising guilt about the times when I have really misjudged a situation – wrecked a fragile relationship with a distressed client; and the anger about the lack of investment in services for those who are the most disabled by their mental health difficulties. I know too the frustrations of working in the mental health system. The frustration induced by directives from above that bear no relation to reality; the myriad rules, far too numerous to remember, that are contained in the ever-expanding volumes of policies, procedures and codes of conduct; the institutional inertia that makes achieving even the smallest change a protracted battle; and the sterile professional rivalries and endless demarcation of each other's roles and place in the hierarchy . . . psychologists don't take cats to the vet, nurses do not clear up after people, occupational therapists do not take people out on trips, social workers do not fill in forms for welfare benefits, psychiatrists do not wash socks . . .

But knowing the world from the perspective of a mental health professional did little to prepare me for my next incarnation as a psychiatric in-patient.

All of a sudden I was experiencing, rather than observing in others, that 'perplexed isolation' of which Trevor Turner speaks (Chapter 4) and so graphically described in the personal accounts and commentaries of service users throughout the book. Those practices that, as a member of staff, I had always taken for granted – barely given a second thought – looked very different from the receiving end. The sense of being a criminal invoked by the unexplained search of one's possessions before being allowed to enter the ward. The formulaic admission checklist of questions read out by a kindly student nurse who was using words that were clearly not her own. The peculiarly degrading experience of being unfit to use the 'staff toilet', of standing in the thrice-daily medicine queue, of colouring in butterflies in the 'art and craft' session. The excruciating boredom relieved only by meal times, medication and an occasional brief 'group'. The fear invoked by the anger and rage of those around you, of waking to find a strange man standing in your bedroom. The dreaded ward round in which your behaviour, thoughts and feelings are related to an audience many of whom are silent strangers. The array of rules whose existence you only discover when you contravene them: no visitors in your bedroom, no hot drinks after 11pm. How many times have I prowled the ward at 3am past sleepy night staff who can barely keep their eyes open to be told that I could not get a cup of tea until the day staff come on? As a staff member I understand how tempting it is to cut oneself off from others' distress, but as a patient I also know the desperate loneliness of pacing the corridors unheeded, too fearful and agitated to sit, or sitting alone, apparently unnoticed, crying with despair.

I have never been the carer of someone with mental health problems. But I did glimpse some of the experiences related by carers in the latter years of my Dad's life when he spent protracted periods in older people's wards. The range of emotions that I experienced when the doting, funny, clever research scientist whom I had relied on throughout my child and adult life gradually became unable to walk, talk, feed, or do anything for himself . . . The constant battle to extract even minimal information from the hospital about what was wrong with him and what treatment and care were planned. The repeated failures to provide support and assistance that had been promised. The way in which so many ward staff treated him as if he were a difficult child, the feeling that I could not complain about the way he was treated for fear that it would make matters worse.

In the pages of this book, the main actors in the psychiatric in-patient world – users, carers and professionals – provide us with a rare and precious glimpse into their differing worlds. They articulate experiences and feelings that too often go unspoken and unshared across the gulf between 'us' and 'them' – providers and recipients of services. It is not always a comfortable read. Repeatedly, the experiences related made me recall my own and once again I felt the guilt, anger and despair that have been variously associated with my experiences as professional, patient and relative. But it is important. Only by bridging the gulf between 'them' and 'us' – by understanding what services are like for those on the receiving end and appreciating the dilemmas and frustrations of those who provide them – can we ever improve the experience and effectiveness of in-patient care.

Efforts to provide alternatives to in-patient care – like crisis and home treatment teams, assertive outreach services and an array of supported housing programmes – have enabled many people who would formerly have spent protracted periods in segregated institutions to live in their own homes and communities. However, we must remember that in-patient wards themselves can have an important role to play in enabling people to sustain their community tenure. I know that I need asylum from time to time, and I am not alone. I am neither nice nor competent when I am ill, and if I cannot get away from my usual roles and responsibilities for a while then I risk losing everything that I hold dear. But to be effective this asylum must make you feel valued and respected, bolster confidence and self-esteem, help you to hold on to hope when you cannot believe in yourself. The accounts provided in this innovative thought-provoking book both provide a stark reminder of just how far we have to go if psychiatric in-patient care is to offer this positive, affirming respite, and identify the steps we can begin to take to get there.

Malcolm Rae, OBE FRCN

Joint Lead, Acute Care Programme, National Institute of Mental Health in England (NIMHE)

I read the proofs of this book whilst on holiday in Switzerland. Being among the awesome scenery and magnificent landscapes may have influenced how I have chosen to describe this book. It may also tell you about my lack of time management skills and difficulties in meeting deadlines!

I found the book to be stunning, fresh, captivating and original. Back home in the UK, with both feet on the ground, faced with the realities of acute care, having read the chapters again I still view the text in such positive terms and feel uplifted as a result.

In recent times, acute mental health care services have been the subject of much bad press, with various reports critical of the poor and in some instances distressing and painful service a user experiences. Various reports have often been critical of the seemingly negative attitude of staff, the barren culture, and the lack of positive engagement of staff in therapeutic activities.

In my view those who have voiced these criticisms have often failed to understand the complex organisational and resource factors, or have not taken account of the stressful circumstances of acutely ill people with different and competing needs, often compounded by illicit substance misuse, all being present in the same environment. An imperative to focus on speedy throughput has also been a problem, causing turbulence, all of which has collectively added up to a varying quality of services and a perceived lack of sensitivity and compassion. Nor, it seems, have they fathomed that repeated criticism of this nature actually makes the situation worse.

Dr Gráinne Fadden, in her commentary (see Chapter 10), asks the pertinent question, 'What have we done to good people, who enter the health professions, to dehumanise them to act in the ways described?' If serious attention was given to the answers to this question, we would achieve significant improvements. I have always been intrigued by the opposite of this question, 'How is it that so many individuals retain the spark of idealism, sensitivity and desire to serve others, despite the overwhelming pressures and absence of leadership, support and empowerment?'

Regular damning criticism seriously undermines the confidence and morale of many highly committed mental health professionals dedicated to improving services. Fault-finding and critical barbs make it difficult to recruit and retain high calibre individuals, and this inevitably leads to some unreliable staff slipping through the net.

So, halleluiah, in this enlightened book we have a bite-sized collection of intelligent, insightful, and absorbing contributions which refreshes the soul.

Whilst problems and awful experiences are analysed and discussed, sometimes with searing honesty and openness, the writers also provide us with many solutions to the problems and imaginative ideas to progress services. The book not only challenges but informs and inspires.

The easy-to-read informal but authoritative style and sequential format of the book, with the occasional added ingredient of humour, significantly moves us on from the current position and encourages us to think and act differently.

The editors have invited service users and carers to discuss their illness and care experiences, to highlight concerns, but also identify positive interactions.

Balance is then provided by commentaries and perspectives from a range of experienced mental health workers, who understand the dilemmas confronting staff, and they have sought within a reflective context to discuss the patient's experiences.

Of special note, at the end of each section questions are posed and exercises for individuals or groups are offered. This process is then reversed with service users and carers having an opportunity to critique the narrative of professionals describing their experiences and aspirations.

I sense all of the mental health professionals share with service users and carers a strong desire to achieve improvements. I also perceive from them a sense of sadness, embarrassment, guilt and frustration, and a compelling motivation to change, put things right, and make better services for patients and their families.

Their efforts will certainly set the pace in pursuit of high-quality services.

I personally, over the years, have been associated with many of the contributors. Reading their observations has revealed to me inner qualities and indications of what makes them tick, their values and motivations, previously unrevealed, and this has reinforced my positive regard for them all.

The editors make considerable use of the experiences of service users, who have been invited to recount their experiences. The contribution from service users and carers on occasions exposes their core raw feelings and painful moments. These sometimes made me shudder, but ultimately their contribution has prompted feelings of admiration and respect for how they have coped with the manifestations of their illness and the inadequacy of the response from services in the past. I was struck by how the service users appear not to have been diminished by their ordeal.

Professionals will benefit from enhanced understanding of the reasons why service users may present as prickly, withdrawn, uncooperative and not always appreciative of what is being offered to them.

The authors collectively make the case for disposing forever of pejorative and hurtful terms, such as manipulative and attention seeker.

The writers discuss the importance of personal quality time being spent with the individual, to find out the content of their ruminations, what might help them in restoring their self-confidence and resilience, and explaining the intent of care and interventions.

Readers will gain from learning what to say and what not to say to avoid knowingly invalidating a person and reinforcing their low self-esteem or hurting their feelings.

The book is a must read for all involved in acute mental health care, including adolescents. Acute care forums should invest in this book and use it as a benchmark to review their policies, in particular medication management, and case mix, therapeutic culture and systems, to revisit their training needs analysis and professional development plans and overhaul their communication and engagement with service user arrangements.

Managers should use ideas from this book in service and individual objective setting, and refresh their audit systems. They should revisit how they collect and act upon feedback from patients and examine how best to motivate and enhance the workforce capability.

Clinical leaders should review their roles in modelling good practice and the support and supervision they provide to frontline staff; encourage staff to listen critically to patients' stories and use the examples, questions and exercises in the book to raise standards and support the development of staff. The questions and exercises should be discussed at staff development groups, community meetings and referred to at handovers.

Higher education staff should weave the learning points into pre and post registration programmes.

Acute Care Forums should also use the messages and examples in the book to creatively engage with those who commission services, and highlight the often serious limitations which may exist locally.

It should not be assumed that all health service commissioners are equipped to understand the issues and dilemmas of modern acute care, and where necessary concepts of recovery and social inclusion should be explained, and how the paucity of resources or the inadequacy of environments negatively impact. Commissioners should be exposed to the realities faced by frontline staff and the traumatic experiences encountered by service users and their carers.

Service managers and clinicians should endeavour to point out to commissioners alternative approaches to the existing flawed systems, the inadequacy of buildings and the resulting deficits in personal care. They should create opportunities to work together in making the hard decisions about increasing the investment in deprived Acute Care Services, rather than other more attractively perceived general services, and make suggestions about how to make best use of current resources.

The impending Health Care Commission focus on Standards in Acute Care makes this book timely and readers will be better positioned to achieve the standards required.

In summary, the book provides a collection of knowledge, wisdom and credible experiences. Combining service user, carer, and professionals' perspectives in a common purpose has impressive results. It has confirmed that sometimes differences count.

For service users, advocates and family members, the book will greatly assist in preventing relapse and sustaining improvements, and will give optimism and hope to many. Aspects of the book will give clear pointers of good practice to be expected and will give additional strength to service users and their representatives in challenging unacceptable practice.

The book should also prompt self-reflection on the part of all practitioners and managers on their personal style and approach in relating to people and spur them on to be fluent in understanding patient needs and be genuinely empathic.

Aspirations and improvements will not be met unless people and teams are equipped to play their part and understand. The purpose of the book is to help to increase their understanding, offer new ideas and motivations to do more, and change mindsets.

A book of this nature, service users, carers and professionals working in genuine partnership to improve services, is an indicator of how far we have come in progressing services and proof of our strength for the future. I not only commend the book but intend to ensure that as many people as possible are aware of its value.

Section I

Introduction

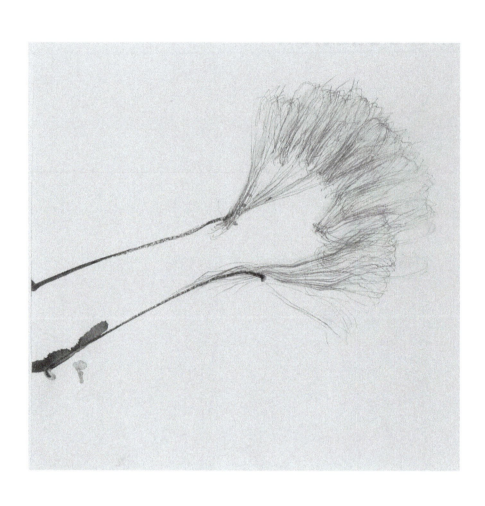

Chapter 1

What is the book about?

David Kennard

This is not a book on new approaches in the treatment of severe mental illness, nor is it the account of one individual's journey into psychosis. You can find excellent examples of both types of book in the libraries. This book presents something that is commonplace and at the same time unique: the experiences of those who live on a daily basis with a psychotic break with reality – in themselves, in their family members, or in the people they work with – severe enough to lead to admission to a psychiatric ward. Commonplace – in that the accounts in this book are a small scoop out of an ocean of similar experiences. Unique – in that such a collection of voices from all the rooms and corners of the ward has never been assembled before. In this respect, the book is like a quilt made up from many individual pieces sown together. Each piece tells its own story, and although there are elements in common, the strength and impact of the quilt is in the combined effect of many different voices and experiences.

The idea for the book grew out of two conferences on making in-patient wards therapeutic, organised by members of ISPS UK. Out of these, the four co-editors evolved a format for the book to complement the policy and research literature on the in-patient care and treatment of severe mental disorders – in particular those with the label of psychosis or schizophrenia – by adding what we felt were the missing pieces of the jigsaw: what it is actually like to receive or provide these services.

The format we developed was to solicit first-hand personal accounts of in-patient care from those in the front line: from those admitted to a psychiatric ward; from those whose relative (usually a son or daughter) has been admitted; and from those who in some significant way provide or contribute to in-patient services. The format of the personal account was chosen as the most direct way of conveying vividly what happens on a ward and the feelings evoked. We then gave each account to two commentators coming from different perspectives, asking them to say what issues they felt had been highlighted by the account and what lessons could be learnt that would improve the quality of care. Some commentators have also contributed their own personal accounts to the book, others are experienced and in some cases leading figures in the mental health field. The aim was to get the best learning we could out of the accounts. Following each account and its commentaries we have posed a number of questions, and in some cases suggested exercises for the reader and teams to ponder, discuss or try.

The book can be used in a number of ways. It can be read by the individual practitioner looking for stimulating ideas and some recognition and validation of their own experience. It can be used as course reading material in the training of mental health practitioners, selecting an issue or topic relevant to a course module. Individual chapters can be used as the basis for a seminar or workshop, asking members to discuss the questions or do the exercise at the end of the chapter. We very much hope that the format of the book will enable it to be used in the training of mental health nurses, clinical psychologists, psychiatrists, occupational therapists, arts therapists and other professions such as social work who still need to know about in-patient services even if their work is largely community based. Although the book is aimed at a professional readership, we are also mindful that it may be read by service users and carers, and we hope that they may find not only some validation of their own experiences here, but may also find it helpful, or at least illuminating, to learn something of the feelings and experiences of those who provide their services.

Sufficient reference has been made to 'we', the editors, to suggest a brief introduction is in order. We come from four different mental health disciplines: nursing (Mark Hardcastle); clinical psychology (David Kennard); art therapy (Sheila Grandison) and psychiatry (Leonard Fagin). Our therapeutic orientations are a mix of cognitive behavioural and various psychodynamic models, both individual and group. This has ensured lively editorial discussion of and with our contributors, aimed at ensuring that the book remains relatively neutral and jargon-free in terms of its theoretical stance. It will be for the reader to decide how well we have achieved this.

It used to be said that mental health was the Cinderella service compared with the rest of the nation's health services. We would add that in the first decade of the twenty-first century in-patient care has become the Cinderella of the mental health services. While we applaud the effort that has gone into developing mental health care in the community, we believe the focus has become too one-sided. A consequence of the emphasis on early intervention, on reaching people in mental and emotional distress *before* they reach crisis point, is that being admitted to a psychiatric ward is now often seen only as a failure. To quote Quirk and Lelliott (2004), 'Today there are no positive indications for admitting a person to a psychiatric ward.' This view impacts on everyone involved: on the person admitted, on their family, and on the staff who work in the psychiatric wards. Lacking in adequate resources, managerial structure, team morale or motivation, the services provided have come to reflect this sense of being a holding situation for failure, where 'too often the experience of acute inpatient care is felt to be neither safe nor therapeutic' (Department of Health 2002b).

The purpose of this book is to help to change this situation, by recognising and exploring the experiences (good as well as bad) of *all* those involved in in-patient care. We seek to understand what creates or contributes to the negative experiences, and to encourage the reader who may work or train on a psychiatric ward to think about how things might be done differently with benefits all round. Although a number of reports have appeared in recent years on the shortcomings of in-patient care and how to improve it, for change to occur there needs first of all to be an appreciation and understanding of the experiences of those involved in the unpredictable, volatile, often anxiety-arousing and sometimes threatening environment of the psychiatric ward. We invite mental health professionals and trainees to hear what it is like to be a service user, a carer, or indeed a fellow-professional working in a different discipline. We want to introduce those who have contact with in-patient services, in all their different capacities, to see each other's point of view. We do not expect this always to make for comfortable reading, but we believe that if all those involved in in-patient services dipped into this book, the result could be a real improvement in the quality of the services provided, and also in the job satisfaction of those who provide them.

How the book is organised

The book is divided into five sections. The first section sets out the historical context of the book, drawing on personal accounts of the care and treatment of people variously labelled as mad, lunatics, insane and mentally ill, over the past two hundred years, and then the contemporary context of practice, guidelines and attitudes.

Sections Two to Four are the heart of the book. These present accounts of personal experience from, in turn, the perspective of the in-patient service user, the relative turned carer, and the service provider. We have given each account a title that highlights the predominant feeling conveyed by the writer, although in many cases the reality is more nuanced than a single feeling. Each personal account is followed by two commentaries written from different perspectives. For example, the account by a service user of being bored on the ward is commented on by a nurse and by an occupational therapist; the account by a junior psychiatrist of feeling helpless is commented on by a service user and by an experienced psychiatrist. The purpose of the commentaries is to highlight the issues raised by each account and identify what lessons can be learnt. Each chapter concludes with some questions or suggested exercises for the reader to consider, or to discuss if the book is being used in a group situation.

Section Two contains personal accounts from six service users of their experience of psychiatric wards. In approaching service users we aimed for a mix of men and women, different ethnic backgrounds, and experiences of voluntary and compulsory admissions. In the context of this book the psychiatric diagnosis given at the time of admission has not been considered relevant, although one writer chooses to open with this. What these accounts tell us most poignantly is that, alongside whatever degree of distress and disorder the individual may be experiencing during their stay on a psychiatric ward, there is nevertheless a still-functioning 'normal' observing part of the mind that reacts as any one of us might to feeling bored, misunderstood, patronised, scared or humiliated, and equally to feeling supported, listened to, befriended or just enjoying the momentary relief of a good laugh. The editors are grateful to our account writers for their courage and openness in sharing these experiences. As in the next two sections, the issues highlighted by the commentaries are summarised at the end of the section.

Section Three takes us into the experiences of five carers. Four accounts are by the mother or father of a young man or woman admitted at the point of crisis, – in two cases, against the individual's will. The fifth account is of a wife recently married to a man with a previous history of psychosis. These accounts do not pull their punches. They convey the gamut of feeling family members go through – anxiety, despair, guilt, relief, bewilderment, frustration, anger – as well as the determination to find a better way. The news is not all bad. There are accounts of kind and caring doctors. But the overall picture suggests that in many cases, as one writer puts it, carers are 'not even on the horizon for consideration' by the ward team. Of course it is not all like this. Our commentators represent the views and practices of those who are seeking a better way, involving the families as partners in care. But there are also important lessons about the small things that can make a big difference – information about what is happening, and why, when someone is admitted, and the offer of a cup of tea . . .

Section Four offers the accounts of ten service providers from (nearly) all the professions and supporting roles that make up what is a surprisingly large team. In addition to the obvious ones – psychiatry, nursing, clinical psychology, occupational therapy – we have also invited accounts from a hotel services assistant (a ward domestic in old speak), a nursing assistant, the chief executive of an independent hospital and a hospital chaplain. We are aware of some significant omissions and limitations. We sought but failed to obtain a personal account of the experience of an NHS senior manager, nor do we have a written account from an arts therapist, though we do have commentaries from both these perspectives, and a personal contribution from an art pyschotherapist of drawings made in visual response to her experience of in-patient settings. We did not seek an account from a facilitator of a support group for ward staff. It may also be pointed out that each account represents only one individual's experience and another member of the same profession might report a quite different situation. We cannot argue that these accounts are representative. We asked people we knew or who were known to people we knew. But we would argue that this collection of personal accounts brings alive in a way that has not been done before what it is actually like for those who work on or in close contact with the world of the psychiatric ward. They may not be fondly regarded by critics of the system, indeed they may *be* critics of the system, but if we want to see improvements we surely need to start by recognising and understanding the emotional impact of the work on the people we ask to do it. Our commentators include service users as well as the range of professionals involved. We think the reader will find their observations stimulating, challenging, discomforting, and we hope at times inspiring.

The final section offers the reader some 'take home' messages of how things might be done better. As one of our commentators says, it is not rocket science. If this book achieves one thing we hope it will be to help overcome the fear of open acknowledgement of how we really feel encountering our own or other people's madness. As another commentator reminds us, we are all much more simply human than otherwise.

Chapter 2

A brief narrative history of in-patient care in the United Kingdom

Leonard Fagin

The world is becoming like a lunatic asylum run by lunatics.
(David Lloyd George, 1933)

I have always depended on the kindness of strangers.
(*A Streetcar Named Desire*, Scene 11, 1947)

The thing psychiatric inpatients value most about being in hospital is their ability to leave.
(McIntyre *et al.* 1989)

Exploring the history of in-patient care through the written accounts of people associated with psychiatric institutions provides a rich seam of experiences, which often have fed the imagination of novelists, playwrights and the general population with descriptions that have created fascination, fear and prejudice about mental illness. Whilst it is difficult to give complete credence to many of these accounts as accurate reflections of what was happening in psychiatric care, in line with our aims in the rest of the book we have attempted to gather representative voices of those who provided or were in receipt of psychiatric care since institutions were set up in the United Kingdom. Needless to say, the collection is idiosyncratic and incomplete.

One way of looking at the history of psychiatric in-patient care is to see it as a recurring cycle of stages, moving from neglect to custodial, repressive regimes, on to enlightened liberal and humane care and then back to a mixture of neglect and highly regimented and controlled environments.

Prior to the mid eighteenth century, the deranged or mentally disabled patient in England was more likely to be assimilated into the group of society's outcasts, the poor, the vagrants, petty criminals and physically disabled. At that time there was no sense of public responsibility and mostly these wretched souls were left to fend for themselves and were at large, relying on almsgiving and Christian charity. The exception to this was the Bethlem, founded in the early fifteenth century with only a handful of inmates as its residents, as well as a small number of almshouses. By the early eighteenth century the rising population, coupled with the commercialisation of agriculture, created an ever-increasing 'army of beggars and idlers . . . the disreputable poor', and attempts to deal with this resulted in the development of houses of correction, 'Bridewells', or 'tolerated prisons', leading Daniel Defoe to comment in 1724:

> there are in London, notwithstanding we are a nation of liberty, more public and private prisons and houses of confinement, than in any city in Europe, perhaps as many as in all the capital cities of Europe put together.
>
> (Defoe, quoted in Scull 1979)

In the affluent classes, by contrast, those afflicted with mental illness were either cared for by their own families, placed with local ministers or medical men, or sent to private 'madhouses', small institutions run for profit. Although in some of these residences patients were well cared for, many such endeavours were set up by those solely seeking financial gain.

> Few speculations can be more unpleasant than that of a private madhouse, and it is seldom if ever undertaken, unless with the hope of receiving large returns on the capital invested.
>
> (Duncan 1809)

In evidence given to the House of Commons Select Committee in 1815, Thomas Monro, then physician at the Bethlem, described the regime imposed on the inmates of the asylum:

> In the months of May, June, July, August and September we generally administer medicine; we do not in the winter season, because the house is so excessively cold that it is not thought proper . . . we apply generally bleeding, purging and vomit; those are the general medicines we apply . . . All the patients who require bleeding are generally bled on a particular day, and they are purged on a particular day . . . Thereafter, of course, patients were kept chained to their beds four days out of every seven.
>
> (House of Commons Select Committee 1815)

John Perceval, brother of the assassinated Prime Minister Spencer Perceval, was first admitted under restraint in January 1831 to the Brisslington Asylum, near Bristol, run by a Dr Fox, an expensive institution which had to be paid for by members of his family. He was then transferred to other institutions, which he bitterly described later in a book on his experiences (Bateson 1974).

> As I was a victim at first, in part of the ignorance or want of thought of

my physician, so I was consigned afterwards to the control of other medical men, whose habitual cruelty, and worse ignorance-charlatanism became the severest part of my most severe scourge.

(1974: 3)

I do not recollect at any time medicine being given to me; neither to purify the blood; neither as tonics; except on two occasions. No! The cheap and universal nostrum was to be ducked in the cold bath; in the depth of winter or not, no matter.

(1974: 107)

An ex-patient, Urbane Metcalfe, mentions corruption among the staff at the Bethlem.

In each of the galleries the keepers pick out one of their patients whose strength fits him for the situation of bully, and when it is not convenient to be at the patients themselves, they cause him to do it, this is great abuse ... It would extend far beyond the limits of this little work to pourtray the villainies practised by the Jacks in office; bribery is common to them all; cruelty is common to them all; villainy is common to them all; in short everything is common but virtue, which is so uncommon they take care to lock it up as a rarity.

(Metcalf 1818)

William Harrison Ainsworth, in his novel *Jack Sheppard* (1839), describes a particular distasteful routine, where inmates were paraded for public entertainment.

But the besetting evil of the place, and that which drew down the severest of censures of the writers above mentioned, was that this spot, which of all others should have been most free from such intrusion, was made a public exhibition. There all the loose characters thronged, assignations were openly made, and the spectators diverted themselves with the vagaries of its miserable inhabitants.

Not everybody's experiences at the time were so traumatic. Late in the eighteenth century, William Cowper, the English poet and hymnist, was placed in the elite St Alban's asylum and had nothing but praise for his doctor, Nathaniel Cotton, for the humane treatment which he said speeded his recovery from serious episodes of depression.

Not only his skill, as a physician, but his well-known humanity, and sweetness of temper.

(Cowper 1816)

The notable exception to these accounts was the opening of the Retreat, in York in 1792, under the auspices of the Society of Friends, the Quakers, and the direction of William Tuke. Patients were to be looked after with gentleness and respect, good food, occupation and friendship, abandoning other drastic measures which simply were not effective. This was later given the name of 'moral treatment' by William's son, Samuel, writing in 1811 about the Retreat in order to spread the experience to other institutions that were beginning to be built at the time. The establishment initially reacted positively to the new methods of treatment, and prompted the setting up of a House of Commons Select Committee examining the restrictive practices described at the York Asylum which led Tuke to set up the Retreat. Tuke's book was very popular, and he was invited to visit institutions across the United Kingdom and Europe, where the philosophy of care was adopted to an extent. The instruction to 'seek the good opinion of the patient and to endeavour to govern by the influence of esteem than of severity' (Tuke 1813) has a modern ring to it. Most remarkably, all the institutions founded in America after the publication followed the same principles. However, the influence of the Retreat on the practice of psychiatry was to be short-lived, predominantly for social and economic reasons (Jones 1996).

The arrival of industrialisation, with its accompanying urbanisation, brought people together in unprecedented numbers. Economic migration separated individuals from their extended families, homes were severely overcrowded, workers toiled for long hours in jobs that were often far away from home; it was therefore very difficult for those families to look after someone who had an acute or chronic mental health problem. The expectation was that this care should be provided publicly (Cooper and Sartorius 1977). By the mid nineteenth century the landscape had changed dramatically, and most of these individuals were to be found in large institutional settings, paid for by charitable organisations and the public purse.

The Poor Law Amendment Act of 1834 had a major impact on this process, setting up an institutional solution to this familial shortage of internal resources. Although some asylums were already in existence, according to some thinkers, new hospitals, asylums, workhouses, prisons and orphanages were being set up as a response to the unsanitary chaos of the eighteenth century, a sort of 'bourgeois discipline' (Foucault 1973; Donnelly 1986). Four waves of asylum building followed the County Asylums Act of 1808 and 1828, the Lunatics Act of 1845 and the Lunacy Act of 1890 as an attempt to divert mentally ill patients, who were difficult to manage in workhouses and prisons, from destitution, neglect or imprisonment into regimented forms of care. Asylums had to be erected in 'airy and healthy situations', which was possible at the time because of cheap land being available, outside major conurbations but within easy reach of towns where visiting doctors were likely to be residing. Asylums became the 'stately homes for the lower classes' (Jones 1991).

An illustrative example of this move to reform was introduced by William Gaskell in the Lancaster Lunatic Asylum, where he witnessed appalling scenes of degradation and squalor among the inmates. The care was predominantly custodial; many patients were in handcuffs, leg-locks or strait-jackets. Some of the patients were chained to box-seats in heated rooms over a permanent sewer, removing the need for patients to go to the toilet. Gaskell minimised the use of restraints, improved the menu by adding meat and tea and introduced recreational activities such as games, slide-shows and dances, with one of the patients playing a violin. He built a library for patients, developed work schemes and encouraged patients to help each other. Purging and bleeding, very common and unpleasant methods of treatment at the time, were abandoned. He selected 40 female patients to take care of an equal number of orphaned children, 'to develop in the women the great principle of maternal love'. Training of attendants was also improved, ensuring that incontinent patients were regularly toileted and that night staff were awake and active at night, which had an immediate effect on violence and suicide incidents (Freeman and Tantam 1991).

Other institutions, such as the Gloucester Asylum under Samuel Hitch, gave strict instruction to 'Keepers' to avoid abuse and maltreatment.

> 9. No Keeper shall at any time attempt to deceive or to terrify a patient; nor to irritate a patient by mockery, by mimicry, or by wanton allusions to anything ludicrous in the present appearance or ridiculous in the past conduct of the patient.

> 10. No Keeper shall indulge or express vindictive feelings, but, considering the patients as utterly unable to restrain themselves, the Keepers must forgive all petulance and sarcasms, and treat with equal tenderness those who give the most, and those who give the least trouble.
>
> (Quoted in Smith 1996: 486)

Early small asylums were more likely to receive patients in acute states, many of whom would have had a good prognosis. These 'convalescent' patients on the whole were treated well: they were allowed a certain degree of freedom, working in the kitchens and gardens, and offered recreation such as music, basket weaving or flower growing. The more difficult patients, however, did not receive this form of care: they were often subject to all manners of restraints, suffered from cold in inadequate cells and had to sleep on straw if incontinent.

Progressively, however, asylums started to grow as a result of the impossibility of finding care for those that did not improve from long-standing, incurable disease processes, the chronic psychoses, dementias, gross learning difficulties, addictions, or organic conditions such as epilepsy or general paralysis. In 1827 there were 1,046 persons in county asylums. By the end of that century numbers had increased to 74,000, and by 1930, to 140,000. From small residential settings providing 50 to 80 beds, asylums grew into large institutions of 2,000 residents, and even then wards started to become over-crowded. Allied to this process, those involved in the care of these patients became increasingly disillusioned in their initial therapeutic expectations, a factor which inevitably must have had an effect on the quality of interaction between professional carers and their charges. Furthermore, public expend-iture on mental health care failed to increase in parallel with the growth of resident numbers, affecting standards of care. Not surprisingly, despite the fact that asylums were attempting to respond in the best way possible with limited resources, they became increasingly unpopular and stigmatised.

Hospital care was hierarchical in nature, with the physician superintendent in absolute, and sometimes dictatorial control, a chief male nurse in charge of the 'male side' and a matron in charge of the 'female side'. Most male nurses were unqualified, recruited from unemployed ranks, whilst female nurses fol-lowed the 'Nightingale tradition', creating a gender divide between the 'barrack' and 'residential home' nature of care for male and female patients respectively.

Life on the ward took place within an internal complex of large dormitor-ies, day rooms and dining areas, and each ward was double locked with a set of heavy keys. Violence was not uncommon, especially before the arrival of phenothiazines, and the ward was seldom quiet, with patients shouting back at their hallucinatory persecutors, in states of profound distress or isolation, and behaving in a bizarre manner. It was a relief for many patients to be given jobs working on the farms, orchards and greenhouses, kitchens or laundry, even staff houses, and paid with tobacco, sweets or small amounts of money.

Diet was unappetising at best,

> . . . weak tea, lumpy porridge, bread and margarine, gelatinous jam, weak-looking corned beef, warm soup with chopped vegetables and small meat fragments, flavoured to create a delusion of strength and nourishment.
>
> (Parfitt 1996: 468)

By the time of the introduction of the Mental Treatment Act of 1930, hos-pital care had liberalised to an extent. Patients could accept a voluntary status, request treatment and be offered 'parole', either in the hospital, its grounds or in the local town, where they could go unsupervised. Patients were allowed to use their own clothes, occupational therapy was introduced and recreational activities included dances (although over-enthusiastic embraces with the opposite sex were discouraged), whist drives, gymnastic sessions and outings to the seaside. The institution had its sports day, Christmas was a big event with the meal being a central feature: some people described going into hospital as an alternative to Butlins, the holiday camp, which was becoming popular at the time. Patients were looked after until their old age and eventual death, and if they had no relatives, buried in the small cemetery on the hospital grounds. The hospital had a community life of its own, and, to an extent, could survive without having to depend on the outside world. The scene was set for the development of institutionalisation, affecting not only patients, but to a similar extent, staff.

> . . . Whatever else the patients were, the majority were clearly harmless; . . . Most were passive, either refusing or unable to carry on sensible conversation, remaining inert, or making inappropriate movements or irrelevant remarks . . . many would be strangely immovable for hours at a time. Some of the staff had given up attempts to develop a friendly relationship, but mostly, they were cheerful and encouraging towards their charges . . .
>
> (Parfitt 1996: 472, *ibid.*)

Even in Broadmoor, a hospital for the criminally insane, some patients experienced humane understanding, particularly from their fellow residents.

> I go so far as to assert that frequently in later years I would have [*sic*] willingly have exchanged the society of my business associates for that of those 'incarcerated lunatics'. Few of these men, accordingly, betrayed the minor pettinesses and idiosyncrasies that are met in ordinary walks of life. Among these patients I made many friends. Many more won my respect alike for patience in adversity, cheerfulness and self-control.
>
> (Warmark 1931)

Following the introduction of the welfare state by the Labour Government and the inception of the National Health Service in 1948, mental hospitals came under the same administration as general hospitals, and as a result a programme of upgrading was initiated by the new regional hospital boards. Despite this, overcrowding worsened, and hospitals started to discharge patients, even before aftercare was secured. Public criticism against asylum care mounted, with reports of the dehumanising and stultifying effect on long-term residents (institutional neurosis), and advocated the need to introduce policies to rehabilitate chronic patients back into the community.

These criticisms were compounded by attacks from a series of writers (Goffman 1968, Foucault 1973, Szasz 1961, Laing and Esterson 1964, and Cooper 1967), describing hospitals in terms equivalent to prisons, or 'total institutions'. The reports arising out of a number of scandals claiming alleged staff cruelty or neglect (Committee of Inquiry into Whittingham Hospital 1972, Kent Area Health Authority 1977), the increasing overhead costs of maintaining large institutions and staff and the rise of community alternatives to hospitalisation led to suggestions to close down large Victorian asylums. By 1961, Tooth and Brooke (1961) predicted that in fifteen years, only half of the psychiatric beds would be required, prompting Enoch Powell's speech (1961) announcing the demise of Victorian institutions. Between 1959 and 1980, the number of hospital residents fell from 159,000 to 79,200. Length of stay also decreased sharply, aided by the introduction of new treatments and the development of out-patient services, so that admissions, which were also rising dramatically in numbers, were seen as opportunities to assess and diagnose, introduce psychotropic medication, make the necessary adjustments and plan for aftercare.

A small number of hospitals, led by charismatic medical superintendents, liberalised rigid institutional practices by pioneering 'therapeutic communities' in, among others, Dingleton, Mapperley, Warlingham Park, Belmont, Fulbourne, Littlemore and Claybury Hospitals, informed by psychodynamic and sociological perspectives which were beginning to gain credence among psychiatric professionals at the time. Previously locked wards were opened, hierarchies between staff and residents were flattened, decisions were made more transparent and more prominence was given to patients' wishes for treatment to be given. Unfortunately, these efforts were short-lived, and to some extent the skills acquired were lost, because the institution itself was becoming increasingly irrelevant. As the medical historian Roy Porter noted, it was a

> 'rich irony' that our age, which has seen the agitation for the closing of traditional asylums come to fruition, has also been the time when many of them have been, at long last, most therapeutically innovative and successful.
>
> (Porter 1996)

The introduction of the White Paper, *Better services for the mentally ill* (1975), raised the hope for 'community care' of patients with mental health problems. Patients were to be treated preferably at home, or if they required in-patient care, they could be admitted briefly to a psychiatric unit in a district general hospital, where mental health problems would be seen as just another medical problem. Financial crises and predominantly negative attitudes from Conservative governments towards social welfare impeded adequate amounts of money being devoted to community care, and in particular the shortage of residential places in local authority homes delayed the closure programme.

Eventually, however, the process of de-institutionalisation continued, to the point that very few of the old Victorian asylums exist in the present day, and now are replaced by a variety of models of care in District General Hospitals or community settings. Many of the hospitals, sitting in prime land and often surrounded by vast tracts of attractive woodlands or arable fields, became the target for property speculators and supermarkets. Long-stay patients were 'decanted' into residential nursing homes or hostels, sometimes without proper after-care arrangements. This massive closure programme has been accompanied by a notable increase of patients who end up in prison, as a result of their dangerousness or law-breaking, some of whom were previously accommodated in the old-style institutions. Another development which has affected the nature of care is the widespread use of illicit drugs, undoubtedly affecting the manifestation of mental health problems and making management an increasingly difficult problem. Psychiatric units have become places where these drugs are secreted and used, often with impunity.

The care of black and ethnic minority patients in the UK deserves some mention here. As a result of Britain's colonial power, ethnic minorities have lived in the UK since the seventeenth century, but little of the experience of these patients when they became mentally unwell has been recorded. Larger immigration flows started in the 1950s, mostly from the Caribbean and the Indian subcontinent, but these were followed by waves of immigrants from Africa, Eastern Europe and the Far East, for economic and political reasons. Only recently has there been any consideration of the special needs of these patients in in-patient settings. This is a particularly important area, as patients from some foreign backgrounds are represented disproportionately highly on the in-patient rolls of psychiatric admission units. Bhui (1977), who has also contributed to this book, summarised the main issues relating to this population, particularly in London and Bughra *et al.* (2000) carried out a survey asking patients about their in-patient experiences. Highlighted was the lack of privacy, the problems with mixed gender units, the assumption that these patients were not 'psychologically minded' and the quality and quantity of food. Many of these patients also resorted to alternative medicine which was not recognised or understood by the formal medical teams.

We leave this chapter with a quote from Morag Coate, who had five breakdowns over 14 years and was diagnosed as schizophrenic.

> The first requirement of a mental hospital is that it should be an asylum in the true sense of the word; as far as is humanly possible it should not only be but should appear to be a place of safety and protection. This is naturally difficult and sometimes impossible to ensure. Acutely disturbed patients whose inner world is divorced from outer reality may need to be forcibly restrained in their own interests and in the interests of other people; they may need to be cared [for] alongside other patients whose different disturbances reactivate and intensify their own; the nature of their illness may be such that hospital is an unhappy and frightening place. The important thing to remember is that they are still human people, and the factors that make for happiness and security in a general hospital apply no less, but in fact more, in a mental hospital.
>
> (Coate 1964)

Chapter 3

Recent times

Mark Hardcastle

In the last section the historical experiences encountered were mostly centred on in-patient admissions to large institutions such as the Victorian and Edwardian asylums. Although the closure programme of these hospitals, which took place predominantly in the 1980s, resulted in an emphasis being placed on community services, the need for hospital provision remained. Very often, this resulted in psychiatric wards being developed alongside mainstream general hospitals close to the centre of towns rather than in the remote countryside. Unfortunately, when staff moved into their new workplaces little was done to prepare those who were previously based in the old hospitals. Staff took their former institutional practices and attitudes from one setting and transferred the same ways of working into the new. In some cases those staff teams that had developed a more creative therapeutic community approach in the large mental hospitals were broken up and their collective group skills lost. Added to this, the new buildings in the 1980s were more cramped and lacked the green space of the hospitals they replaced. The poor quality of in-patient care was becoming a focus for vociferous complaint from an emerging and strong service user movement supported by a *zeitgeist* of consumerism that demanded better from its mental health service. Reform was required.

Contemporary mental health services in general have experienced an unprecedented level of scrutiny and subsequent reform and in particular the care of people in hospital settings has received more than its fair share of interest and comment. The former Director of the leading mental health charity, The Sainsbury Centre for Mental Health, Matt Muijen, remarked:

> It would be surprising if a public service was tolerated when it was feared by its customers (whom it puts at risk), unable to show evidence of its effectiveness and paying its staff uncompetitively. It would be astonishing if, nevertheless, such a service could not cope with demand. Yet this is a recognisable picture of acute mental health care in the NHS.
>
> (Muijen 2002)

This strident statement was made after a number of influential studies conducted in the late 1990s had concluded that in-patient care nationally was in a very poor state indeed. *Acute problems* (SCMH 1998) was the first of these major reviews of the quality of care in acute psychiatric wards. It surveyed 38 services spread throughout the United Kingdom in which 215 patients were asked about their experiences of admission, care and treatment received and the discharge process. Among the findings it was shown that therapeutic input was minimal for many and multidisciplinary care was absent for most. Patient contact with staff other than in-patient nurses and doctors averaged one contact per patient per stay and nearly half of the patients had not received enough information about their illness.

The report concluded that among the problems of acute care were:

- No clear goals for acute care
- The setting was neither pleasant nor therapeutic
- Staff were not delivering targeted programmes to improve users' health or social functioning based on individual needs
- Acute in-patient care had poor connections with community services.

Remarkably, despite these conclusions, the study acknowledged that 'Most patients leave acute care in a better mental state than when they came in' (SCMH 1998). In a similar study of service user experience by the mental health charity Mind it was found 56 per cent of people who use in-patient services describe the experience as untherapeutic, over half said they didn't have enough contact with staff and two thirds had problems getting a restful night's sleep (Mind 2000). The third major study, *Addressing acute concerns* (Department of Health 1999a), commissioned by the Department of Health (DoH) and led by the Standing Nursing and Midwifery Council (SNMAC) was carried out by a panel of nurse experts drawn from education, management, commissioning, research and practice. Their role was to review research literature, examine policies, and consult with service users, carers and professionals. Despite using wider and more varied sampling methodology, not exclusively focused on data drawn directly from patient experience, the results of this study repeated many of the findings of *Acute problems* (SCMH 1998). These studies were important as they provided evidence and a high degree of consensus that would support the rationale and need for reform. This had to address the manifest issues of poor patient experience and a demoralised workforce, which remains the largest challenge to modernising mental health services that we face today.

Significant among policy initiatives were *The national framework for mental health* (DoH 1999b) and, more specifically for in-patient care, the supporting *Mental health policy implementation guide: Adult acute inpatient care provision* (DoH 2002b). These documents urged modernisation of in-patient care that relied on the development of therapeutic cultures, systems and practices which enabled user empowerment and evidence-based practice. Very much in the style used by this book, The *Mental health policy implementation guide* highlighted the issues facing in-patient provision by including direct quotes from service users and professionals.

A poor physical and psychological environment for care including lack of basic necessities and arrangements for safety, dignity and comfort.

Lack of involvement and engagement in the planning and reviewing of their own care and how the ward is run.

Do something about the dreadful ward rounds and the queuing up for medication like naughty school kids waiting to see the headmaster.

A lack of clarity of purpose.

The use of such statements drawn from personal experience provided a clear context for a large number of the reforms and associated targets addressing practice issues, service user involvement, the organisation of services and improvement of physical environments. The achievement of these targets would be closely monitored by commissioners for mental health services and audited by the then Commission for Health Improvement (CHI). As an incentive the funding of services would be partly determined by the achievement of these reforms.

To support the implementation of the *National framework for mental health* (*ibid.*) a number of initiatives were launched. A regional network known as 'Development Centres' was formed under the auspices of the National Institute of Mental Health NIMH(E). Many of these regional centres set up so-called 'in-patient collaborative programmes' to identify and support improvement in in-patient care. The Sainsbury Centre for Mental Health started their own initiative, 'Acute Solutions', which identified four pilot sites which would take part in a three-year programme of service development and which hopefully would then be used as exemplars of practice to inform other services. Universities that had previously provided very few opportunities for in-patient staff to study relevant issues appropriate to in-patient mental health services had now started to produce modules following the publication of the National Service Framework. As a further element of reform, new roles were developed, such as 'Modern Matrons' who would be responsible at a clinical level for fundamental aspects of care during an in-patient stay. Another new role, the Support, Time and Recovery (STR) worker, would convey concerns raised by service users which would then be addressed by professional workers, and who would have the time available to help them in important practical ways. A programme for building new hospitals or, at the very least, improving the existing ward environment was also supported.

Have these reforms and developments resulted in better experiences for service users? It is perhaps too early to say but certainly there is an impetus to improve that has now been sustained for over six years. There are many examples of good practice, some outstanding well-designed buildings, and the service user voice is more clearly heard through advocacy services and a growing acceptance of service user empowerment in general. Despite this, in-patient services continue to attract high-profile controversy, either born out of tragedies such as the death of Rocky Bennett when undergoing restraint, or media reporting, such as the issue of the high incidence of illicit drug misuse occurring inside hospitals. Pessimistically, a recent audit of service user experience of acute in-patient wards conducted by the Sainsbury Centre for Mental Health (2004) continues to highlight similar issues that were of concern in the earlier reports.

Perhaps the most recent initiative will be the most significant yet in transforming in-patient experience. The adoption of value-based care described by Woodbridge and Fulford (2004) will provide the opportunity to consider collaborative and recovery-based practices within a framework of values that imparts among others, hope and respect. The recent Chief Nursing Officer's Review of Mental Health Nursing: *From values to action* (DoH 2006) is a clear indicator of such intent. How values are adopted into practice is uncertain. It will require far more than NHS Trusts producing a list of good but glib intentions in the form of value statements which they require their employees to conform to. Values cannot be enacted through dictat. To imply a value statement without it being authentically believed is reminiscent of another similar initiative in the 1980s and 1990s when it was *de rigueur* for each NHS organisation to have its own *mission statement*: a statement that was supposed to ensure employees would (it was assumed by managers) go about their clinical work espousing quality and excellence.

Finally, it is interesting to note that such value-based practice harks back to the times of William Tuke at the Retreat in York and the notion of 'moral therapy', which informed and improved the care of people with mental illness in the early nineteenth century. An earlier missed opportunity to generalise and sustain good practice, perhaps?

Section 2

Service users' experiences

Introduction

In allowing these stories to be shared, the authors who have contributed to this section of the book are courageously revealing highly personal and at times traumatic material. The motivation for their disclosure is the hope that it will help others. The accounts are drawn from experiences in a variety of in-patient settings, most are contemporary recollections, however, some experiences are older but the memories are no less vivid. Whilst, the majority of the accounts are first hand and focus on adult acute care there are many issues, experiences and lessons to generalise and learn across history and all care groups including children, adolescents and the elderly. The stories that are told may give the reader a mixture of feelings; anger, sadness, pain as well as hope and joy. There is evidence within the accounts of care and compassion and other times extreme harshness and inhumanity. Sometimes all these observations can be witnessed within the same experience.

The commentaries that follow each service user experience are from different professionals who have been chosen because of the relevance of the themes contained within the accounts or because of the professional's own field of work or experience. The commentaries are stimulating and as you would expect varied in the perspective taken, which may give you reason to question and debate the stance of the commentating writer. The questions and exercises at the end of each section will allow you to engage with the issues presented by both the service user accounts and the commentaries. It is hoped that you will be stimulated to think, discuss and take action in your own places of work.

Chapter 4

Feeling misunderstood

Nigel Short

For years I've been fascinated with my 'Desert Island Discs'. There are a few favourites that always come up, 'If paradise is half as nice' by Amen Corner and 'You know my name, look up the number' by the Beatles. The remainder are influenced by my mood at the time. Memories of being in hospital change each time I think about it.

I'm sure we have all experienced being with people reliving an event we have all been at and realised we all have different memories of the same event. My experience of sadness was at the same time both typical and untypical of how other people would experience sadness. I wasn't sleeping or eating well and sometimes I had some very strange ideas, some I acted on. For example I spent many evenings trying to cut my left thumb off. I thought this would make me feel better, and for short periods it worked. I did feel better. How can you begin to explain that trying to cut your thumb off makes you feel better? How would that be appraised by other people?

The way I was feeling my sadness was mine. When I was in hospital, staff rarely took time to find out what this was like for me. Not taking the time often fuelled what I was thinking: 'I'm not worth finding out about'.

When I first arrived on the hospital ward two male staff took me to a side room. I desperately wanted to go to sleep. I hadn't slept well for two months and what little sleep I did get was alcohol-inspired.

What did the staff want to do? Check my belongings! They could have taken everything, I wouldn't have cared at all. Whilst I somehow appreciated what they were doing, it seemed odd, as I could have had many other opportunities to harm myself earlier in the day. One was clearly more senior than the other and he wrote in the book whilst the other went through my belongings. It felt like they were invading me. What did they think about what I had brought in? After this job had been done, the junior one [who later told me, he was a bank nurse, 'What's a bank nurse?'] stayed in the side room with me. 'Why?' He started chatting about his personal difficulties. He may have thought this would be helpful. I didn't want to hear about anything, I certainly didn't want to hear about his problems.

I wanted to sleep.

Having someone in a room watching your every movement was uncomfortable. I eventually got some tablets to help me sleep. The medication soon took effect. He continued to talk. I was worried that if I told him to stop he wouldn't like me. This was a recurring theme throughout my stay. The fear of saying something wrong and the impact that this error might have on the staff and how they might behave towards me later.

Interestingly, as I hadn't slept properly they had given me a sleeping tablet BUT still insisted that I woke up at about 6.30am! Daft!

The room door had a small window, about 12 inches by 12 inches. On the outside of the door was a small curtain that covered the glass pane. People could peep at you. Not only staff, but other people. Anybody could look at you. Knowing this kept me awake. Eventually I fell asleep.

I woke to find yet another 'bank' nurse. He sat very close. Perhaps two feet away. I could hear him breathing and smell his breath. I rolled my body away from him. What more did I have to do to let him know that I didn't want to talk? I wanted to sleep.

Then the domestic came into the room and started hoovering. How dirty had I made it overnight? The staff used to knock on the door and then walk straight in. Why bother knocking?

The room was sparse. A bed, a sink and a wardrobe. I spent many hours thinking of ways of hanging myself. I didn't want to kill myself but it kept my mind busy.

The nursing staff had the unenviable task of 'getting me to eat and drink'. Hearing their different tactics was interesting: some would blackmail me, 'You won't be able to go home if you don't eat', some would leave the food and some would tut and tell me it was good for me, 'come on it will make you feel better', and leave.

A sandwich wrapped in plastic cling film is not appetising. Coronation chicken in square processed white bread. Green unripened bananas. I went for ten days without food; or so they told me. I was drinking from the cold-water tap in the room. Once I asked a male nurse if he could do something about the cold water in my room, it was coming out warm. He came into the room and put his hand underneath the water to check. I felt humiliated. Would I lie about it, was I deluded, did he think I was deluded? This theme of invalidation surfaced many times.

Asking for a drink at night was difficult. The response was usually something like 'If we give you one every one else will want one'. This reply seemed contrary to the messages I had been given during the day about the importance of drinking. So when I wanted a drink I was refused.

The ward rounds were distressing events. The meeting usually involved about eight people; I might have known two or three. I was introduced to people who couldn't possibly help me, people from local social services and the local council. The nursing staff would talk about me, in front of me. Their descriptions of me were often in conflict with my experiences.

There was one person who seemed particularly interested in me, the senior registrar. He dropped by each day and spoke with me, not at me. He tried to help us both understand what was or what had gone on. He would often say things in the conversation that we had spoken about the day before. 'Hey this bloke is listening to me.' This helpful approach was in stark contrast to many other members of staff who made, perhaps innocent, mistakes, but nevertheless, important errors. For example one doctor asked me how I felt when my mother died. She was still alive. He also took lots of notes without ever asking me if it was OK. I became very worried about what he was going to do with all the information I had given him. It sounded like he was completing a checklist of questions.

One further difficulty was that each member of staff had their own ideology. Some would be 'cruel to be kind'; a sort of pull yourself together approach. Some were kind and tender and some were rude and unapproachable. One of them called me a 'lazy c**t'.

These differences of opinions occasionally caused me problems. Once I had been given an hour's unescorted leave off the ward. I was enjoying my walk and was paying little attention to the time. As I walked back through corridors of the main hospital I realised that I would not be back on the ward in the allotted time. I rang the ward on an internal phone and explained the situation. The member of staff who answered the phone said 'Thanks for letting us know, see you when you get back'. When I got back a few minutes later I went to the nurse station to let them know I was back. A senior member of staff chastised me for using a hospital internal phone, in front of all of the nursing staff. A man of 46 being told off. I felt humiliated. I thought my problem solving was a sign that my mental health was improving! Clearly not.

Medication was a horrible ritual. We all had to line up at the door of the clinical room and put our hands out. Limited communication went on. It felt like a chore, something that had to be done. Interesting when one thinks about the importance that psychiatry puts on medication and the little emphasis put on checking out whether it's helping or not.

All the long thin fingers of the people looked very similar. If people didn't attend they were invariably referred to as manipulative or attention seeking. The clinical room was in a small corridor with very little space to manoeuvre. This area was the scene of much confrontation and most incidents of aggression that I witnessed happened here.

After a few weeks the room door would get a knock every week-day morning at about 9.00am and a member of staff would enter and they would shout 'Art Therapy'. No explanation was offered. One morning a member of staff entered my room and told me that I 'wouldn't get better if I didn't help myself'. 'You're down for Art Therapy.' I did eventually go. I went to keep the staff quiet and also to find out what this therapy was about. The therapist was a pleasant bubbly woman in her mid twenties. We sat together for a while. Nobody else came. We started. She gave me a piece of paper and asked me to draw my family. I drew some lines on the page. Random lines, different thickness and different colours. The therapist studied the lines and began to tell me about my family. 'This line represents your father, you don't seem that close to him', she said. She then continued with this interpretation for a little while. I didn't go again. I would have been happy to go and chat with this woman each morning. She gave me time, seemed interested in me and it was distracting. It also gave me a chance to get out of my room. It was her interpretation I didn't like.

Commentaries

Trevor Turner (Consultant Psychiatrist)

Thinking through one's list for 'Desert Island Discs' is a delightful introspective standby for all Radio 4 aficionados. Such lists are bound to change over the years (has anyone kept an annual one?), different songs reflecting key passages of the journey from youth to maturity. Likewise the notion of a 'desert island' seems an apposite metaphor for an acute psychiatric ward, reflecting a transformed space, fraught with psychological and physical difficulties, and needing some sort of therapeutic music to deal with the loneliness of depression, confusion or psychosis, or whatever has generated the admission. The theme of 'Feeling Misunderstood' seems to be that of perplexed isolation, the ward an archipelago of lonely souls, set in an organisational ocean that can be threatening, can be gentle, but is never quite comprehensible. How can we, the appointed carers, whatever our strange titles (RMO, CPN, ASW) help find the right pieces of music, and while providing the routines of 'Shakespeare and the Bible' still get to the 'luxury item' that should of course be the return ticket to home and happiness.

The stigma of mental health pervades so much of what happens to Nigel. So many patients and their families feel ashamed at getting ill, and can easily feel talked down to or demeaned. Stigma creates a Cinderella service, denial of illness (by everyone including sufferers, carers and many NHS staff) and the ready resort to phrases such as 'pull yourself together'.

Nigel experiences differing and/or selective memories, which is quite the norm, particularly when someone cannot concentrate, feels depressed, or is having strange psychotic experiences (e.g. trying to cut off a thumb!). Having nurses give descriptions 'in conflict with my experiences' or feeling that no one is checking that the medication is helping are entirely understandable cognitions. Making things clear, all the time, over and again, should be a priority for all ward staff.

There are few explanations, of what's going on, the routines, the acronyms and the checklists. We have our technical phrases, as every profession does, such as 'bank nurse' and 'SHO' (sweetly explained as 'senior hous officer' on my current ward photo list), and we get so used to them we forget how strange the world is in which we work. Telling someone 'I'm a see pee en (CPN) from the see em aitch tee (CMHT)' is essentially gobbledegook. Whether it's what we're writing down or what is meant by 'art therapy', we shouldn't be afraid to explain and to use plain English (e.g. I'm here to 'help you leave hospital' not 'to facilitate your discharge').

Hospitals are designed around routines. By definition hovering on the edge of anarchy they have to have rules, defining how a group of individuals (some carers, some patients, some in between) live and work together. The numerous guidelines and policies (many Trusts even have a policy on policies) mean that checking belongings, handing out medication, vacuuming floors and using checklists (especially reinforced by CPA and risk management) can dominate ward activity. They are, however, vital to running an acute ward, which can be seen as a kind of psychosocial operating theatre, but unfortunately the drilling and the cutting too often overwhelm the music and the therapy. How do we humanely routinise? How do we empathise, sympathise and organise rather than, say, hypnotise or even terrorise?

Acute wards certainly carry out 'unenviable tasks', and this shouldn't be hidden, especially from carers, managers and visitors. Such tasks are part of the stigma problem, create differing memories, demand explanation and require routines. Wards can be noisy when people want to sleep. Getting people to eat and drink can be tiresome, boring even, and unrewarding. Smells, incontinence and washing people are undignified. People from an enormous range of ages, cultures, classes and expectations are mixed together. And of course their musical appreciation differs as does their knowledge, insight and level of illness. Such needs require the best qualified and most experienced staff, not those left over by the allures of sexy new teams and pleasantly limited social interactions, somewhere in 'the community'.

What are the lessons to be learned?

There is never a comprehensive answer to all the issues brought up, but if we always keep in mind the sense of perplexity and isolation of each individual patient, and ban entirely terms such as 'manipulative' or 'attention-seeking', then we should be able at least to improve the atmosphere on any acute ward. We need to grasp at the essential fact that there will by definition be misunderstandings between patient and carer, and our task is to reduce that gap in everything we do and say.

Patients should have their key nurse talk with them daily, about things they want to talk about, if they want to, the nurse perhaps keeping a diary of what's going on, or having a medium (a patient's favourite newspaper) to talk through things. Helping people relax, with simple relaxation techniques and cognitive strategies about what's going to be done today, should be part of that.

Tired phrases like 'cultural sensitivity' need real actioning. Confused, young African-Caribbean men often respond well to older, pragmatic, African-Caribbean women (are these mother figures even?). Paranoid/depressive white middle-aged males need someone of their age and education to talk to and trust. Vulnerable women need empathetic sisters, and trained interpreters should be available at a much easier level.

Every patient needs their personal space and should have their own bedroom. One-to-one nursing is known to be a dilemma, and the way nurses dress, smell, look and talk to people should be carefully monitored.

Ward rounds, with 'people who couldn't possibly help me' are inevitable, but can be made better. The nurse and patient should talk through the core issues, as should the ward doctor, before the round, so that it can be used simply as a practical organising event. An advocate/carer/relative should routinely be present.

Staff attitudes have to be made more positive and interactive. Senior staff, especially doctors, need to model their approaches, and agency/bank staff should be closely reviewed, before and after their sessions. Patient and carer feedback, looking for both complaints and compliments, on a routine basis, must be built in to the admission and discharge process.

The environment, in terms of what the ward looks like, the furnishings, the paint colours, and the food, is as important as the quality of the auto-steriliser in an operating theatre or the soundproofing and equipping of a lecture theatre. If difficulties and untoward behaviours occur, we should look at where and why these are happening. Medication queues always look depressing, so why do we have them? And readily available hot and cold drinks, and snacks (healthy of course) are not difficult to arrange.

Therapy workers should be multi-skilled, able to do art, music and relaxation work, as well as organise a quiz, run a scrabble or table-tennis tournament, assess people's self-care or social skills, and enliven their lives generally.

In conclusion acute wards are difficult places to run and be on. They should be people-focused rather than paper-focused, with one-to-one interactions at the heart of the process. Staff working there should be given additional pay, with encouragement to acquire additional skills (e.g. cognitive approaches, relaxation training, exercise workouts), and they should ensure that their methods of communication skills are honest and unambiguous at all times.

Mark Hardcastle (Mental Health Nurse)

'No management problems, rather aloof and dismissive in communication, spent most of the morning in bed. Not motivated to take part in activities.' So begins a shift handover describing a patient like Nigel at any number of acute psychiatric hospitals. Nigel describes many of the issues that have become legion in the various reports that have singled out in-patient hospitals as 'verging on the un-therapeutic' (SCMH 1998). Nigel's experiences are authentic and painful and do not make for easy reading if your chosen profession is a psychiatric nurse. Yet such narratives are not uncommon and often form the basis for the sort of written complaint that every ward manager must have read.

What's to be done? The things that seem to create and maintain such poor experiences shouldn't be difficult to solve. Many of Nigel's experiences appear to be due to the attitude of staff who he feels have interpreted him in a way that was unhelpful. Unfortunately, obvious and straightforward answers such as training and disciplinary procedures are not sufficient to bring miscreant staff into line. The solutions to better in-patient care experiences lie with people, their relationships, buildings, environments and the systems, which, together, create the cultures and associated values that transform experiences. Achieving such a transformation is a complex non-linear process requiring investment of a wide range of resources and skills as well as the support and motivation from all levels of an organisation. Not easy!

People

Nurses make up the bulwark of in-patient personnel. They staff the wards 24 hours a day, 52 weeks of the year. Without nurses the wards would close. Most are committed, skilled and compassionate, many are not. Nurses are engaged in work that ranges from care to custody and everything in between. They are the ones you see first thing in the morning and last thing at night. They are the ones that sometimes don't say hello and fail to show an interest in you that makes you feel like nothing and worse. Yet they are also the ones that care enough to sit, talk and connect with you about your deepest fears.

Compared to other nurses, in-patient nursing staff are the worst paid and receive the least professional investment. They work the most unsocial hours and serve in positions that are staging posts before a job in the community. It is one-way traffic – community staff very rarely leave their jobs to be in-patient nurses. These factors have a significant effect on self-esteem and it can lead to a closed institutional behaviour that is both protective and defensive. Power, control, subordination and rule-bound behaviour are the cultural orders of the day in such environments.

Nigel highlights many examples of poor care that had a direct effect on his mental state. 'Staff rarely took time to find out. Not taking the time often fuelled what I was thinking, "I'm not worth finding out about".' His depression was such that communication was difficult; his appraisal of situations prone to depressive distortions and his subsequent behaviour reflected his assumptions and negative thinking. Staff also held assumptions and made appraisals about Nigel that also reflected in their behaviour towards him. One member of staff called him a 'lazy c**t'. Goffman (1968) describes how staff deal with the low status of their job caring for the mentally ill by dehumanising people in order to stress the differences between them and their charges in an attempt to avoid stigma by association.

There were staff that would make time to speak to Nigel. The account of a senior registrar who would drop by each day seems to suggest a collaborative and healthy adult relationship. The simple act of the doctor remembering facts that had been mentioned in conversation the day before appears to have had a remarkable effect on Nigel, 'Hey! This bloke is listening to me'. These simple yet validating experiences contrast readily with other inter-actions when Nigel would report feeling distressed at impersonal ward rounds, refused nutrition and being unbelieved.

There are no occupational health hazards such as molten metal, volatile chemicals or dangerous machinery in an acute mental health in-patient ward. A different occupational health hazard does exist that takes a more emotional toll. In order to offer the type of care and attention that Nigel wants and deserves, staff need to give so much of themselves personally that they make themselves emotionally vulnerable. Such stress is well documented (Hannigan *et al.* 2000), however, beyond organisations providing limited employee assistance and occupational health facilities, little else is done.

Buildings

Whilst most in-patient care has moved from the old county asylums of yesteryear, the newer venues built in the 1980s and 90s arguably have been a let down. The design for these units was often based on design notes for hospital buildings that were intended for medical and surgical use rather than the needs of someone with acute mental health needs. Complete with features such as six-bedded bays, sluice rooms, poor sight lines, ligature points, communal toilets and bathrooms, these buildings were not appropriate.

On admission Nigel was given a side room that was sparse and lacking in privacy. Living in such conditions cannot engender feelings of being valued. Nigel spent large periods of time in his room during which time he frequently thought of ways of killing himself, although he did not actually want to die. The Department of Health (DoH 2002a) has identified the prevention of suicide as an important goal. This has led organisations to identify and remove potential ligature points in all its hospitals. Much effort has gone into this activity and has resulted in safer environments through, for example, the adaptation of collapsible curtain rails. Newer, purpose-built hospitals that are well designed and pay attention to natural light, space and ergonomics are gradually replacing the inadequate hospital facilities that are often less than twenty years old. These newer hospitals have far more patient and carer involvement in their commissioning and it should be no surprise that as a consequence attention has been paid to comfort, dignity and safety. Unlike Nigel's 'side room' the newer facilities are en suite, complete with toilet and shower, thus putting an end to degrading, shared and often dirty facilities at a stroke.

New facilities should result in greater patient satisfaction, better mental health, improved recruitment and retention, and a corresponding increase in staff morale. These benefits should not be assumed to take place purely on the basis of a move into a brand new hospital. It is what goes on inside the hospital that ultimately matters and that will depend on staff, their practices and the ward culture. The fillip of a building fit for purpose should, however, make the achievement of better practice expressed through shared values a little easier.

Systems and cultures

Nigel describes a catalogue of rituals that for the most part are not questioned by staff who engage in activities that serve to humiliate, dis-empower and anger people who use services.

- Medication routines
- Ward rounds
- Observation
- Admission practices
- Cleaning
- Early morning calls
- Mental state examinations
- Petty restrictions.

Very little activity in a psychiatric hospital setting is based on evidence in the strictest sense of the word, be it randomised control trials or even professional consensus of what constitutes good in-patient care. Moreover custom and practice dominate in a culture which is task-centred at best and at its worst serves the demands of convenience made by professionals at the expense of patient need and dignity.

The importance of creating therapeutic cultures that truly are compassionate, needs-led and empowering cannot be overestimated. Nigel observed that each member of staff held their own ideology and related to him in dramatically contrasting ways. Disparity of attitudes of this kind between closely knit staff is confusing and distressing for patients who would expect (not unreasonably) that teamwork and consistency would be apparent during their admission. Teamwork and the cultural norms and values such as the recovery values defined by the Chief Nursing Officer's Review of Mental Health Nursing (DoH 2006) characterise the systems and practices on a ward and are a corollary of strong leadership.

Boredom features highly in the list of complaints by patients about their stay in hospital. Boredom is not an emotion without consequence for psychiatric patients. Boredom creates the medium for depressive ruminations, thoughts of suicide and aggression. Creating opportunities to develop cultures of therapy and activity that can assist in the achievement of mastery, pleasure and diversion are worthy endeavours. Yet frequently therapy and activity opportunities are rare in hospitals. This is partly due to the self-serving routines and rituals that mitigate against staff having time to run groups, make music, garden or even talk. It is also indicative of cultural norms that do not place value on such important pursuits. Where activity and therapy does exist it is often uniformly offered (Short *et al.* 2004) in a routine programme without due regard to individual needs. It is often left to the non-ward staff to provide outlets of therapy that are not medical. Nigel recounts his experiences of art therapy, which held some potential for him to explore his issues with a member of staff, but the opportunity was lost.

Questions and issues for discussion

1 Nigel highlights many abbreviations, routines and structures that impacted upon him during his time in hospital. In your view, what routines in your place of work are patient-centred? Are any unquestioned rituals or practices regularly highlighted as being unhelpful? Can things be done better?
2 What are the values and beliefs that inform the care and treatment of your ward? Can they be observed as evidence?
3 If an assessment of ligature risk is carried out, is emphasis given to the ward culture, activity and therapeutic practice as well as environmental issues and observation policy?

Exercise

During a ward round/review or a shift handover list the words used to describe the personal characteristics of patients. What is the frequency of pejorative labels such as 'manipulative' or 'lazy' compared to positive phrases such as 'resilient' or 'motivated'? What do you think is the impact of describing patients using such language?

Chapter 5

Bored on the ward

Janey Antoniou

There are two sorts of 'boring' on the ward. One is caused by having lots of hours to fill and not having the things one usually has to fill them up with because one is not at home. The other is a side effect, or a series of side effects from the medication(s). It is possible to be bored on the ward even when there are activities planned every hour, and not to be bored when doing nothing. The trouble with boredom is it makes slow hours go even more slowly.

Years ago, sometime after my first few admissions, I read a book called *I never promised you a rose garden* by Hannah Green which described the boredom of the psychiatric ward in terms of the physical characteristics of the building:

> . . . The number of cracks on the cold corridor floor was nineteen, the wide way, and twenty-three the long way (counting the seam). When Deborah was in the world of the ward, she walked with the moving frieze up and down the corridor . . . into and round the day room, out to the nursing station, past the front bathroom, past the banks of seclusion rooms, past the dormitories (where wandering was not allowed) . . . When she was not real enough to walk, she lay on her bed. The ceiling was nineteen holes by nineteen holes in its soundproofing squares. (Excerpted from *I never promised you a rose garden* by Joanne Greenberg. Copyright © 1964 by Hannah Green; Copyright Renewed © 1992 by Joanne Greenberg. Used by permission of the Wallace Literary Agency, Inc. as agents for the author, and Henry Holt and Company, LLC, publishers.)

And by what was happening:

> Then there was to wait for the lunch trays. Then there was to wait for the end of lunch. Then there was to wait for change of shift. Then there was to wait for supper. Then there was to wait for the sedative line. Then there was to wait for bed. (Excerpted from *I never promised you a rose garden* by Joanne Greenberg. Copyright © 1964 by Hannah Green; Copyright

Both of these passages really strike a chord about how time goes by in the ward and what there is to do in the absence of specifically planning for it.

Although I've never counted the cracks in the floor (I have always been aware I would be copying someone else), I have counted new leaves coming out on the tree outside the window, gossiped about the staff, timed people in the lavatory and regarded other patients' symptoms as a floor show. I've also measured the day by drugs and tea. I would play Scrabble games knowing they would take between an hour and ninety minutes to finish; play the whole of Mozart's *The Magic Flute* on my Walkman which takes about three hours. Probably the most extreme thing I did was to have my husband bring all his washed shirts into the ward (about fifteen) so I could iron them. In fact I would do anything that would make it so I did not have to watch the minute hand of the clock crawl. And for a while I even had a hallucination of the clock making faces at me and laughing because of the time it took for the minutes go by.

For me there was a feeling of panic at the hours stretching away in front of me, and the frustration of not having any way to defeat it. Of course I've been bored at home but have been able to find something to do – my present way of passing time is to play spider solitaire on the computer or read the newspaper from front to back.

It can be difficult to provide occupational therapy when the patients on the ward are at various stages of being ill or getting well, and all are interested in different things. There are usually problems finding the space to do things too, especially if some people have to stay on the ward. At different times in past admissions I've found cooking, pottery, art, relaxation, salsa dancing, yoga and various quiz groups an interesting way of passing the time. I've taken part in knockout scrabble tournaments, read various newspapers every day and gone for group walks to feed the local ducks. However, since a friend brought me some watercolour pencils and a drawing pad, I have spent most of my time sitting on my bed (with a Walkman playing) and drawing. In the past I have also found that the easy-read novels (Agatha Christie, Jilly Cooper, Dick Frances, David Eddings, etc.) and craft materials I found on the ward were really useful just to pass the time. I've drawn the line at some things, such as table tennis, women's groups and puzzle books, but there are other people who do like these things.

Perhaps the greatest addition to my local psychiatric unit over the last few years has been the forming of a garden where we can go and sit, or play rounders. It is enclosed so patients on higher levels of observation can go down with a nurse. In this area we could have peace and quiet away from the public and the ward and in the fresh air.

The other sort of boredom in the ward is caused by the side effects of various medications. It can be exceptionally annoying to want to read the newspaper or play Scrabble and not to be able to do so because either my legs don't want to sit still or there is what feels like thick fog or cotton wool in my head. Some medications give a nasty kind of feeling that precludes settling down to anything. When I was on the depot version of haloperidol I found that if I was walking around I would want to lie down and if I was lying down my legs would want to walk around. I could never get my body comfortable and was intensively aware of it all the time. I couldn't even start thinking of things to make the time more interesting. It became agony and followed me out to the community.

Perhaps my worst experience of boredom was caused on two different occasions by two other drugs, lithium and chlorpromazine. They interfered with my mood so there were no ups and downs in my life, everything was grey and I wasn't actually interested in anything. The hours stretched away from me and I could not conceive of ever being interested by anything again until I died. It was very frightening, because having no hope of things ever changing for the better was a part of the experience. I think the medical people call it dysphoria.

During my time on chlorpromazine I most vividly remember going on an outing to Kew Gardens from the ward. When I got there I was not sure how to pass the time so I went into a small museum they have there and read all the captions for the exhibits because that was a tangible thing to do, in a way that walking around and enjoying the plants was not. I remember nothing of what I read but I passed the time (as I saw it then) constructively. There was also an occasion when I was reading an Anita Brookner novel and thinking to myself 'how did the heroine manage to pass all that time and can I do that?' I was thinking about looking for diversions all the time but did not have the interest or energy to actually find them. This state also followed me out into the community and affected those around me. I was not interested in anything and could not share other people's pleasure in activities.

Obviously, in the ward, people deal with physical and chemical boredom in different ways. The most common way in the ward is to try and stay asleep or doze through the days. It is great when three or four hours have passed by between the closing and opening of an eye. The downside of this is the possibility of not sleeping during the night-time when there is even less to do, the staff won't have a conversation (policy) or allow the making of a cup of tea (more policy). Conversation can also cause time to pass, either with visitors I like or from making friends with my fellow patients. It is a well-known fact that all the best conversations in a psychiatric ward always take place in the smoking room!

In the end though, hospital is going to have its moments of boredom. But I've found they happen less often now that I understand what is happening and can guard against it with watercolour pencils, a Harry Potter book and medication that doesn't flatten out all my experience!

Commentaries

Len Bowers (Mental Health Nurse)

I'm a psychiatric nurse researcher in acute in-patient psychiatry, and Janey's account of boredom rang lots of bells for me – both from my research and from my clinical nursing experience. This doesn't surprise me. I have met Janey at several conferences where she has spoken most eloquently about acute in-patient care from the patient's point of view. I've been impressed by what she has had to say before – and learnt from it.

Most of my research is in the area of conflict and containment. By conflict, I mean those patient behaviours that put them and others at risk, and by containment I mean those things the staff do to keep patients and others safe. Part of what my research has indicated so far is that the existence of 'structure' on the wards is important in the maintenance of a safe, calm environment. Structure is made up out of the rules for patient conduct while they are on the ward through the ward routine. It is that latter part that we are referring to when we talk about ward activities for patients. When I interviewed over a hundred nurses (Bowers 2002), they told me that the ward structure had several functions and therapeutic benefits in its own right. Because it promoted stability and reduced friction, it meant that patients were able to engage in and attend to getting better. The structure also provided scope for rehabilitation – it provided a framework of goals for patients, for example to attend a group, that were stepping-stones towards discharge. That same framework allowed nurses to assess whether patients were ready for discharge, and were able to live within the wider social structure outside the hospital. The nurses also spoke about the structure providing predictability and a sense of purpose, both of which had a direct therapeutic benefit for patients.

Other research I have conducted into absconding by patients has shown that boredom is a motivator to leave the ward without permission (Bowers *et al.* 1999). One of the absconding patients we interviewed told us that there was nothing to do on the ward except watching TV and going to sleep. Coupled with lack of access to freedom, fresh air, and the other irritations of living on an acute ward, these things gave patients reason to vacate the premises. Janey has, in many ways, been lucky. She describes a huge range of activities that have been available to her as an in-patient, and has had access to an enclosed garden. Unfortunately this is not the case on many wards. Many wards do not have such garden access, do not have the equipment for all these (and other activities), or do not have enough rooms for those activities to take place. Activities require money and investment, not just staff willingness and action. Wards have to be adequately resourced with the right environment and equipment. That equipment has to be regularly and quickly replaced as it breaks, gets lost, etc. Sometimes staff get blamed for poor-quality care in this respect, when in fact resources are at the root of the issue (Brennan *et al.* 2006).

The need for structure on acute wards can challenge current boundaries between staff groups, particularly nurses and occupational therapists. Recognition of the importance of ward activities has led to occupational therapists spending more time on the wards themselves, providing those activities. However, in many places nurses are also involved in the provision of ward-based activities, leading to some overlap – in some places this perhaps creates tensions, in others to role blurring and a huge strengthening of the ward team as a whole through the integration of what occupational therapists have to offer (Simpson *et al.* 2005).

All of this begs the questions of what activities are appropriate and helpful and for which patients. Patients on acute wards often are, by definition, acutely unwell. They can be psychotic, undergoing hallucinations, irritable, unable to concentrate, overactive, underactive, confused, cognitively disorganised, etc. The occupational therapists we have interviewed have remarked how difficult it is to engage such patients in activities and that as soon as patients start to get better and are able to engage in activities properly, they are discharged (Simpson *et al.* 2005). From time to time I still work on acute wards, and have observed: a drumming group come in to engage patients in making music, without getting any response or participation at all; and games of various sorts being started with only transient, minimal and passing participation from patients. On the other hand I can recall one patient of African origin who, despite being acutely psychotic, managed to engage me in detailed political debate about colonialism, whilst trouncing me at draughts – a feat he managed repeatedly over the course of a week, in between retreating to his bed to hallucinate and ruminate on his psychotic ideas.

There have also been many patients whom I have been unable to persuade to do anything, despite repeated attempts. This may have been because they have been too ill, or it may have been because the right activities were not on offer. It could have been because they were suffering some of the medication side effects Janey mentions, or the other, most common one that she did not: sedation. Or it could have been because they were long-standing sufferers from negative symptoms, apathy, withdrawal, etc. However, this raises the issue about how much persuasion can be used to get patients to engage in activities that are thought to be therapeutic. For example, patients can be repeatedly asked and told the benefits of participation, they may even be told that it is part of their treatment, or that it is required of them to participate. I have two answers to the problem of non-participation. First, I think the benefits can be explained to patients, and they may be told that they are expected to join in, but that they should not be harried into participation. Second, the range of available activities needs to be large, so that patients are drawn into activities out of their own desires. Lastly this is where activities blur into normal nursing care, where patients can be drawn into doing something with a nurse, e.g. being asked to help the nurse with some clearing up, or being asked to carry a cup of tea to another patient. These are the constant small ways that nurses use to induce activity and human contact between patients.

And what is the purpose of ward-based activities? Are they just to pass the time and reduce boredom, as Janey implies, or are they for that purpose and to provide the structure I have described above? Or should they be therapeutic in their own right. Should some of those group activities be specifically about preparing for discharge, or about medications and the promotion of compliance, or about learning from group process, in short should they be educational, psychotherapeutic, cognitive behavioural and the like (Bowers *et al.* 2005, McCann and Bowers 2005)? There is real scope in acute in-patient psychiatry to deliver a more therapeutic programme, one that consists of more than waiting for drugs to take effect or the illness to remit. However, developing that programme will need new ideas, and new research evaluations to discover what works. I'm looking forward to seeing acute care develop in this way over the next decade.

Rachel Christian-Edwards (Occupational Therapist)

There is a sadness to reading this personal account of boredom not just for its author but also because I recognise that I have heard of similar experiences many times in my career. It is something, however, that has not gone unnoticed judging by the number of significant and influential publications that have highlighted the need for acute in-patient mental health services to address the issue of boredom and therapeutic engagement of service users, DoH (2002b), Sainsbury Centre for Mental Health (1998) and Mind (2000). All clearly identify that wards need to do far more than provide *custodial care*; engagement in therapeutic activities including leisure and diversional activities should be an integral part of all service users' experience of an in-patient setting.

One could very easily ask why that is so difficult to fix. Nurses, doctors, occupational therapists, clinical psychologists and other professionals are all able to contribute to the engagement of service users in an in-patient setting. Unfortunately it never seems to be that simple. Therefore it is important to recognise all the contributing factors.

Environmental issues identified by the Royal College of Psychiatrists (1998) have been addressed in the newer units, with the move towards single en suite rooms providing some personal space for service users. However, therapeutic space on the ward is also essential if therapeutic work is to have a chance of being established. The older in-patient units tend to have only lounges as communal spaces. These rooms are not the right setting for group work. This is the patients' space and it is difficult to go in, turn off the television and say 'it's now group time' – patients will vote with their feet. Communal meeting and social groups can work in this space but need to be part of the routine of the ward if they are to be readily accepted.

From an occupational therapist's perspective an individual away from their home environment will be affected by their lack of opportunity to perform occupational tasks or the activities that would be part of their normal day. Their motivation for occupational performance may also be impaired and this is clearly demonstrated through the work of Kielhofner *et al.* (2002). All of us in our daily lives have routine, for example the familiar pattern of getting up, having breakfast, going off to drive or catch the bus to college or work. These tasks all require skills we not only take for granted but are motivated to do. Being on a ward you are away from your familiar routines and have to conform to the ward structure and routine, as Janey clearly illustrates. This can be disempowering and contribute to institutionalisation. The example Janey gives of getting her husband to bring in shirts for ironing could be viewed as an example of her need to have familiar tasks which she can achieve and gain some satisfaction from doing. This activity would be part of her usual routine at home. Establishing routines and engaging in tasks that the service user has choice in is an important part of maintaining a sense of self. An occupational therapy programme or the work of activities staff can contribute to this although resource limitation always means that you cannot suit everyone.

There is no one profession that provides all the therapeutic input to acute wards, but occupational therapy has provided therapeutic engagement through activity and psycho-educational work for some considerable time. As occupational therapists working in acute environments, we have to be very aware that the activities and interventions we provide have meaning and relevance to the patient. Duffy and Nolan (2005) highlight the valuable role that occupational therapists have in in-patient acute care. Through client-centred practice they are able to empower service users and develop self-esteem through the three core areas of occupation: self-care, productivity and leisure. Dutton (2004) also highlights the role occupational therapists can play in the ongoing process of engaging through partnership with service users. There is a view that occupational therapists and nurses can be in conflict over this role; however, where occupational therapists are part of the ward team there is an opportunity for greater collaborative working.

All group and individual work provided by the occupational therapists needs to be accessible Parkinson (1999). This may require being creative in the way and place that treatment is provided. For patients on a high level of observation, occupational therapy provision may need to be on the ward. Alternatively the patient may need a staff escort to enable them to attend occupational therapy off the ward. The security needs of the patient should not prohibit engagement in occupational therapy. The reality is that staffing levels and the need to respond to the immediate ward situation often result in the escorting of patients being a lower priority. This is frustrating for service users and staff alike. For the service user it can affect their motivation to engage, which may already be limited. Teams need to look creatively at staffing if they are to enable the more well patients to be engaged as part of their treatment plans and recovery.

The activities provided by the occupational therapy service need to reflect the varied and changing interests of the community. Mee and Sumsion (2001) found that having a choice of activity and how long to engage in it played an important role in generating motivation and a sense of purpose. One example of a valued activity is access to computers. For many service users computers provide a valuable link to the outside world – giving them the ability to check emails and keep in touch with family and friends, as well as looking up the myriad interests that are out there on the Web.

Creative activities also still have a place, a view confirmed by Perrin (2001). However, many occupational therapists wish to move away from their creative past. For many patients, concentration, motivation and the ability to make decisions are difficult in the early phase of their admission, and creative and leisure activities can have an important place both in structuring time and contributing to recovery.

There is no one answer to boredom on in-patient wards but central to relieving it is staff getting to know their service users as individuals, encouraging participation and promoting motivation for therapeutic engagement.

Questions and issues for discussion

1   In your experience, what do you think are the effects of boredom in the in-patient environment? What are the benefits of addressing this issue?
2   How well do activities and therapies available to you meet individual needs?
3   What are the possibilities for closer joint working between nurses and occupational therapists? Should professions other than nurses work across shift patterns including at weekends?

Exercise

Consider setting up a daily planning meeting each morning to discuss the day ahead.

Chapter 6

Feeling out of control

Kevin Norwood

My name is Kevin Norwood. I was first diagnosed with manic depression many years ago at the age of 17 when I was admitted into hospital in a very manic state. Previous to my admission I was doing some very strange things which I did not realise were strange at all. I will briefly explain what led to my first admission. One day I was fishing on a river in Hertfordshire with a younger friend. It was getting dark towards the end of the day and instead of packing my fishing tackle away I jumped into the river for a swim. Afterwards I walked into a nearby pub without my trousers on and asked if I could use the phone to call home. When eventually my dad, brother and uncle arrived at the pub to take me home the landlord of the pub said to my brother, 'I think your brother is slightly mad'. We went back to the river bank to collect my fishing tackle, then headed for home.

When we arrived home I could not sleep and went out on the balcony of my flat and started to cut out the mortar between the brickwork with a hammer and plunging chisel. The only way to stop me from what I was doing and get me off the balcony back into the flat was for my mum to say that it was tea break so I could come in. After this I managed to go to sleep for a couple of hours; however, I woke up early the next morning and left the flat without my parents knowing. I went for a run and a walk to the local ponds in my pyjamas.

When I returned home there was a doctor and social worker waiting to take me to hospital. On the way there we passed a new roundabout being constructed and there were men using theodolites. I thought they were filming me with TV cameras.

My admission into an old Victorian asylum was very frightening because I did not understand why I had to be there. I tried to run away from the ward but was restrained by two nurses and brought back. I was in a very manic state for quite some time, constantly singing and running about the ward. I found it hard to understand when the nurses kept telling me to keep still and be quiet.

I was put on lithium and Largactil, and over a period of time my mood started to come down and the Largactil made me very slow and tired. With

Largactil you should not be exposed to sunlight because it irritates the skin badly. I found this out for myself when I went out in the open air one day when it was sunny.

During the time when I was very high, one particular nurse used to take me off the ward for walks in the grounds. He was very understanding towards my condition. There were other nurses on different shifts who were not so understanding and I remember being restrained and injected, which was very frightening. To be a psychiatric nurse you have to have a lot of patience and love; with some nurses I did not experience that.

Over a period of about four months my mood changed completely and I went into a deep depression. I wondered how being kept in such a large hospital would get me well and help me face the real world again. I felt that nobody understood how I felt and I thought the depression would never end. My consultant at the time asked me to consider having electro-convulsive therapy (ECT). He told me it was a good treatment in helping lift depression. I was scared about this treatment because you have to be put under a general anaesthetic which frightens me. My mum helped me and told me that if it could help me out of such a deep depression it was worth a try. So I went ahead with the treatment. It only took one ECT to really lift my mood. After a lot of love from my mother and encouragement I gained my confidence and started back at technical college to carry out my apprenticeship in bricklaying.

On another occasion I was admitted to a new acute psychiatric unit. To me, that unit was like a pressure cooker because there are not enough green spaces for patients to walk in, which is helpful when you are in a high state and are allowed to release energy. I found this a very hard environment to be in. When I was manic I remember being kept in a locked part of the unit. I felt like a caged animal. The new ward was a small compact unit and because of this it was hard for patients to get on with each other because of their different types of psychiatric illnesses. For example, people who are very high can feed off each other's illnesses and make them even higher, and a depressed person having to be around someone who is very high can be very distressing. On my last admission into hospital back in 2001, I was in a severe depressed state and I found the new unit's environment very depressing with its narrow corridors, low ceilings and drab lifeless walls which had no pictures on them. I was on the other side of my illness and found it hard to cope with patients who were high or in another psychiatric state.

The old hospital had such wide open spacious grounds with lovely quiet spots where a person in a depressed state could be taken out for a walk and be listened to and encouraged by a nurse in helping them get well. I found this more so in the old asylum than in the new unit.

When I look back at my previous admissions into hospital I have had some very caring nurses helping me. On occasion, however, one particular nurse had no time for my high state and I can remember being restrained and injected by him and two other nurses. His attitude was very military-like, with no compassion or understanding.

For myself and I believe others, two areas of great importance for the road to recovery are group psychotherapy and occupational therapy. Patients can help each other in groups by expressing their feelings through art, pottery and other crafts. This is an important part in helping patients focus their minds on doing something which can help lift depression. This has been my own experience of admissions into hospital.

Commentaries

Maria Cañete and Arturo Ezquerro (Group Analysts)

Kevin provides an honest personal account of his in-patient admissions over a period of his illness. The clear and vivid memories that he keeps of his first admission as a seventeen-year-old adolescent are particularly striking. A breakdown at a young age can leave a life-long impression. Kevin's story is a good example of a need for early intervention psychosis teams.

Manic and depressive states are two sides of the same coin. We talk of being high or being low in comparison to being even with others. The latter is a level of ordinary relationships where sharing and understanding can develop more easily. Kevin writes about his manic state: 'I was doing some very strange things which I did not realise were strange at all'. His manic symptoms became a form of communication which could not be shared or understood by other people, including his family.

Following his first admission, it seems to us that Kevin's need for communication and understanding was often unmet. In this context, he felt under increasing pressure to express his symptoms. We can imagine that he did not have sufficient and adequate therapeutic opportunities to feel understood and to understand himself, in order to transform his symptoms into a socially acceptable language. Instead, he was often restrained and sedated by injections.

Symptoms can also be an expression of distress. People vary widely in the extent to which they can cope with distress. Two things are crucial: the magnitude of the distress and our own confidence in our ability to cope with it. Sharing our distress helps us to keep engaged with others and not to retreat into ourselves. Following months of trying to communicate through manic states, Kevin retreated into deep depression.

For such a young person on a psychiatric ward a long admission on an adult psychiatric ward is far too long. The long stay in a sub-optimal therapeutic environment (apart from the open spacious grounds) also appeared to be depressing in its own right. At least, Kevin's mother was involved in some of the important decision making about his treatment, which seemed to be more reassuring for him than the medical opinion itself. We believe that this maternal understanding became an important factor in his recovery.

Kevin also refers to the support he received from his mother to make another important decision, when he returned home: 'After a lot of love from my mother and encouragement I gained my confidence and started back at technical college to carry out my apprenticeship in bricklaying'.

In spite of the disturbing nature of his first psychotic breakdown, Kevin retained (as Bion [1957] put it) a non-psychotic part of himself that helped him to survive. For example: he telephoned home from the pub and, when outside on the balcony, he was able to respond to his mother's invitation to come into the flat.

Therapeutic interventions can take many forms that can be beneficial in their own right. Kevin positively recalls that an understanding nurse took him for walks in the grounds of the old hospital outside the ward. He perceived this nurse and others as caring and helpful, which was a therapeutic experience for him.

The NHS executive's review of psychotherapy services in England gives a framework for psychological therapies, which includes three types of provision (NHS Executive 1996). The work done by some of Kevin's nurses could be included today as 'type A' psychotherapy: psychological treatment as an integral component of mental health care. It might be too much wishful thinking to believe that during Kevin's earliest admissions he was receiving a well co-ordinated care plan. In fact, he did not seem to have explained to him the side effects of Largactil.

During subsequent admissions there is a repetition of communication problems through manic symptoms. This leads again to physical restraint and sedative injections by nurses whom Kevin perceived as 'military-like, with no compassion or understanding'.

As the old hospital closed, he was admitted into a new acute unit. This new environment was, in his own words: 'very depressing with its narrow corridors, low ceilings and drab lifeless walls which had no pictures on them'. Sometimes he felt like a 'caged animal'. Kevin has a point. Modern psychiatric units can be as depressing as the psychiatric institutions of the nineteenth century if not more so.

Kevin also refers to the negative influence of other patients when there is no therapeutic context: 'For example, people who are very high can feed off each other's illnesses and make them even higher, and a depressed person having to be around someone who is very high can be very distressing'. However, he appreciates the value of group psychotherapy and occupational therapy: 'Patients can help each other in groups by expressing their feelings . . .' We gather that it was important for him to work therapeutically with fellow patients who know what it is like.

We feel curious about what happened in between admissions in terms of follow-up or psychotherapy for him. Therapeutic insights can help to prevent or delay relapses as well as to maximise the capacity to live well.

Richard Morriss (Psychiatrist)

Kevin's case illustrates many pertinent points about the in-patient care of people with bipolar 1 disorder (manic depression). It is a complex disorder characterised by episodes of mania and depression that can even occur at the same time in the form of a mixed affective episode. The subjective experience and mental health care of each of these different mood states is quite different. Like many people who first experience mania, Kevin did not understand what was happening to him or even appreciate he was ill.

Mania is a complex disorder and experiencing mania is a significant barrier to the patient's understanding of what is happening to them. For example, some aspects of the condition are inherently enjoyable and rewarding while other aspects are distressing and frightening.

There is therefore a need for a supportive and psycho-educational approach to the in-patient care of a person with mania. The psycho-educational element of care should start from the beginning and gains momentum as the patient recovers and is more able to attend and make sense of what has happened. There is a lot to do if we expect the patient to have sufficient insight into their condition which will allow them to be able to take a full part in discharge planning before they leave the ward. Unless the patient does develop such insight and take responsibility for their care, then aftercare may break down quickly leading to readmission.

Kevin raises the issue of needing to make sense of what has happened to him. He gained benefit through expressing himself in art and pottery, and by sharing and listening to the experiences of others. There is increasing evidence of the value of group psycho-education with other patients and families (Colom *et al.* 2003, Miklowitz *et al.* 2003). The process of psycho-education in a patient with acute mania or depression has to be low key, given frequently and in small chunks. There is evidence that intense psychotherapy can be associated with increased relapse if given when the patient is not stable (Scott *et al.* 2006).

Kevin's comparison between the in-patient unit and the old asylum is illuminating. While the space of the old asylum with its lovely quiet spots can be beneficial to contain the energy of mania and lift the spirits of depression, it also raises significant challenges in terms of monitoring risk. These secluded spots are difficult for nursing staff to observe. Suicidal acts and ideas can arise within hours or days in bipolar disorder, partly because acute bipolar episodes can take many forms and be unpredictable (Fagiolini *et al.* 2004).

The issue of medication for mania is clearly important but the amount required can be influenced by the ward atmosphere and environment. Patients with mania can mop up huge amounts of medication because they are over-stimulated by a hostile, disturbed or excessively busy ward environment; patients with depression respond more slowly in such an atmosphere. The presence of more than one disturbed patient with or without mania can contribute to the adverse ward environment.

Negative attitudes of staff may contribute to increased ward disturbance. A more positive, supportive approach can reduce the need for restraint and injected medication, foster a more co-operative relationship between the patient and mental health service, and substantially reduce the amount of medication given. In turn these will benefit the patient and service because of the lower risk of adverse physical health problems from high dose antipsychotic medication such as sudden death and reduced readmission.

A sometimes neglected feature of a supportive ward environment is the use of distracting pastimes and the chance to release energy that has built up. However, too much stimulation from activity can be counterproductive again increasing the severity of mania or the presence of dysphoric symptoms or irritability. Similar benefits from distraction and a supportive ward environment are reported for people with severe depression where it is particularly important to activate patients by getting them out of bed first thing in the morning. Patients with mania and depression stabilise more quickly and do not relapse so rapidly if they get into a predictable daily routine in terms of regularity of sleep onset and waking, meals and dispensing of medication on the ward (Frank *et al.* 2005).

Today there are options for fast control of the symptoms of mania that do not require injections, such as medication that dissolves easily in the mouth and other antipsychotics which can reduce symptoms of mania within hours and days. In randomised controlled trials the use of only one such medication reduces manic symptoms by 50 per cent in 50 per cent of patients. It is therefore helpful to use combinations of treatments (preferably only two drugs to reduce the risk of unanticipated adverse drug interactions). This may include benzodiazepines in the short term as well as lithium. Benzodiazepines are sedative rather than anti-manic, but the sedation can be reversed with drugs such as flumazenil. Some anti-psychotics, as well as valproate and lithium, have anti-depressant effects that may reduce the chances of a switch into depression. Switching from mania to depression and vice versa can contribute to long hospital in-patient admissions.

The propensity to switch from mania to depression and vice versa means that contact needs to be made during leave from the ward and in the week after discharge. A patient who seems to be recovering from mania may be sliding into depression and suicide risk while the patient who seems to be lifting out of depression may become manic within days. Often insight lags behind recovery from other symptoms of mania so unfortunately adverse incidents can occur if discharge occurs too soon after symptomatic recovery.

Questions and issues for discussion

1 To what extent does the mix of patients and their illnesses affect the experience of being an in-patient?
2 What does recovery mean to you? How important is medication?
3 To what extent are people with mental illness attempting to communicate something through their symptoms?

Exercise

Speak to colleagues who have worked in mental health services for over twenty-five years. How have their views and practices changed over this time? What has been for the better and what has suffered?

Chapter 7

Restraint: a necessary evil?

Clare Ockwell and Capital Members

While no one would claim that being restrained is a therapeutic experience for the person at the receiving end, it is often argued that restraint is only ever used where there is no alternative and therefore it is ultimately in someone's best interests. However, for many people the experience of being restrained is traumatic and leaves lasting psychological scars. This chapter tells in their own words the experiences of members of the CAPITAL Project, a service user-led training and research group. These collected experiences raise questions about whether restraint can ever be justified or whether the time has come to develop more humane ways of reacting to challenging situations.

Use of restraint on an acute ward affects not only the person being restrained but also those who witness it, provoking reactions of shock and fear.

When I was in hospital in 1999, there was a girl who was frequently restrained. What they did was hold her so she was bent double and moved her to another room. It took about four of them to hold her down in this position. She was potentially quite volatile but I never saw anything that prompted the nurses to act in the way they did.

. . . I certainly didn't get a debriefing . . . It wasn't very nice to witness. And it is a bit frightening because you think 'there but for the grace of God go I'. And I have actually been restrained myself.

Another witness described an 'absolutely abusive' incident involving an old woman with Alzheimer's disease.

She was sunbathing in her bikini in the garden and two female nurses were there gossiping among themselves. She wanted to go to the lavatory. She got up and attempted to walk across the ward where everyone was sitting. The two nurses woke up and realised she shouldn't do that because there were men present. She was a withered old woman and they physically restrained her. They didn't try and calm her down, they just shouted at her. Held her quite inappropriately too. Not with arms down and theirs around her, but by her arms at the back of her. I was very upset and complained about it. One of the nurses ... said that she was flaunting herself in front of the men, but she was seventy-nine.

Neither of these accounts shows any consideration for the reactions of other patients witnessing restraint, despite the fact that inevitably this experience will be at best unpleasant and at worst traumatising. However, being on the receiving end of this form of treatment has deeper more lasting effects.

The first time it happened I was in this hospital I'd got transferred to. I was really frightened. I went to leave my room and the bleepers went off and six nurses jumped on me ... If someone had sat down and talked to me and explained what was going to happen it would probably have been different. I'd rather know it [being restrained] was a possibility so I could explain to myself how it was going to make me feel.

It was years ago and I still remember it like yesterday. The first time was very traumatic ... I'd never been in a psychiatric hospital before, I refused medication and I was held down and injected by six staff. What I feel really strongly about is that no one gave me a choice ... They might have said to me you need medication, but no one said if you don't take the medication we will have to force you to have an injection. If someone had talked to me instead of leaving me on my own in a room, and explained what my choices were ... There would have been no need to hold me down and inject me which I interpreted as a physical assault ... added to the trauma that I'd already experienced in my home, being yanked out to an ambulance ... it was a very nasty experience.

I was a voluntary patient, but I was on a red dot which meant you were not supposed to leave the ward unless someone was with you and to be fair my intention was to try to run under the nearest bus, but I only just made it out into the grounds when I was rugby tackled from behind by a six foot something male nurse. At the time I accepted it, you do, you don't think you deserve humane treatment but it has haunted me ever since. He could have easily got in front of me and talked to me. I only weighed about seven stone at the time and I was already a victim of rape ... I re-live both experiences to this day.

These last accounts raise the issue of re-traumatisation. For someone who has in the past been a victim of violence or abuse the experience of being restrained is likely to re-enforce feelings of worthlessness and violation.

At the time I accepted it. When you are that low you don't think you deserve to be treated like a human being.

I felt violated.

In these days when we talk about service users and professionals working in partnership the use of restraint also throws up issues about the power imbalance between us.

People think seclusion is all about being on your own but to me it's not ... It's about power ... What if someone did something more frightening to me in this room? I had a mattress and nothing else and the power they had was that they could do this to me.

In none of these accounts is there a sense that restraint was the only course of action available to nursing staff. In each case the key problem appears to be lack of communication when people are feeling at their most vulnerable and desperate for compassionate human contact.

No one spoke to me about what was happening to me ... I wanted someone to talk to me.

If they explained what they were doing I wouldn't have wanted to escape. I think they should have spoken to me in a better way and explained rather than injecting me like they did.

If someone had of sat down and talked to me and explained what was going to happen it would probably have been different ... On the odd occasion they've let me get to the point where I've been restrained and they've told me later that was what they were going to do. So they've let me do it and then restrained me. They didn't want to interact ... I've asked them why they didn't interact with me. They've just said that they know the restraint is going to happen.

When I'm that wound up I can't say 'help'. Acting out is the only way I can express how awful I feel. You want someone to pick up on that, to be prepared to talk to you. Instead they treat you like a naughty child and you end up feeling far worse.

I wanted someone to show me some compassion.

Those of us who have experienced being restrained seem to be left wondering why things happened as they did. Why did no one pick up on our distress before it erupted as it did? Even then why react with brute force rather than seek to diffuse the situation with calm words and reassurance? From our point of view what happened to us was wholly avoidable and in the long run certainly did more harm than good. Neither do I believe there is any other area in society where restraint is used as a first-line defence rather than a last resort after attempts at mediation have failed.

I don't believe that anyone should be restrained . . . and they don't take into account your experiences of being held down.

In an acute psychiatric ward patients are almost by definition people who have had damaging experiences. Being restrained re-enforces that damage and should have no place in any model for humane treatment in the twenty-first century.

Commentaries

Kevin Gournay (Mental Health Nurse)

I was asked to write this commentary just a few months after the publication of the National Institute for Clinical Excellence (NICE 2005) *Violence: The short term management of disturbed/violent behaviour in psychiatric in-patient settings and emergency departments*. This guidance took three years to develop and I am honoured to say that I was the Chair of the Guidance Development Group. Previously, I had conducted a number of research studies on the topic of violence in mental health care and have been involved in policy development. Over a period of eight years, work on this area became a significant part of my life. I am sad to say that this period was also marked by the death of a patient during a restraint episode. This patient, Rocky Bennett, probably died as a result of a combination of incorrect restraint, over-prescription of medication and inadequate resuscitation procedures. The inquest into Mr Bennett's death delivered the verdict of 'Accidental death aggravated by neglect'. In turn, the case of Rocky Bennett became the subject of a Public Inquiry and the publication of the report of that inquiry in 2003 brought to the attention of the wider public a broad range of issues in mental health care, including the vexed topic of institutional racism.

Also of significance during this time was the work of the Joint Parliamentary Committee on Human Rights (2004) *Deaths in custody*. This report also focused on restraint-related deaths. As a special advisor to this committee, I was provided with the opportunity to examine issues beyond mental health care in the British Prison Service, the Police Service and immigration centres. One of the striking findings of this work was that the twin issues of restraint and mental health problems were prominent in all settings, not just in mental health units.

Power imbalance

Therefore, when I began to read this chapter, I was fully aware of the problems associated with restraint in persons with a mental health problem. Nevertheless, when I read the specific accounts, I was, despite my experience in these matters, very shocked and saddened by the very graphic descriptions of restraint. In this commentary, I will attempt to address some of the issues mentioned.

The accounts rightly draw attention to the power imbalance that exists between staff and service users and I hope that, to some extent, the NICE guidance addresses this important issue. The guidance now clearly states that, if at all possible, the service user should be able to write an advance directive which goes into his/her care plan for all to see. To explain further, if a service user has a history of violence or disturbed behaviour, they should be provided with an opportunity to provide instructions about their preferred method of management, should they become disturbed/violent in the future. Service users have different preferences for the way that they are managed and the only way to deal with this issue is to ask the service user directly. Quite often they will provide a preference that will very much reduce the possibility of the situation getting out of hand and restraint being needed. Therefore, for example, a service user may be able to say that, if they become disturbed, they would prefer to be provided with the opportunity to sit in a quiet, low-stimulus room or, alternatively, to be offered a mild tranquilliser to be taken by mouth. Such strategies may prevent the situation escalating.

Trauma

The accounts reinforce for me the endless problem of re-traumatisation and I have heard on numerous occasions that women with a history of abuse have suffered very grave psychological consequences when being restrained. Such an episode might lead to even greater mental health problems in the future. I should add, on a more general note, that my work with NICE confirmed for me that women receive a very poor deal when in receipt of in-patient treatment. It is worth adding that the women who have complained about the re-traumatisation that accompanies restraint, also commented that they felt very unsafe in the mixed-sex accommodation, which is still so prevalent in our mental health services.

Service user involvement

I would like to provide some comment about how service users should now be involved in issues connected with the management of violent behaviour, including restraint. NICE guidance was developed with very considerable service user involvement. Therefore, two members of our Guidance Development

Group had a service user background; the guidance process utilised the Patient Involvement Unit of government and we were able to obtain considerable additional input from focus groups that particularly targeted service users from ethnic minorities. I hope that the guidance goes some way to address the issue of power imbalance because, if the guidance is implemented as it should be, future mental health services will need to involve service users at every stage of the development of policies.

In addition, the guidance makes it clear that service users should be involved in teaching and the development of training. I am pleased to say that the National Institute for Mental Health (England), which is now responsible for training initiatives across the NHS, has taken the issue of service user involvement very seriously and the aspiration is that service users will be actively involved in the development of future policy and training initiatives, and work at a local level with Trusts will ensure that best practice is implemented across all services.

In conclusion, I would like to emphasise that there are very positive developments unfolding across British mental health services. Having said that, at the same time I must acknowledge that the mental health system is one where, by definition, service users will always be at risk of suffering as a result of the power imbalances that exist. As professionals, it is our duty to ensure that the risks associated with this imbalance are reduced to an absolute minimum.

Bill Turner (Mental Health Advocate)

I step on to the ward making sure the door is locked behind me. I look around for the patient that has asked to see me and then I feel it in the air . . . . . it almost cracks with tension and distress. My client can't be found so I walk into the staff office behind the toughened glass. By contrast, the atmosphere is cool and calm yet a hive of activity. A nurse is writing up notes, another is on the phone, the OT [occupational therapist] is planning the weekly programme and another is tapping at the computer. I am told the patient I'm looking for is probably lying on his bed so I step out of the office and head for the male dorm. The air cracks again, something is going to kick off . . . .

My perspective on the issue of restraint is that of a mental health advocate. Our job is about empowering people with mental health problems, ensuring that they are fully informed by providing information, advice and guidance surrounding their issues. We work alongside our clients and assist in helping them work out their options. In addition we provide support for our clients at meetings such as ward rounds, care planning and other meetings to help them to express their views, needs and wishes, hopefully aiding them to exercise their gift of choice.

Having read the service users' experiences of being subject to restraint coupled with my opening to this commentary I am keen to make the following observations and suggestions, and raise the occasional question.

Sadly, all too often the open psychiatric ward is locked, thus making for a pressure cooker environment. I feel the first positive step forward could be to return to the open ward system with robust measures in place to manage the risk of a patient absconding. In short, by creating a safe, unrestricted environment we can help to release the tension so often felt on the psychiatric ward. After all, to lock people in is restraint in itself.

Most in-patient units have a booklet full of local information, ward routines and local services, etc. Could not a very carefully worded page be inserted informing all new admissions on the potential for the use of restraint? The booklet can clarify that it can very occasionally be used to help people if they become very disturbed whilst in hospital in order to ensure that they and other people are safe, but would be used only as a last resort if it were really necessary and after all other options had been explored.

Throughout the piece, service users highlight that communication, information and compassion are perhaps the key elements which can be used to avoid the use of restraint in the first place. These for me are the central roles of the psychiatric nurse and compassion should be the main reason why many people go into the nursing profession in the first place.

As an advocate I often see good staff caught up in so much red tape and administration that they are too busy to talk to their patients. This hardly affords much space for the nursing care that would facilitate the use of their skills which could be used to de-escalate situations that may otherwise have led to a situation requiring restraint. What, I wonder, could be done to shift this administrative responsibility that would then lead to more time for genuine nursing care?

One of the accounts from a service user mentions that 'I went to leave my room, the bleepers went off and six nurses pounced on me.' I don't doubt for a minute that an awful lot must have been going on in terms of this person's mental ill health but from his perspective all he was doing or trying to do was to leave his room. This raises the question for me, what could have been done at an early stage to talk to this person to ensure that he was aware that the nursing staff had the sort of concerns that would eventually lead to six of them pouncing on him? Communication with information and a pinch of compassion would for me seem the right recipe.

Another service user explains that the only way to express (him/herself) is by acting out, and then being made to feel like a naughty child for doing so. It makes me wonder, if people feel this is their only option for expression, what could have been offered as an alternative? And then, should a person be made to feel guilty for becoming ill? Where is the compassion in that?

Over the years working as a mental health advocate and from personal experience I am fully aware that many distressed people requiring restraint as a result of their behaviour do so involuntarily. In psychotic conditions, for example, an individual may be experiencing intrusive, unwanted and distressing thoughts not of their making. Is it therefore kind, fair, therapeutic or helpful in any way for them to be treated as though they have done something wrong, or were responsible for becoming ill? I suggest that to be treated in this manner is often a confirmation for the individual of the very worst and frightening aspects of their mental condition, which can thereby cause lasting detrimental effects. I know of one individual (and I am sure he is not the only one) who as a result of his mental illness lives in constant fear that he is living life beyond the pale. He has received such negative treatment at the height of his distress that being subject to restraint has made him feel guilty about his behaviour to the extent that this has compounded his views and he is now convinced that he will be eternally damned.

Restraint, from my viewpoint, is the opponent to empowerment. What can be offered to patients on a psychiatric ward by way of nursing care, a therapeutic environment and culture, communication, information and compassion which could lead to this evil called restraint becoming unnecessary?

Questions and issues for discussion

1   What have been your experiences of being involved in restraint situations? Have you had opportunity to attend management of aggression and violence training? How does restraint fit with other values and beliefs you might hold?
2   What do you think have been the effects on other people witnessing restraint who are not directly involved in such situations?
3   Have you known people to be traumatised after restraint? What can be done to minimise a traumatic experience?

Exercise

Ask a service user representative organisation to facilitate some training or be involved in developing operational policies that address issues of restraint.

Chapter 8

Feeling alone: experiences of a female teenager

'Gina'

I was nearly fifteen and despite having problems for some time things began to change around the summer starting with sleep problems. Frequently I would lay awake worrying about my concerns. Alone and scared inside there seemed to be no one who I could turn to for help. As well as losing my appetite I lost a general sense of caring about myself. Socially, I became withdrawn from everyone around me. I began to fantasise about having a different life as well as make-believe things that children believe in. For a while I had control over the dreams but then the dreams took over me. Looking back now I can see my mind had broke.

My mind was exhausted and it started to play tricks. I was hearing things and seeing things that were not there. I was in a world of my own with all the pain and fear manifesting itself through voices. The madness was unbearable and I could not think or focus on anything, my thoughts were all over the place. I thought some one other than me was listening to what I was thinking. The voices began to scream and shout and persecute me. There was no peace inside my head and I was driven on many occasions to attempt suicide. After several trips to the hospital Accident and Emergency department I was seen by a psychiatrist who put me on medication which didn't help. The voices continued becoming more aggressive sending me crazier to the point that I became so angry at home that the police were called.

I was taken to the police station and put in a cell; the police were not very nice to me. All I could do was cry. I felt so alone and was wondering what I had done and what was going to happen to me? I was alone in the cell for ages before anyone came to see me. I found it hard to answer the questions the police were asking. The person who spoke to me was aggressive, I remember him hitting me on the forehead. I never told anyone that the police had hit me. I was a child, I had no power, no rights and who would believe me.

The following morning I had to appear in young person's court. I found out that the police had advised my mum to press charges against me. My mum would have if my social worker had not been there. He and the solicitor explained to the court that I was experiencing a break-down. The court decided that I should go to an assessment centre so that they could decide what was the best course of action to take.

Eventually, I was hospitalised and taken to an adolescent unit just outside of London. The hospital was located in the countryside away from the hustle and bustle of city. The adolescent unit was in the grounds of a big mental hospital for adult patients. The hospitals were big grey buildings with long corridors like the kind of images you see in old black and white movies of old Victorian mental asylums. The wards were surrounded by lots of trees and flowers and it was peaceful and quiet making it a nice place to rest.

Despite the nice scenery I was confused about everything that was happening to me. I had changed from a child that did have times of laughter and fun into a sad withdrawn person. I did not want anyone around. I just wanted to be by myself. I remember sitting in the dining room and thinking to myself that I was being punished.

Once there was a sense of a glowing light surrounding me. Then all of sudden there was this shouting coming from the corridor. It was another child, a boy shouting about the same things I had been mumbling about. A smile came to my face and somehow I could identify with him. I felt a sense of relief; I was not on my own. Many of the other children were white and I was one of only two children of mixed race. I never found my colour created any problems for me as many of the nursing staff were of different nationalities.

The entrance to the adolescent unit led on to a long corridor and along each side there were rooms that were used for different functions. There was a large dining area where we had our meals, each side of this area were two sitting rooms with a television and chairs. There were two dormitories, one for the girls and one for the boys. The dormitory was divided into cubicles with only a curtain for privacy. I found sharing in this way difficult because although there was a curtain you could still hear everything most of the time. Frequently, the music centre was on and some of the girls would sit up chatting late at night. All I wanted was the peace and quiet. I suppose I could have asked them to keep the noise down but I did not feel it pertinent to do so.

Most mornings before going off to school we had daily chores to do. We had to vacuum our dormitory, clean the bathroom and at meal times we had to wash our plates and cutlery. For me such routines were important, as I was always someone that took pride in my surroundings and myself. After becoming ill I found it hard to even get out of bed and go to the bathroom but once I was given medication I was able to resume control over my appearance.

After our daily chores were done we would all gather in one of the sitting rooms with the nursing staff and doctors for our daily community meeting. The day's events would be discussed and any other business. The meeting was generally relaxed and afterwards we went to school.

The school was in the hospital grounds. Classes would begin at nine and finish at three. I cannot remember being taught anything in school. At the end of the year there was a meeting with my social worker and teaching staff to discuss the future for me. After the meeting had taken place I spoke with my social worker and he told me that the teaching staff felt that I was backward. I found that statement hard because no one paid any attention to the fact that I was experiencing emotional problems which left me feeling that I was incapable and it had an effect upon my confidence. I think some professionals like teachers get things wrong in their assessments, for some reason all the facts are not taken into account. Despite the opinion of the teaching staff my social worker did everything in his power to help me.

The care plan I received consisted of monthly meetings with my social worker, the nurse assigned to me and my family. The meeting was a place for me to talk about the things that were troubling me, however, it was difficult to talk about how I was feeling because I shut so much of me away. Talking to people I hardly knew was hard and I think looking back now I did not trust anyone, although having the meetings was important as it did bring some sense of safety. I was given medication as part of the treatment, which helped to stabilise my condition. At the time I was not told what my diagnosis was, I suppose I was too young at the time to be told and did not need that information.

All the children at the unit were on some form of medication. Usually it was given to us twice daily, once in the morning after breakfast and again after tea. We lined up outside the treatment room. Taking the medication was never an issue for me at the time until an incident involving one of the charge nurses.

It was the evening and every night before we went to bed we had hot chocolate and toast. Most evenings I would prepare this for everyone. That evening I didn't so one of the other patients prepared the hot chocolate. I was feeling uncomfortable and did not want to sit with the others. The charge nurse was there; he was quite strict and did not seem to show much emotion. I became very uneasy and got up and ran to the dormitory. I was frightened. The charge nurse came after me with two of the other girls I had made friends with. I decided to run and lock myself in the toilet. A scuffle broke out between me and the charge nurse and I was brought back to my bed. I was angry and upset at what had happened. I did not really understand at the time what was going on in my head. The next day after my medication was increased I found myself disliking that particular nurse. I questioned the increase in medicine and the fact that it made me very sleepy and my weight increased. I remember that I was told that the amount of medication I was given was to do with my body size as well as the symptoms I was experiencing.

Looking back at what happened I could see that the actions of the charge nurse were right because I was ill and anything could have happened to me after locking myself in the toilet as I had a history of trying to take my own life. He was doing his job as a caring professional.

Another situation that I and the other children had to deal with was the death of the nurse who was assigned to me and my family. It came as a great shock to all of us and the nursing team. I remember that we all gave some of our pocket money to buy flowers. That was the first time I experienced death in my life.

As well as school and family meetings we had group sessions two or three times a week. These were small mixed groups with about six to each group; one of the doctors led the groups. We talked about whatever came to mind. I remember we had a conversation about whose doctor was more senior. This was important as being children there is a tendency to get jealous of each other if one feels someone else is getting more attention. We also had psycho-therapy once a week. We would do role-play sometimes and we would act out each others' lives. I remember my friend was given a set of questions about me. How did I see myself in relation to nationality? Where did I feel I belonged? How did I feel as a person? I found this difficult to deal with at the time and ended up leaving that group.

Being teenagers there came a time when we had a talk about the birds and bees. I remember us sitting round in the girls' dormitory and along came some of the nurses. They started asking us what we knew about sex. The nurses explained to us the physical and emotional changes and how at times things can be frightening and uncomfortable. I found this helpful as I was not sure about being a teenager. We talked about never going into each others' dormitories and it was explained that us girls had to be careful about getting into compromising situations with the boys. Although this was explained some of the patients did indulge.

Our leisure time was not always spent sitting around, one evening a week we would be taken out to the cinema in the minibus and drive up to London. That was usually a good evening. Sometimes we went into the local town centre, or we would just go for a long walk around the grounds. In the summer we went camping and once we went on a day trip to France, most weekends I went home to my family.

Looking back on my in-patient experience which lasted over a year I think it was a good one. I needed to be there, it gave me time and space to just be. The day-to-day routine and the boundaries that were set were important; it made me feel secure inside. There were moments when things did not go too well but if the adolescent unit had not been there things might have turned out a lot different for me.

Commentaries

Sarah Goodfellow (Mental Health Nurse)

Although Gina's story took place several years ago her experiences are not totally unlike those a young person in her position may experience today.

Gina's description of her illness is one easily recognisable to me. I liked her child-like explanation that her mind broke as this allows for the idea that it can be mended. It is a far more hopeful metaphor than a static label such as 'crazy' or 'mad' can impart.

It is concerning, though, that she had lived with these symptoms for some time. It's unclear what sort of intervention she was receiving from the community service. Whatever it was, it was not sufficient to prevent a crisis for Gina. It is possible that she was being monitored by Child and Adolescent Mental Health Services (CAMHS), as it is often the case that some of the behaviours described by Gina are signs of 'normal teenage angst' rather than an emerging mental illness. Adolescence is the time for new thoughts, feeling and responsibilities which are part of the emerging adult personality. When a mental illness occurs during this vulnerable time the dynamic between the two blurs the whole picture. Once Gina was in a crisis though, things seem to have quickly spiralled out of her control and started her on a journey to an in-patient service via police custody.

Unfortunately, there was no outreach or community team made available to support Gina intensively at home in order to prevent admission, as would be made available to many children and young people today. Such a service would have been able to make 'follow-up' appointments after her visits to the Accident and Emergency department, or offered daily contact to help her feel contained during the trial of medication she was put on. However, an admission might still have been necessary but she would at least have had the opportunity to become more familiar with some of the staff and possibly even visit the hospital ward prior to a more planned and less crisis-led admission.

Though the behaviour of some young people does still bring them into contact with the police, hopefully the unsympathetic response to the situation experienced by Gina is not typical. Gina's treatment by the police was terrible. It was made even worse by the fact she was so vulnerable. She was experiencing voices and as a result of this and her delusional beliefs her ability to make sense of her experience and surroundings was perceptually distorted.

It is a source of great concern that this was Gina's access point into the so-called 'tier 4' CAMHS (specialist child and adolescent mental health services including in-patient facilities). Her abusive experience at the hands of the police could have quite easily become associated as part of the culture of the unit she was about to be admitted into. Her feelings of powerlessness, being 'done to', are well evident and could have had a negative impact on her ability to develop informed and working alliances with the care staff. CAMHS should be a young-person focused service, which enables young people and their families to take a central role in the planning of their care. The circumstances of Gina's admission placed this endeavour at risk.

Whilst Gina seems to appreciate the calm surroundings of the parkland unit, some young people would find it very disconcerting being removed from their urban environment. It is unclear how far the unit was from her home but this can affect parents' ability to visit and can make a massive demand on both their time and finances. The ease with which parents can visit is particularly important for many children and young people; for some this may be their first time away from home.

Many units have traditionally found themselves sharing a site with adult services. I think it may have been a frightening prospect for some young people to be exposed to unwell adults, albeit on a highly segregated basis. As well as possible child protection concerns, there must also be the risk that the young person starts to imagine themselves with a mental illness future ahead of them.

Gina said she felt relieved when she met young people who were having the same problems as hers and this is something the young people I work with echo. Even when the accommodation is on a dormitory basis and lacks a degree of privacy, many of the young people whom I work with, particularly the girls, say they like it and cite the camaraderie it instills as a helpful aspect in their recovery. It is unfortunate that Gina did not feel able to address her need for quiet with her peers who were noisy. Community meetings are generally good places to bring up such issues, with staff supporting a young person if needed. Through communal living young people can learn self-worth and respect for each other by sharing the same facilities whilst also ensuring that their own individual needs are met.

Gina points out that admission to an in-patient unit for a teenager will coincide with lots of novel but profound experiences. In Gina's case she explored sexual relationships and death.

Even though young people are in hospital it is vital that they remain in close contact with the families, friends and communities, and it was heartening to read that this was the case for Gina as she went home most weekends. Going home at weekends is commonplace in CAMHS, leaving the units virtually empty.

It is good that Gina did not feel her skin colour or race was ever an issue on the unit and that she had contact with staff from a variety of ethnic backgrounds. It sounds as if Gina had a very positive relationship with her social worker who was a constant presence, both prior to and during her admission. All too often community-based tier 4 CAMHS workers do not maintain their relationship with the young person during their admission.

Whilst the relationships she formed with staff were largely helpful and she acknowledges that it was necessary for her to come into hospital, she felt her need to be involved in determining what sort of therapy she received was overlooked. There were no interventions that would have helped her to understand her experiences. The incident with the charge nurse, which appears to have directly resulted in an increase in medication, and her experience with the school's 'diagnosis', could have had life-long consequences and confirm her sense of not being able to influence her care through personal involvement. Today CAMHS, like mental health services in general, is developing ways of working which place a greater value on ensuring that people who use services are more involved in their care. Whilst many aspects of Gina's account are similar to today's experiences for young people, it is hoped that at least in this one aspect teenagers like her may have a better experience.

Trish Barry (Social Worker)

Gina makes a fundamentally important contribution to our understanding of what it means to be psychologically distressed and subsequently ill through the experience and eyes of an adolescent. Considering her words from a child care/child protection/child and adolescent psychiatric social work and psychotherapeutic perspective, Gina manages to help us think about the complexities of the inner world of the adolescent as she slips further into mental illness and gives pointers about how practice should have picked up earlier signs of severe distress and should have been more sensitive.

The first part of Gina's narrative draws the reader into a reflective space where the isolation and loneliness she started to experience could be imagined. Recognising that she was withdrawing from others into a world of make-believe Gina eloquently describes a sense of needing to flee from the internal and external pressures around. I was left asking myself the question, 'who noticed?'

We are taken further into the terrifying world of auditory and visual hallucinations and the presence of intrusive voices which drove Gina to desperate measures. She describes vividly how she suffered from delusions and how she felt her only avenue of escape from this experience and the persecutory voices was to deliberately self-harm. Gina attempted suicide on several occasions.

Safeguarding children

I was left wondering where the child protection process started in Gina's case. How was it that she presented on several occasions to the Accident and Emergency department and was not assessed by a child and adolescent psychiatrist and social worker on her first presentation? The child protection process in relation to deliberate self-harm should identify key areas of risk in the contexts of Accident and Emergency departments, child psychiatry, paediatrics and social work. I was sorry to read that; I think she was badly let down here.

It is disheartening to note that Gina's need for a comprehensive mental health assessment at a time of crisis was not heard. Instead of professionals trying to understand deliberate self-harm as an attempted solution to her distress, it appears she did not have a psychiatric assessment until some time after she had dipped further into her 'illness'.

Workforce issues

A possible explanation is that the reality seems to be that there is a short-fall nationally of child and adolescent multidisciplinary staffing. Approved social workers are relatively rare and rarer still are those who have extensive experience and are trained in issues specific to CAMHS.

We know from research that 170,000 young people a year present at Accident and Emergency departments after an episode of deliberate self-harm accounting for one in five adolescents and that as a society we have a serious problem. The National Institute for Clinical Excellence has published guidance and recommendations on self-harm (NICE 2004) which it is hoped will improve services to those presenting with an episode of this in Accident and Emergency. Gina assists us greatly in understanding the urgency of the need for general hospital services to be more knowledgeable and respon-sive to the needs of young people presenting with an episode of deliberate self-harm.

While the 'mental state examination' is vital, so equally is the role of the social worker in carrying out the 'social state examination' (Souter and Kraemer 2004). If Gina was presenting to an Accident and Emergency department today, a local authority social worker should undertake an initial assessment which would combine therapeutic and statutory roles in a core assessment using the Department of Health's (2000) *Framework for the assessment of children in need and their families*.

Therapy

I was pleased to read that Gina was admitted to an adolescent unit at a time she needed it and where it appears she had a period of respite, care, contain-ment, group work, psychotherapy and structure which provided her with a 'holding' environment (Winnicott 1965). Holding and ego support, according to Winnicott, continues to be a need of a growing child, adolescent, and at times the adult, particularly if there is a strain which threatens confusion or disintegration.

It is of some concern to note that while there are approximately 1,100 child and adolescent mental health beds in the NHS in England (Lindsey and Griffiths 2004) there is still a shortfall of approximately one third of the required in-patient beds needed. This is my experience as an out-of-hours approved social worker trying to find adolescent in-patient beds for young people made the subject of a section under the 1983 Mental Health Act.

I enjoyed reading what Gina had the courage to offer. I found myself creating a contemplative space to think through and take on some of the challenges we as professionals need to address.

Questions and issues for discussion

1   What has been your experience of people with developmental issues portrayed through their behaviours and emotions which may resemble a mental illness, particularly at times of crisis? Are people with such presentations any less deserving of care and services? How should we respond?
2   What can adult wards learn from children and adolescent mental health services (CAMHS)?
3   What difference does a social worker's perspective and contribution make to in-patient care?

Exercise

Visit an in-patient facility associated with a different care group from your own. What are the similarities and differences in terms of culture and practice? What can you take away from your visit and use?

Chapter 9

Feeling humiliated: experiences of a black man

'Joe'

There is a stereotype that seems to go with people like me, a person of colour who has a mental health label. I seem to be still learning about it as I go through life and as much as I try to be a righteous individual it seems an uphill struggle to buck the trend. Sometimes I think there is a them and us! I feel I am a person of good balance and judgement, the fact that the government is trying to encourage people in my position to get more involved in their care is one of the things I find gives me a lift. One way of being involved is for me to write about some of my experiences.

My time in hospital was not too pleasant. On entering its gloomy stale air all your rights are no longer yours. Staff telling you – do this, do that. I start feeling upset on entering the system. Police, remand, hospital. I just cannot get my head around what is happening, I feel fraught. While being transported from remand with some guards I felt so fraught I pissed myself. Everything was just so alien, so unfamiliar I just cannot explain. I walked into the hospital soaked in piss with a guard either side handcuffed through all those doors. I entered the ward and staff approached the guards who explained what had happened. Whilst the handcuffs were being taken off I was ushered into a bathroom to change. I was a new arrival, eyes looking at me. Looking back on that emotional time I think the guards and the staff felt for me. *Documenting this I am feeling emotional so I will stop now* . . . .

Sometime later. . . . You're locked in time and time moves very slowly, nothing to do, everyone's watching your every move. You enter into an environment you're not used to and everything is strange. You seem drawn to the people that seem to make you laugh and they help relieve the pressure. They might be staff, or patients, you do not care who they are just as long as they take you out of that space and time, however, you are still wary of people and where you are. Some staff and patients though want to keep you in a doom and gloom frame of mind as they feel you're having too much of a good time. They seem to resent the fact that you're in hospital, getting as they see it free board and lodgings while they have to come to work. Whenever I enter hospital my only goal is to get out as fast as possible.

I was angry about something and I went to a staff member who I felt was approachable. As we were both talking another member of staff approached me from behind and grabbed my wrists which were at my side. The rest of the staff got involved supporting their colleague, which I understand as a team player. In that sort of situation they have to support one another. I have heard that a lot of people die in situations like that. The bigger you are the more force they think is needed. There were bodies on each limb, knees in each shoulder blade and I was unable to breathe with all that weight on the back of my chest. No one ever came and spoke to me and explained what was happening or tried a more gentle approach, which would have been beneficial for me and the staff. I see it as a form of bullying. I am not saying there may not be some situations that may warrant that type of treatment but this has got to be when all other options have failed.

If I get a visit from my mother the impression is given that she is pleased that I am in hospital. She brings me so much food that I have to give it away. It is an occasion for her, as if she is on show. My mother's face is that she is coping, she has a big smile. Deep down I feel otherwise.

I remember once going up for my medication and was given the wrong stuff, which I spat back into the beaker. The nurse who gave it to me pleaded with me not to say anything. As a man with a family myself I could see he was concerned that he may lose his job, so I said nothing, as I would not want his family to go hungry.

There can be a funny side too. One time a French guy who was in hospital with me missed his meal as he was asleep. He could not speak English very well but could get by. By the time he woke up he was hungry and wanted something to eat. He decided to order Chinese food which was a minimum of twenty pounds with free delivery. Twenty pounds of Chinese food would feed three of us. So we clubbed together, as the third person was paying his share the ward manager got involved and took us all to a side room. The French guy was just saying he was hungry and was showing her the menu, explaining the situation to the ward manager. She started trying to explain something to the French bloke. I just could not help myself and started to laugh, the manager did not see the funny side, which made me laugh even more, and that was when she went absolutely ape shit. I must explain the manager's native tongue was Chinese; her accent was so strong I had to leave the room. We all had a good Chinese meal that night.

Commentaries

Leonard Fagin (Psychiatrist)

After reading Joe's account, and having worked as a clinician for many years, I asked myself : 'How can we, as responsible and more often than not, caring professionals, find ourselves in the position where we are blinded from recognising how humiliating an experience a hospital admission can become?' Joe describes in just a few poignant sentences how the process of humiliation emerges even before he has made an entry into the unit. He has to contend with the fear of being manhandled by guards and policemen, undoubtedly the response to his own attempts to come to terms with his own breakdown, which provokes a standard counter-response by those charged with taking him to a 'place of safety'. Although this might be perfectly supported by justified notions of protection for all concerned, the procedures often completely misread and ignore the frightened individual trying to make sense of what is going on. And he is black. As if the colour alone adds to the impossibility of others making contact with the internal fear. Joe pisses himself. Further humiliation.

And then Joe speaks about the right to be in hospital. He perceives that staff do not make him feel welcome, in fact, he picks up messages that he is a 'sponger', someone who is enjoying his stay in hospital and using badly needed resources unnecessarily. The only way he can justify his stay is if he shows symptoms of incapacity or serious mental illness. Interestingly, when I have spoken to staff about this feeling of being taken for a ride by patients I am often surprised at how pervasive it is. I think it is also true that many patients treat staff despicably. In this regard, the act of humiliation is not one-way traffic. Staff will often report feeling abused and unacknowledged by their patients. We can see here the start of a spiralling course of events, where the 'them and us' differentiation begins to take root. This feeling can rarely be discussed openly with patients: it is seen as unprofessional and poor form, and yet it poisons possible therapeutic relationships.

Even when Joe makes an attempt to discuss his anger, his efforts, in his eyes, are inappropriately understood as an act of aggression in itself. He approaches a member of staff who he thinks will help him with his anger, and he is met by a response from another member of staff that is not in keeping with his intentions. He feels misunderstood, and again humiliated. It is not inconceivable that the way he expresses his anger is rooted in his own culture, and we have extensive evidence to suggest that black men's behaviour, in particular, meets with harsher responses by the police and mental health services, simply because, I contend, it stirs up fears and stereotypes of the unknown, of untamed aggression. Once again, rarely can staff discuss these fears openly in their own support groups, for fear of being accused of racial prejudices.

And the process of humiliation does not constrain itself to the dyad of staff–patient relationships. Visits from his mother awaken feelings of rejection and being ignored, something that Joe hints runs deep in making him the person he is. The fact that he reads his mother's visits as self-serving rather than attempts at offering consolation and support must come as a deep blow when he is at his most vulnerable. It seems he is telling us he has never been properly cared for or understood. This leads me to think how often the interaction between staff and patients reproduces early emotional experiences of trauma or neglect, and how an awareness of these issues can allow an admission to be therapeutic rather than a repetition of previous injuries. Staff can become sensitised to these subtle interactions by discussion and feedback, recognising how feelings are projected onto them, which can then be worked on with patients when they are ready to absorb these insights, either in one-to-one sessions or in therapeutic groups.

Two comments Joe makes stand out for me. He cares. He cares about the possible impact on the career of a member of staff who has made an error when dispensing medication, even though one can question the fact that the nurse has included him, inappropriately in my opinion, in a collusive act. He cares enough about another patient who has gone hungry after missing a meal, and joins him in a spontaneous whip-round to buy a Chinese meal. And he cares enough to allow himself to laugh at ludicrous situations. Caring about others can become a natural healing process, and again, there are myriads of opportunities to witness events in in-patient services where patients help each other, and even, dare I say it, where patients are helping staff. Two-way inter-actions of this sort, as well as laughter, are probably the most effective way to break down the barriers that foster the humiliation spiral.

Kamaldeep Bhui (Psychiatrist)

Feeling humiliated is a moving account of one man's struggle to use help and available services for recovery whilst having to overcome experiences of alienation, coercion and at best disrespectful treatment whilst an in-patient. Several words might be used to describe the overall experience of this service user: fear, sadness, confusion, perplexity, injustice, assault, hurt, ridicule, 'off balance' and 'no peace'. Such an experience is not an intentional part of the in-patient experience, but how does an environment that is supposed to provide skilled care come to engender such powerful feelings?

Discrimination

At the core of the disquiet is an intense personal experience of struggle with professionals and providers, their institutional cultures and the adverse impacts of practice. The perception is that staff are not aware of the service user's experience of being dehumanised. Particularly troubling was the per-haps too prompt use of restraint. More importantly, miscommunication culminates in the account of confusion, laughter, ridicule and all 'feelings of discrimination' between the Frenchman and service user and the Chinese manager.

This account shows how intense and passionate racial dynamics can lead to a muddle or confusion; all feel wounded and traumatised whilst none foster and apprehend a therapeutic environment that is nurturing, nourishing, and caring of staff as well as service users. The account goes to the heart of what it means to have a different skin colour from the majority, of the meaning of felt and enacted stigma, and what might distinguish it from felt and enacted racism.

Stigma and prejudice

Stigma and prejudice against those with disability is well known and seen in all walks of life. There is a specific stigma around mental illness as people are perceived to be 'crazy, out of control or potentially violent' and 'not in charge of their own faculties' perhaps being uncontrollable. This is a popular portrayal of mental illness but clearly it does not do justice to a whole range of types of mental distress from very mild states of anxiety and dysphoria and natural experiences of sadness (e.g. due to bereavement), through to more severe episodes of depression or psychosis. The Recovery movement and service users have shown clearly that recovery is possible in a personal sense and, indeed, between 20 and 50 per cent of people do recover fully from a first episode of psychosis. Population studies also show psychotic phenomena are not uncommon in the community. The question arises what is it that sustains psychosis and why is such a state stigmatised?

Stigma has two components:

1   A felt experience of being excluded, treated differently including the assault on personal identity and feeling different.
2   An experience of being discriminated against (enacted stigma).

There are real consequences beyond the personal experience. This is not to understate the personal experience of feeling different and feeling excluded as this itself is known to be associated (e.g. in the racism literature) with common mental disorders. There is at least one prospective study showing racism is related to psychotic symptoms at follow-up.

How does stigma then differ from discrimination and racism, particularly around experiences of ethnic groups and people of colour? Clearly, stigma begins for those with mental illness at the point at which an illness begins and becomes sustained so that they then identify with a particular group that is socially excluded. This is not to underestimate the disabilities of some forms of mental distress and illness but illness experience does not always follow the same course as the 'disease' process in Eisenberg's terms.

In contrast, those exposed to racism might be exposed to it at a very early age in their early development at school, relationships between parents and the outside world. This means the felt component and possibly enacted components of it are prominent at a very early stage of maturation when an individual (a child) is not fully or is possibly partially aware of cultural, racial and ethnic differences and prejudices. One could argue also that there are felt and enacted components of prejudice and racial discrimination. The felt components of perceived discrimination are as noxious and damaging as actual episodes of discrimination which are more obvious and apparent for scrutiny. Of course, discrimination (as opposed to racism) and social exclusion don't appear to take such a dramatic form and are often subtle and consist of micro-aggressions and micro-episodes which culminate in a growing lack of resilience and ability to cope, or at least greater effort required to overcome obstacles.

Both stigma and racism share a conceptual problem: they might be globalised explanations and used too frequently to describe all sorts of obstacles to access the services. Indeed, that is one way the words stigma and indeed racism have been used, to explain ethnic disparities irrespective of intentions of practitioners or policy makers or service providers or managers. However, understanding the underlying processes both at an experiential level for the individual with mental distress whilst experiencing stigmatised treatment, as well as at a systems level in services is essential to remedy and eradicate injustice. The perceived integrity of the healer is as important as their technical skills.

Questions and issues for discussion

1   What has been your experience of race issues in your work?
2   Should patients be enjoying their stay in hospital?
3   How can communication with people whose first language is not English be assisted?

Exercise

Conduct an audit of when control and restraint techniques have been utilised on your ward. Are there any racial differences? If so what does this mean?

Summary of the main issues in Section 2

Communication and values

These accounts start with a piece written by Nigel Short of his experiences in an acute psychiatric ward where on many occasions he felt misunderstood by staff caring for him. This issue of communication is repeated in many of the other narratives presented in this section.

In its strictest sense communication might be defined as 'a meaningful interaction between a sender and receiver'. However, it is the word *meaningful* which changes the emphasis from a rather linear process definition into something more complex and at the same time more human. Meanings can be both shared and understood within groups of people but they can also be very idiosyncratic. The communication from a sender may be intended to mean one thing but it might be received as meaning something very different. This difference in the perception of meanings is reciprocal and can directly result in the *misunderstandings* that Nigel and others write about. Meanings are also affected by the environmental and situational context and also importantly, culturally located in the beliefs and values of groups and individuals. The beliefs that people hold about one another are an important variable in determining not just interaction through communication but also behaviour more generally.

The therapeutic interpretation of behaviour and communication is fraught with such subjective difficulties, not the least being the stigma and prejudice that Professor Kamaldeep Bhui highlights. For this reason the accurate communication of someone else's meanings is extremely difficult. Nigel benefited from meeting with an interested and kindly art therapist; however, he found her interpretations gave him further evidence of being misunderstood. Maria Cañete and Dr Arturo Ezquerro interpret Kevin's illness symptoms and behaviour as a form of communication in order to convey issues for which he had no socially acceptable way of expressing himself and as a result found himself restrained by staff.

The proper and judicial use of minimum restraint is an important part of managing a situation when someone is so distressed that there is no other alternative to preventing someone from harming themselves or others. Professor Kevin Gournay in his commentary of the restraint experiences of Capital members written by Clare Ockwell acknowledges the power differentials that exist between staff and service users as being a factor in the use of restraint. Power differentials are expressed through verbal and physical communication. Clare Ockwell pleads for staff to be more compassionate in their interactions with service users when they are at their most vulnerable and advances the notion that the demonstration of such values as compassion would reduce the incidence of restraint. Similarly, advocate Bill Turner feels that many restraint situations can be avoided by someone caring enough to allow communication at times of distress.

Professor Gournay suggests communication between staff and service users through collaborative care planning and advance directives as being one way to reduce the differential in power that leads staff to practise in such authoritarian ways. Whilst the use of restraint to illustrate power differentials in practice is an extreme one, it is by no means uncommon experience, as evidenced by the accounts of service users Kevin, Gina, Joe and others.

Perhaps a less traumatic example of poor communication is highlighted by another commentator, consultant psychiatrist Dr Trevor Turner, who illustrates how service users can be maintained in a weaker position when communicating with professionals because of the use of acronyms as a shorthand statement between professionals.

The use of professional language and forceful action are demonstrations of how sets of beliefs and values held by staff, inserted in a cultural system, about what they think of service users, themselves and their roles, are acted out in practice.

Practice

Changes to the structure of hospital routines and functions can have an impact on practice. Gina's admission lasted a year, a somewhat longer period of time in hospital than described in the other accounts. As an adolescent she appears to have had a different experience to adults, including attending a hospital-based school, group therapy sessions and going home most weekends and during end-of-term holidays. This practice of frequent home leave is acknowledged by child and adolescent mental health nurse Sarah Goodfellow, who recognises the significance of time spent at home as a designed practice which enables family relationships to continue to grow and develop. It also highlights the importance of trying to avoid the inappropriate admissions of young people into adult mental health wards, as Kevin Norwood experienced as a 17-year-old. This is an issue recognised by commentators Maria Cañete and Dr Arturo Ezquerro, when they state that the developmental needs of a young person are unlikely to be met in such an adult environment.

Based on his research into conflict, Professor Len Bowers (Bowers 2002) has noticed that wards which have a structured programme of activity had greater stability and a reduction in perceived friction. Only if activity is meaningful, respectful and appropriate will service users want to engage and gain benefit. Activity is not just the province of an occupational therapy programme, it should be something which all professionals are involved in and can be expressed across a continuum from diversion to formal psychotherapy depending on need. Let us not underestimate the usefulness of diversion as a therapeutic activity, particularly as a potential life saver when it inhibits suicidal rumination.

The benefits of practices that inform service users and allow them to take more responsibility over their care is advocated by Professor Richard Morriss who recognises not just the power of medication but also the importance of collaborative medication management. Being able to communicate Janey's experience of *medication induced boredom* through such a collaborative practice would be a good practice development issue.

Social worker Trish Barrie suggests service users should have a 'social state examination' as well as a mental state examination. This is an interesting idea and would chime with practice issues that serve as evidence for adopting recovery-based values (DoH 2006).

Some of the practices highlighted by service users serve as a useful reminder that even trivial actions such as early morning vacuuming can have a real impact on a patient's experience. Some practices appear petty or vindictive; others are more based on ritual, tradition or habit such as ward rounds or queuing outside the clinic for medication. Most of these practices could be rendered obsolete if the ward was organised on practices based on communication, information and compassion as advocate Bill Turner encourages.

Environment

The physical environment in which people are cared for is highlighted by nearly all of the service user accounts. Kevin Norwood had experienced being a patient in both a Victorian asylum and a more modern unit. Similarly Gina's adolescent in-patient unit is within the grounds of a Victorian mental hospital where she describes the typical side rooms leading off a long corridor. Both Gina and Kevin remark positively about the hospital grounds in the old hospitals, which were characterised by a sense of fresh air and peace as opposed to the 'pressure cooker' enclosed facility that Kevin later resided in. Janey also highlights the beneficial impact of a garden which has been a recent addition to her local psychiatric unit. It appears that local services are rediscovering once again the therapeutic benefits of a green lung in their building designs. This was something which was known by the Victorians and then forgotten in the 1980s when many psychiatric units were attached to general hospitals and designed not unlike the wards of the nearby medical units.

Surprisingly, only Nigel mentions the poor quality of hospital food in his account, although Joe is amused by an incident involving a Chinese food takeaway order after a fellow patient had missed his hospital meal. There is sense of camaraderie in Gina's remarks about sharing hot chocolate with the other teenagers before bedtime. Beverages are also mentioned by Nigel and Janey who are denied a hot drink after a certain time in the evening despite being encouraged to eat and drink at other times. Tea breaks also represent something by which Janey measures the time of day.

Occupational therapist Rachel Christian-Edwards, in her commentary of Janey's account of boredom, mentions the difficulty of being able to find space on wards for formal therapeutic activity such as group work or the educational sessions that Professor Richard Morriss suggests. Very often such activity has to make use of lounges and other spaces that have another communal purpose. Janey, however, points to another communal space, the *smoking room*, as a place for the 'best conversations'. Smoking rooms will become something of the past as new health-related legislation imposes a prohibition of smoking in public spaces. Perhaps service users and staff who are smokers will shortly find that they will have similarly interesting conversations with non-smokers as they had done previously in what were invariably nicotine-stained walled rooms.

New building design is now being based on the purpose-built requirements of the needs of people with mental health problems. Particular attention is being paid to therapeutic and outdoor spaces. These accounts serve as an important reminder to ensure that there is comprehensive service user involvement in the design of such buildings; after all, they have had first-hand experience of using them.

Section 3

Carers' experiences

This section presents us with the experiences of the members of the immediate family of someone who is admitted to a psychiatric in-patient unit. Usually the first admission takes place in a crisis situation when the family members – soon to become carers – are full of emotions – anxiety, guilt, fear, relief – and desperate for help, support and information. What happens next is a rollercoaster ride that can go on for weeks, months or even years, which you are about to join. Psychosis, especially schizophrenic psychosis, commonly develops first in late adolescence (Harrop and Trower 2003) and four of these accounts are by the mother and/or father of someone in their teens admitted for the first time. In two cases this required compulsory admission in which the parent had played a part. The writers say many similar things about the experiences surrounding the admission and following it, yet each account is unique and eloquent. The other account, which we have placed in the middle to give the reader a varied perspective, describes the experience of the young wife of a man admitted not for the first time but following a period of stability when everything seemed to be going so well. Her account raises particular questions concerning hospital attitudes towards service users and carers' relationships. All these accounts honour the writers' courage and openness, and their commitment to improving the services that in varying degrees fell short of what they and the person they cared for needed.

Why us?

David Shiers

This question preoccupied us for most of the three years that our daughter resided on psychiatric in-patient wards. I will outline her pathway to Monica's first experience of in-patient services as a context for describing some of our feelings as parents.

The illness emerged from an increasingly difficult adolescence, falling school performance, some difficulties with speech, some clumsiness of movement and increasing social isolation. An attempt to harm herself led, at the age of 16, to receiving a specialist domiciliary assessment at which a diagnosis of schizophrenia was made. Our initial naïve acceptance of this diagnosis was followed by twelve months of increasingly chaotic home life. The local Child and Adolescent Mental Health Service (CAMHS) supported us over this period. Subsequently Monica, at age 17, commenced a series of in-patient stays. Six months in an acute adult admission ward of a large district general hospital (DGH) was followed by 2.5 years in a rehabilitation service sited in a run-down asylum. From there she spent two years in a small community residential resource offering 24-hour nursing care before moving five years ago to her current situation in a supported housing scheme.

As parents, we experienced various emotions linked with key transition points for Monica's journey from the age of 17 to age 20 through three continuous years of hospital care. We have chosen to highlight our emotions when Monica entered the acute adult ward aged 17.

On entering the acute adult ward aged 17

This was Monica's first experience of an in-patient setting, precipitated by a crisis one Mothering Sunday when her paranoia extended to the whole family. Our ability to cope had finally become exhausted. As parents, we had developed an increasing sense of personal failure at not containing Monica's symptoms in those first twelve months of illness. This was associated with a rising tension at home from the day-to-day pressures and huge adaptation of our way of life. The CAMHS service exhorted us to cope at home, apologising for their lack of a suitable service and fuelling our increasing expectation that Monica, once old enough to access the adult services, would discover a service specifically geared to deal with psychosis. It was thus with a certain sense of relief that we all arrived at the acute adult admission ward.

For the first 48 hours we relaxed free from the responsibility of providing constant observation and support. For the first time in twelve months we had some time for our two sons and ourselves. And then the reality began to dawn on us. Monica had exchanged a CAMHS service that '*didn't do psychosis*' for an adult service that '*didn't do young people*'. That initial sense of relief and expectation disappeared within days. We became fearful for her vulnerability in this chaotic and at times physically threatening environment. She rapidly became much more ill and required very heavy tranquillisation to control her psychosis.

Two feelings are easy to recall from those harsh times – guilt and fear.

Guilt

We assumed blame for somehow failing to cope with this illness at home. We had let her down. We would struggle to sleep at night, conscious that Monica's bedroom next door to ours was empty and that we had left her to sleep in some unfamiliar hospital ward. An overwhelming sense of guilt swept over us. We must be awful parents – and yet we had two other lovely children who had had no difficulties? Perhaps she was emotionally neglected – but our children had always been central to activities within an apparently happy family blessed with grandparents, aunties and uncles? As health professionals we visited many, many families with apparently far more difficult circumstances – and yet ours seemed the most unhappy family we knew. And there was Monica, drugged up almost to oblivion though still terrified by my presence, requiring intensive nursing to eat, drink and the most basic self-care. Far from seeing her improve, this chaotic environment seemed to make her more frightened and indeed more ill. We kept returning to the 'Why us?' question.

Fear

Simply walking on to the ward reminded us of the completely new and strange world our daughter and ourselves now found ourselves part of. Monica's grandmother commented on how frightened she felt about some of the other patients. She seemed a child among a far older group of patients – we feared for her vulnerability and the inappropriateness of this environment. We sought fellow family members for comfort and advice as we attempted to find out about and make sense of the ward environment and routine. Sometimes visiting hours would be punctuated by the ward alarm sounding – someone had 'made a break for it' and several members of staff would run off the ward in pursuit of a patient. Different drug regimens were tried but failed to control her illness and we began to fear that nothing was going to work. The staff's efforts to assure us that she would soon respond to treatment, or that she could resume school or college seemed hollow. Previous certainties in our family life became replaced by confusion. As parents we had lost control over the process. The present felt grim but we feared even more for the future. Articulate, middle-class, knowledgeable of health systems – it counted for nothing. We felt totally disempowered.

Monica left the acute adult ward after six months to move to the rehabilitation ward, sited in an old asylum. We were greeted with an immediate choice: for her to sleep in an eight-bedded dormitory without curtains or carpets, or alternatively a single accommodation consisting of a long narrow room with a tiny window at its end and an inspection glass in the door. It took little imagination to realise what this room had once been used for. It was thus with a sense of disbelief that we found ourselves standing in a ward setting that we had thought had been consigned to history.

Despair

A single emotion easy to recall from this time and perhaps the most difficult emotion of all those we had to deal with. Long corridors with shuffling elderly men, little clusters of patients huddled in corners smoking, a pervading boredom, a canteen where many of the most enduringly disabled would gather to pass time – and this was the environment that was going to rehabilitate Monica. We could see no future for her. She was in some sort of cultural limbo, lost outside time and sentenced to life in a ghetto of disability. The unavoidable question for us had now changed from 'Why us?' to 'What had we abandoned our daughter to?' Initially our personal feelings had the quality of an emotional roller-coaster but as despair set in we found ourselves becoming exhausted and without hope.

Anger

To complete the sequence of emotions there is one important final twist. From this point of despair two things happened in short succession. Monica commenced taking clozapine and almost miraculously the psychosis at last began to diminish. And her psychiatrist advised us to complain, with the result we had one memorable meeting where a local senior health manager in effect told us off for complaining. The combination of these two things provided us with a turning point. Our despair turned to a raw anger which we focused on the local health systems and managers. Monica began to ask about when she could leave the ward. Thus even though there was no tangible change we all began to entertain the possibility of improvement. We began to focus our anger purposefully on influencing changes in the local health systems.

In conclusion

Our complaint was eventually rewarded by the commissioning of a new community-based service for seventeen other young people like Monica. She eventually left the rehabilitation ward to move into this service three years after her first admission to the acute adult ward. Subsequently often tiny but incremental improvements have combined to achieve remarkable progress. She now lives in a supported home, remains well integrated with her family, and leads a full and happy life.

Despite being experienced health professionals, nothing had prepared us, as parents, for the level of distress and despair of those early years. 'Why us?' had dominated our thinking. And yet now, seven years on from Monica leaving hospital, that question seems less important, reflecting our success as carers in integrating the raw emotions generated by those initial troubled times.

Feeling invisible

Father of young man with psychosis (submitted through the Meriden Programme)

The worst thing that happened in my life was having my son admitted to hospital against his will. Things had been getting out of hand for some months, and we were all exhausted in the family trying to handle it and work out what was wrong. He was involved with drugs, there were unsavoury characters calling to our home looking for him – people we would never have had dealings with before. He became more and more bizarre in his actions and ideas, and really paranoid – thinking that people were coming to get him. It all escalated – the GP got someone to see him, he wouldn't cooperate. The police were called, and it was clear that he was going to be hospitalised. He thought that the mental health staff who assessed him were agents of Satan, and fluctuated between being terrified and aggressive. The hardest thing I did was to help the police put handcuffs on him. It was the only way to help him at the time, but the memory of doing that will stay with me for the rest of my life.

This was the backdrop of my first contact with an in-patient unit – weeks of anxiety, worry, sleeplessness, not understanding what was going on. I wasn't at my best. I followed my son onto the unit on the day he was admitted. I couldn't work out what was going on. It was really hard to work out who was who, or to find someone to ask. Somebody else who was on the ward kept pestering me about something that had been in the news, and I thought I would hit him if he didn't leave me alone. I feel bad about that now, as I wasn't tuned in to the fact that he wasn't well.

It was hard to work out who the staff were, and nobody came up to me. I felt that I was invisible, as nobody seemed to notice me. Maybe I was feeling disorientated myself through lack of sleep. Eventually I found someone, and they said I would have to wait, that they couldn't tell me anything yet. I didn't know where to wait. I asked if I should leave it for an hour or so and they said it was up to me. I walked around outside for a while, and phoned my wife. She couldn't stop crying, and I felt I needed to be there to support her, but wanted to find out what was happening. I felt really torn, feeling in need of support myself, but having so many people who needed my support.

Having gone back onto the ward, it seemed to take ages to find someone again – everyone was busy, rushing around. Eventually I stopped someone, and they said they couldn't really tell me anything, that the doctor would need to assess my son who was sleeping because of the medication he had been given. There was no signposting as to what I should do. Was there anyone who could talk to me, or anything I could read?

That was my first experience, which was repeated in various ways several times over the weeks my son was in hospital. Contact was not made with me, rather I always had to initiate it. I always felt I was being treated with suspicion by the staff, although I didn't know why this would be. My son had lots of odd ideas about what had being going on in the weeks before he was admitted, some of them relating to other family members. What I found really odd was that nobody ever talked to us in the family at length to ask us for our account of what had been happening. My son, because of these odd ideas, did not want us involved or told about what was happening. Whenever I asked for information therefore, I was usually told that they couldn't tell me because of confidentiality. I didn't know what this meant, and it was never really explained to me. It was just a term they all seemed to use.

At one point, one of the staff suggested going to a support group for relatives. I'm afraid I wasn't really at a point where I wanted to talk to a group of strangers about the traumas of our family life. I just wanted to know what was happening with my son.

Eventually after persisting, I was told I could come to a ward round, which I didn't find very productive. It was a bit intimidating with so many people there that I hadn't met. I clammed up, and forgot what I wanted to ask – it came back to me afterwards.

The first time that the ward proactively contacted me was when my son was being discharged. I felt let down that I had not been more actively involved in the whole of his treatment, and the overall feeling I had was one of being excluded. I was surprised that, on the whole, the staff seemed disinterested in my son's life before he was ill, or in the whole of his world outside of hospital.

One of the things that surprised me most was that they seemed to find it very hard to understand all the reactions and feelings that we had as a family. We had been through so much. I know we did not always come across as reasonable, but at the beginning we were in shock, and later on we couldn't understand what was happening. I would have thought they would have understood our emotions better. The other main problem area was around the whole area of confidentiality. I still don't understand the ins and outs of this, but think it could have been handled differently as it resulted in us not having the information that would have helped us to cope.

Commentaries

Mike Shooter (Psychiatrist)

Reading these two heart-rending accounts, I went through some of the same emotions as the carers themselves – guilt (that the system I work in should have been so appalling), anger (that we seem to have done so little to change things) and despair (i.e. where to begin). The difference, of course, is that I could shut off after writing this. Carers cannot; their job is for life.

Here are just half a dozen big issues that both accounts raise so eloquently.

Service structures

Too often we cram people into traditional service frameworks instead of fitting services to their needs. Young patients with an emerging psychosis need the maximum amount of continuity during these critical years. They should not be passed like a relay baton between Children's Services (that 'don't do psychosis') and Adult Services (that 'don't do adolescence'). This is an argument for Young Persons Services, both for better treatment and for the emotional needs of patients and carers whose identity is undermined enough by the psychosis, without further disruption from foolish service demarcations.

In-patient conditions

Many of our hospital wards are now frankly scandalous. We can only guess at the horror of patients and carers as they walk (or are dragged) into a ward that is filthy, offers no sexual privacy and has an atmosphere of predatory violence. Partly, this is a matter of resources. The impression has grown that community care equals success and in-patient care equals failure; so all the fancy new money and creative thinking has gone into community teams. Hospital staff and patients alike have been left behind, demoralised and institutionalised, cut off from the world outside the walls. Ideally, hospital and community should be complementary parts of one mental health service, equally well resourced, with integration of patients' and carers' needs, across the boundaries. And there are plenty of examples now of in-patient care broken down into smaller, modern, short-stay units nearer to patients' homes.

We should not have to put up with old-style, isolated 'bins', where I did most of my training decades ago. But it is a matter of attitudes too, and I will come to those.

Carers' feelings

In the face of all this, it is hardly surprising that carers, as well as patients, should struggle with a range of disturbing emotions. Far from rejecting their loved ones, most families have been brought to their knees with exhaustion before seeking help, then feel guilty for 'failing' to cope. They are terrified by the illness that has shattered their life and the intrusions it brings with it. They are bewildered by the system they are trapped in. They are confused by the way they are shut out of their carer's role one minute and have responsibility thrown back at them the next. And however articulate they may be, they may become patients themselves because of the stress of it all. You can see from these accounts how easily these feelings can get converted into anger that is directed at themselves, at staff, or is played out between members of the family. So professionals, patients and carers become divided by mutual resentment, instead of working in partnership for everyone's benefit.

Communication

None of these feelings would be prevented by talking things over, but they would certainly be helped. More than that, it is difficult to see how anyone – staff or carers – could do their job properly without the regular passage of information between them. Staff need to know what the patient was like before the illness, what he/she is like between episodes of illness, what scary behaviour the carers see between CPN visits, what stresses the family are under and what imminent events might affect their caring role. Carers need to know who is who in the staff team and what they do; they need to know who to talk to, day to day and in a crisis; they need to know about the illness, the range of treatments available, the good and bad effects of medication to look out for, and prospects for the future. They need to know their rights and responsibilities and how best to exercise them: basic information – but often not given at all or only grudgingly given in the glare of the ward round. And the problem, it seems, is 'confidentiality'.

There must be some boundaries around what patients say to staff, across which carers may not trespass; but this should not prevent the passage of information with which confidentiality is confused in a legalistic world. However, the carers in these accounts, like so many others, feel that confidentiality is being used as an excuse to hide behind by staff who are suspicious of them at best, feel they are part of the cause of illness rather than its cure, and fear being overwhelmed by the carers' needs.

Complaints

Carers' anger, when it occurs, should be validated, listened to and acted upon as appropriate. It is no part of a manager's job to avoid that anger, to dismiss it or to get angry back. Some of the anger will be a natural response to the unfairness of illness – and carers may be helped to see it as such and supported with it. Some of it will be justified anger at mistakes made even in the best of services. Paying it credit begins with a clearly advertised complaints system that is more than lip service and is not used to scapegoat individuals for faults in the system. And who knows, patients, carers, staff and managers may use a complaint together to persuade commissioners (or even governments) to make changes.

Training

This is the key to attitudes. Resources are important. No one functions well where facilities are awful, where there is no money to put them right, and where too few staff have too little time to talk. In such circumstances, diagnosis is rushed and treatment is reduced to the drug trolley. Carers get no attention at all. But even then, there is no excuse for some of the behaviour described in these accounts: behaviour that springs from attitudes that set in early and which can be addressed in training. Patients and carers, properly selected and supported, should have a role in that training – and at long last we seem to be on the point of making that happen.

   It is difficult to believe that any trainee, in any profession within the mental health system, could not be affected by listening to the distress of a father helping to handcuff his own son. Or, better still, to role-play the agony of it directly. Harrowing though these accounts may be, they might just be what changes the attitudes of trainees, that encourages them to treat more sensitively the carers' needs and to act upon this in future practice. For that I offer both these writers my thanks.

Dr Gráinne Fadden (Clinical Psychologist)

I read these two accounts with a growing sense of discomfort as the nightmarish scenes unfolded. As I immersed myself in them, the 'hairs on the back of your neck' feeling changed to an uneasy feeling in my stomach. Direct and honest stories such as these have a way of triggering emotions – their content certainly makes it clear that this is needed for many of the managers and clinicians who work in our current mental health systems. 'Why us?' triggered memories of my first real exposure to residential institutional settings as a young psychologist at the age of 21. It took time to get used to the scenes similar to those described in this account: the shuffling men often unfamiliar with the sight of a woman, the people looking for cigarettes, the alarms, the people talking about things that didn't make sense to me. I tried to imagine how I would have felt if four years previously at the age of 17, I was told I would have to stay there and sleep there. The feeling is one of horror. Having gone back in time, I then thought ahead to what it would feel like if in a few years' time, like the man in the 'Feeling invisible' account, I had to put handcuffs on my own son. These are nightmarish accounts, but the biggest horror is that they are current, not past.

Following my initial emotional response, I was left mostly with questions. Most ordinary members of the public would have tears in their eyes listening to these accounts. My biggest question was, 'What have we done to the good people who enter the health professions, to dehumanise them to the extent that they act in the way described in these accounts?' I will come back to this issue later.

And so, to the common themes of these accounts: the first has to be the trauma experienced by families when facing mental health problems for the first time. It is clear from both accounts that the onset of mental health difficulties transported these families from the comfort of normal family life into a range of unfamiliar worlds – coping with their own child who saw them as the enemy, dealing with self-harm, contact with drug dealers, having a child effectively 'arrested', police involvement, contact with disturbed and distressed people, in-patient environments with primitive and threatening conditions. It is not surprising that this gives rise to a range of powerful emotions – confusion, fear, anger, despair and total bewilderment.

Perhaps the most striking feeling is the description of guilt, the sense of having let their child down, even though in both cases they had been dealing with a whole series of problems over a period of months. It was only when things reached crisis point that they asked for help. These families have such high expectations of themselves – to deal unaided with very unfamiliar and troubling circumstances. What is also clear is the impact of these difficulties on the whole family – parents, siblings and grandparents, leading to people feeling 'torn' trying to meet the differing demands. Their worlds had changed from being safe and secure to being unfamiliar, stressful and uncertain.

The second common theme is the way in which health systems are set up with the expectation that people will fit their criteria, rather than respond to the need as it arises. The classic example of this is that of the child and adolescent/adult divide referred to in the 'Why us?' account, though this can also happen at the adult/older adult end as well. How confusing this must be for families, to be told you are not the right age to receive particular services. The message clearly is that you must fit the system rather than that the system will meet your needs. It brought to mind for me my time working in the Buckingham Mental Health Service which provided high-quality Adult Services. It was a frequent occurrence that GPs would time referrals so that they would arrive on a young person's sixteenth birthday, which was the earliest age at which people were seen in the Adult Services. There is something very wrong with our systems that create rigid boundaries that are not responsive to need. Other examples of this are in the 'Feeling invisible' account where the staff couldn't tell the worried father anything at the time when he most needed some information, and only initiated contact at discharge when it suited them.

The third issue is the total unsuitability of some in-patient settings as therapeutic environments. They can be threatening chaotic places that exacerbate the anxiety of the experience of mental health difficulties. Too often, admission to an in-patient unit is seen as a treatment in itself, rather than a location which provides an opportunity for therapeutic interventions to take place. As a psychologist, one of the things that is most striking for me is the apparent total reliance on medication as the sole treatment. Where were the cognitive therapy, psychotherapy and family therapy?

The in-patient units, as described, retain a very institutionalised feel, evidenced by the lack of interest in the world of the individual outside. There appeared to be no sense of people existing in a social context, and nobody asked the family about their experience. There really is a sense of seeing the person as an 'illness' rather than a many-faceted, interesting human being. The arrogance of making a diagnosis of schizophrenia in a 16-year-old following one domiciliary visit really struck me. All the other features of the institution are present – seeing families only in the stressful context of a ward round, the power of holding onto information under the pretext of a misunderstood 'confidentiality' concept, the language, the systems that only those on the inside understand. It is not surprising that those entering the system feel hopeless and disempowered.

And so back to the staff issue mentioned earlier. Why is it that the staff described seem unempathic, unable to put themselves in the other's shoes, to tune into emotion, or to act in a way that is not defensive? Mental health staff should bring a calmness, a reassuring presence, should be the holders of hope for those in distress. People become 'dehumanised' when they are in difficult circumstances over which they have no control. Perhaps more than anything these accounts reflect the issue of the forgotten staff group – in-patient staff who cope with underdeveloped services, high staff turnover and sickness levels, and are frequently neglected in terms of training and support.

The appeal for mental health staff now appears to be to work in specialist community teams. The specific needs of in-patient staff need to be addressed. This includes innovative methods of training such as *On the Edge*, an interactive play exploring mental health issues developed by the Exstream Theatre Company with the support of mental health service users and professionals. I have a sense that those working in dehumanising systems need powerful methods such as this to bring back their humanity and ordinary human responses.

Questions and issues for discussion

1 What are the likely feelings of parents when their son or daughter is first admitted to a psychiatric ward?
2 What feelings do you think ward staff have in relation to family members visiting on an acute ward?
3 What facilities or support could be provided for carers visiting the ward?
4 What information do you think ward staff should provide for the family members of a new admission?
5 What information is confidential and why?
6 What information would it be useful for staff to seek from carers?

Exercise

Role-play a first admission. Different roles will include: the young person being admitted for the first time; their mother and/or father; a busy ward nurse; at least two other patients in various states of distress. After the role-play, take time to explore the feelings generated by each role.

Note

1 This chapter combines two personal accounts. The chapter was constructed before the format of the book was finally decided, but we felt the quality of the commentaries was such that we should leave the chapter as it stands.

Chapter 11

No sex allowed

'Charlotte'

Peter and I met in Cardiff in the 1980s and were immediately attracted to each another. Quite early on in our relationship Peter told me he had been diagnosed with schizophrenia six years earlier, at the age of 17. I found this, and him, fascinating. He explained to me that he was an undergraduate, studying biochemistry, and that he was having a year out from his studies, having suffered a 'psychotic episode' a few months previously. This was something I knew absolutely nothing about, and when he described it to me, my interest was fired.

Within a few months, Peter and I had fallen in love, and it was to be the most powerful relationship I had ever had in my life. Peter, in his everyday life, seemed quite 'normal' to me, and so did his friends, two of whom, both undergraduate students, he had met in hospital. They were bright young men who enjoyed comparing and laughing about their similar episodes of psychosis (which they nicknamed 'the cosmic wars').

I had never actually known Peter or any of his friends when they were in a psychotic state, and I only dimly registered that they were all on antipsychotic medication. The first time I began to ask about medication was when we started to have a sexual relationship. Peter was embarrassed because, although he had no difficulty maintaining an erection, he couldn't ejaculate easily. He worried that I might think he was not turned on by me. It took a while, but we eventually discussed what was happening and, encouraged by me, we got his medication changed.

From the start our sexual compatibility was a joy and a reassurance to both of us. I look back at this period in my life as one of truly great happiness. As lovers do, we felt we could conquer the world together, and I noticed that the emotional benefits of a brilliant sex life brought calm and a sense of 'groundedness' to both of us. Making love seemed the perfect therapy for feelings of stress and anxiety, as well as an affirmation of the deep and healing bond we shared. We moved in together, Peter returned to university to finish his degree, and we planned to get married.

Our happiness was to be severely tested when, one year down the line, everything seemed to crumble. In our naivety we had reasoned that the love we experienced would prevent Peter from ever being mentally unhappy again, and two months before our wedding he began to reduce his medication. At the same time the stress of his degree made him unable to sit his Finals, and gradually Peter was overcome by a hugely frightening psychotic state. He was admitted to hospital six weeks after our wedding, and my whole world seemed to fall apart.

Peter was put in a typical hospital room which had a lino floor, a single chair, and a glass-fronted door. Peter was to be in hospital for nearly four months, and I visited him every day after work. It was a period of terrible sadness, confusion and despair for me. The man I knew and loved seemed to have disappeared under a great cloud of bizarre ideas, hallucinations, and strange mood swings. His speech was slurred and his hands trembled under the effects of medication.

The ward was noisy and there were constant interruptions. In order to have some privacy we would walk in the grounds together. I did not know how to respond to him and resorted to a sort of amateur psychoanalysis, and desperate pleading and reasoning, which I now realise was the worst possible thing I could have done. The stress for him was enormous, as was the frustration and guilt for me.

The one thing that would have really helped us, unravelled our anxiety, and grounded both of us, would have been the chance for us to be physically close. We both needed skin-on-skin contact, stroking, warmth, reassurance, and a chance to express our love for each other. We needed nights together, sleeping side by side. We missed that terribly. What we got were those chilly walks in the grounds.

As for making love, that was out of the question. We couldn't even sit side by side and have a cuddle, with just one hospital chair in the room. When, after a few weeks, I did join him precariously in his single bed, we felt like naughty schoolchildren, with one eye constantly on the door in case any staff should see us or come in. We managed once, furtively, to make love this way, but understandably it wasn't the most thrilling sexual experience of either of our lives. As I left the hospital after my daily visit, I used to compare myself enviously with staff going home after their (possibly stressful) shifts to the human comforts I was denied.

As Peter's mental health improved, our relationship reappeared and we both became less anxious. This was when our longing for each other really returned, but it was to be many weeks before we could spend the night together, when Peter had a couple of weekends at home before finally being discharged.

There were to be many subsequent admissions to hospital for Peter in our married life together. Sex and the importance of intimacy was never once mentioned to us or discussed by staff. It remained always something outside the realm of hospital admission. It was something we just had to deal with on our own, and yet often, something, I am convinced, which could have helped our stress, facilitated Peter's recovery and comforted both of us.

I don't know exactly why the subject was never broached with staff. I am usually able to talk openly about such subjects, but in the context of the ward this seemed to be unthinkable. Not only could I not talk about our needs as a couple, no member of staff ever approached me to ask if we had enough privacy or chances to be intimate. It was a completely taboo area on both sides.

With hindsight, I think it may be that staff (consciously or unconsciously) see an in-patient purely in terms of their mental condition, and, perhaps more significantly, as existing within a work environment. Of course, for the in-patient who has to sleep there for weeks or months, endure confusion, fear, distress, interruption, noise, hospital heating, cleaners, plastic chairs, their environment is neither work nor home. Instead it is like some strange hinterland outside of the world, where distinct rules apply that are entirely different to normal life.

In the ward, concepts of healing, comfort and recovery are linked inextricably to care plans, multidisciplinary teams, occupational therapy, medication, and 'therapeutic' routines of one sort or another. Everything is recorded, analysed and discussed. One's very humanness is professionalised. Touching, stroking, cuddling and (dare we mention it?) sex fall way outside the boundaries of the staff–patient relationship. Is this why staff are able to 'blank out' these ordinary, vital aspects of human need, because there is no way they can supply them professionally?

What a strange double-think exists in these circumstances. It is as if those who go home after an arduous shift on the ward, needing the emotional and sexual release and comfort of their own partners, are unable to imagine that those they leave behind might be longing for exactly the same experience. Do staff imagine that professional approaches meet all human needs? They didn't meet ours as we clung on to each other in those cold and windy hospital grounds.

Commentaries

Lis Jones (Nurse)

This is a very moving account of a couple struggling to face the unbearable, frightening and painful reality of the male partner's mental illness. 'Charlotte' starts by saying that 'Peter' had been diagnosed as suffering from schizophrenia six years previously and that she found him fascinating. Indeed she says that her interest was fired up by his account of his psychotic episode a few months before they met. Psychosis in such a young man is a tragedy and the disintegration of the mind is a disturbing and frightening thing. This fear of mental disintegration can be defended against by various psychological defences that protect the individual from the full implications and meaning of the breakdown. Charlotte may have dealt with her own feelings of anxiety, fear and disappointment by turning them into fascination and excitement. The full implications of the illness are pushed out of her mind as she only dimly remembers registering that Peter and his two friends are on anti-psychotic medication.

As can happen in many areas of life, the sexual relationships can act as another form of defence, functioning as a psychological retreat from the fear of madness and catastrophic collapse. Charlotte and Peter's sexual relationship seemed to them 'the perfect therapy for feelings of stress and anxiety', and as lovers they felt they could conquer the world together. Unfortunately this ideal solution breaks down as Peter breaks down into a frightening psychotic state and the idealised relationship breaks down. As she says so poignantly, 'the man I knew and loved seemed to have disappeared under a great cloud of bizarre ideas, hallucinations, and strange mood swings'.

The description of the stark room Peter stayed in, while no doubt an accurate description of the external environment, may also have represented the dawning of a depressing reality that the ideal relationship she believed she had established with Peter was breaking down. The noises are the depressing voices of reality that interfere with her picture of herself and Peter as a 'brilliant' married couple. Charlotte feels resentful that the hospital does not allow access to opportunities for physical intimacy, especially as Peter's mental health improves.

However, a hospital is not a home. It is an institution that mainly exists for the diagnosis, treatment and care of people who are suffering from a physical or mental illness. In such states patients are often regressed and in a state of dependence on others for psychological and physical care. In these regressed states patients are often very vulnerable as they may not have full command of their senses. Vulnerable and ill patients can fall in love with their doctors and nurses, and must be protected from others and sometimes from themselves. It is for these reasons that doctors and nurses are forbidden from having sexual relationships with their patients. Patients suffering from a mental illness can be particularly vulnerable to these processes and need protecting from their own actions as well as the actions of others. For example, a mother recently wrote a complaint that her young daughter who was suffering from manic depression had been seduced by a man with a personality disorder while she was on an in-patient unit. She rightly believed that her daughter was not fully responsible for her actions and was entitled to be protected while under the care of the hospital. Patients and staff need boundaries that protect them from all sorts of mistreatment including sexual mistreatment.

Nevertheless, Charlotte's experience regarding the absence of any acknowledgement of an issue that was so central in their relationship is significant. We talk of 'engagement' and 'holistic care' and 'recovery' – yet the way in which our institutions operate risk excluding the 'humanness' that Charlotte talks about. One of the main challenges for staff on the ward is to maintain the boundaries that protect patients, but also protect the staff – yet create an environment that is safe and that can allow healing.

The capacity of the staff team to create the potential for therapeutic opportunities will be influenced by their understanding of the dynamics at play in the ward, and in the experiences of each patient. Lacking confidence and competence, and often subject to externally imposed controls and constraints, staff defence mechanisms can lead to a distancing from patients and their families. The lack of opportunity for reflection, supervision and thinking about the patient can reinforce a culture in which complex and sensitive issues such as Charlotte and Peter's sense of loss and despair, and its focus for them around the intimacy of their sexual relationship, are too difficult to even acknowledge let alone explore.

Cultures that can support opportunities for dynamic reflection that shape professional approaches are more likely to be able to create those therapeutic moments that might have made a difference to Charlotte and Peter's experiences.

Jan Olav Johannessen (Psychiatrist)

> We are all much more simply human than otherwise.
>
> (Sullivan 1953)

Charlotte and Peter's story shows us the humanity so easily forgotten when we treat people with psychosis. For one reason or another, we tend to distance ourselves from the deep subjective suffering experienced by patients with such a confusing disorder as psychosis. It is they, not us. Sullivan's words, that 'we are all much more simply human than otherwise', seem somehow to slip from our minds.

When training as a young doctor in a department of psychiatry, my supervisor informed me that it was no use trying to make a joke when talking with patients with schizophrenia. They had lost their sense of humour; in fact, they had never been able to develop the sense of humour that so-called 'normal' people did. Their psychological mindedness was incapable of dealing with the complex task of understanding an ironic remark, and as for self-irony, well, need I say more?

This reductionist point of view has been prevalent within many therapeutic ideologies, psychological as well as biological. We are all aware of the early psychoanalytic masters who deemed the psychotic conditions to be 'unanalysable', as we today encounter those who look at human minds solely as chemical factories with some disturbance in the signalling systems. I think all this is rooted in our need to defend ourselves from the potential suffering embedded in human nature, in the pure existential fact of acknowledging our humanity and aloneness.

This fundamental human experience, the feeling of 'aloneness', is compensated for in different ways; we all have our strategies to avoid it. And, in some life situations, we need the closeness of others more. When feeling down, we need to be held. When falling apart, we need someone to keep us together. When feeling confused, we need someone to help us sort things out. When feeling alone, we need someone who can be with us. And, if we love someone, they, or he or she, are the ones we want to be there.

Charlotte tells us about affection, love, compassion, more than just a simple need for physical love, or sexuality. But she also tells us an important story of the person behind the psychosis, a person with the same needs and capabilities as any one of us. She tells us the story of two human beings, where one for a period of time is deeply confused, or psychotic, but none the less as human as any one of us.

I hope we all have learned some lessons, but none of us should confuse our professional predecessors' lack of insight with bad intentions. The physical surroundings, the buildings, the crowded wards; in the early 1980s they didn't encourage individuality. The treatment ideologies intermingled with house rules, however humanistic they may have been, in most cases did not permit sexual relations between patients or between patients and visitors. Some of the reasons for this are still valid, and obvious. In some cases, the very dissolution of what we call ego-boundaries, that is the capacity to experience oneself as an integrated person, separate from the rest of the world, makes close physical (or psychological) contact very threatening. What today we would call need-specific, or need-adapted treatment would take such aspects into consideration in each individual case. And one of the lessons that has taken us longer to learn is to talk with the relatives, and in most cases to work together with relatives. I hope that in today's psychiatry mental health workers would have talked with Charlotte and Peter. I also hope that the material conditions we offer people with psychotic disorders have changed for the better, at least in our part of the world. But I know that we do not have to travel far to discover worse experiences than Peter and Charlotte's in the UK then and now.

Humour and sex. Sadness and joy. Hope and despair. These are all ingredients of everyday life, of human beings' daily lives. In the caricatures of the press, psychiatrists are portrayed as preoccupied with sex. Charlotte has effectively demonstrated to us that we, mental health workers, still struggle to handle this topic within our wards, within a therapeutic setting. Why is that so? I have touched upon some of the reasons in the above. If I should choose one, the most important, I end up by pointing at our need to distance ourselves from, and have control over, the in-built fear in each and every one of us of the profound anxiety behind and inside serious psychiatric disorders such as the psychoses. By admitting that, we can come to terms with this fear, and hopefully dare to acknowledge that 'we are all much more simply human than otherwise'. If we can manage to understand the other person as a real person, with the same feelings, wishes, capabilities, needs and hopes as ourselves, then we have formed the basic platform for helping each other.

Questions and issues for discussion

1 What are the main differences between a hospital and a home?
2 Why do you think the staff didn't talk with this couple about their sexual relationship?
3 How would you approach the topic of a patient's sexual needs while in hospital?
4 How would you draw the line between minimising risk of harm or exploitation, and supporting personal relationships between patients on a ward?

Exercise

Set up a role-play of a CPA review one month after admission based on this account. Roles include the male patient, his wife, the psychiatrist, the ward manager and the patient's named nurse. You may include other professionals.

Chapter 12

Frustrated and angry

'Felicity'

My reactions to in-patient services have almost always been definite, personal and intense and I think this reflects the high stress associated with my daughter's admission to the ward. My emotions, sensitivities and awareness at such times are raw and exposed, and I feel very vulnerable, so kindness is really appreciated and indifference really hurts.

The worst situation for me was the week preceding and the early weeks following my first encounter with the psychiatric ward, and I think this is true for many carers. Nothing in my previous life had prepared me for this experience; I was as lost as my daughter.

As a single parent, twice over, I am used to facing difficulties on my own, at least in the fifteen years since my last parent died. Even when my parents were alive I made my own decisions, though their background support had always been invaluable and I never doubted their love. In this new situation of a mental health problem, I had neither love nor support, and did not know where to find help. There was no one with whom I could share this burden. The whole territory of mental health problems was strange, unpredictable and frightening; my world had become as surreal as my daughter's. At the same time, I recognised that to everyone else, the world was still normal. It was something like a perpetual bereavement, which might outlive me. My daughter, the person I used to know so intimately, and whom I loved and wanted to rescue more desperately than I'd ever wanted anything, was beyond my reach and everything which had seemed stable and reliable so recently was not. Her actions, emotions and discourse, and therefore my own responses, were unpredictable, shifting even from minute to minute. My girl had become a stranger to me and I was a stranger to her. I was no longer her loved and trusted mother, but often seen as 'the enemy' (a view sometimes clearly shared by ward staff). Any action, the mildest question, even something so innocuous as offering a cup of tea, might provoke an angry response or a vacant or frightened stare. So, it is perhaps not surprising that in-patient services were the lighthouse signalling both support and help which were so desperately sought, and also the dangers of a terrifying future.

Clearly there were some very sick people in the ward. I was alert to the patients, and to the staff and their body language. Were they friendly or disinterested, or even exploitative? Were these strangers going to add further insult, help my daughter or see her as a lost cause? Would they see the special and talented young woman I had known? Or would they see just another 'druggy' who had blown her mind in overindulgence? Never before had I been in such unknown territory, or had to leave my precious and vulnerable daughter in this situation where she could not be responsible for herself, and I felt uncertain of the staff and patients. Because of the silence surrounding mental health, I did not know where to seek help and information, and I had never needed it so desperately. I had never known anyone facing a similar situation. I felt completely isolated, and my daughter's health, even her very existence, at least as we had known it to that point, seemed to have ended.

The psychiatrist who admitted my daughter to the ward was from Africa, and from a country in which I had lived for some time. I came to like and respect him very much during the next months. He was unfailingly kind and courteous, showing warmth, humanity and listening respectfully to my daughter and myself. He answered my questions and was the first to tell me that a third of people who have a psychotic episode recover completely, another third would have several episodes but were able to continue to live fairly normal lives and the remainder often had recurrent relapses. He offered me the first glimpse of hope. I shall never forget his dedication to his patients and the kindness and support he offered to both patients and carers. I never met a carer who did not like him immensely. Later I came to hear he was criticised by his colleagues for empathising too much with patients and carers! Sometimes he spent the night attending to emergencies and went straight into the next day's appointments without a break. After my daughter had returned home some weeks later, I had an opportunity to take her to France and he approved our excursion. A few days before we went, I wondered whether it was wise for us to leave the UK. He is the only consultant I have ever met who reminded me I could return quickly if necessary (and he didn't think it would be), and in any case, I was most welcome to phone him from France should I need to do so.

(Some months after her first admission, and when the first psychiatrist had left, we were assigned a temporary consultant. He also was a humane man and well liked by patients and carers. He had a policy of meeting carers for two hours/week and said he could not manage his patients properly without drawing on their insights and knowledge. He did not know how other consultants managed without using this asset. All the carers knew themselves to be valued by him.)

Returning to my daughter's first admission: in contrast to the psychiatrist, the ward staff were almost without exception disinterested. Later, I learned they were mainly temporary agency staff, by way of explanation. My daughter was upset and very angry that I had caused her to be sectioned; she and I were both in tears. I recall a nurse standing by irritated and impatient that we were not just getting on with it. They intended to bath my daughter, a male nurse was designated to the job, I said I would prefer to help her and this was agreed with some annoyance. Later, another nurse commented that I seemed to be very interested in what was happening to my daughter, as if this was rather odd behaviour! I was offered no information about mental health conditions, support organisations and local contact numbers, no useful reference list, there was no named nurse to whom I could address questions, not even a note of ward phone numbers, visiting times, ward rounds and routines, etc. Later, I saw the scene that became very familiar, with the nursing staff in the office, behind the reception desk and with the door shut, chatting together. No one offered me a cup of tea, or a word of comfort; and this too was a common scene; carers leaving the ward after a new admission completely grief-stricken. I left the ward feeling very ambivalent and without confidence in the quality of care my daughter would receive. The consultant psychiatrist was the one person I trusted.

There were lots of petty regulations on the ward, e.g. snooker could only be played until 6.00 pm, after which the balls and cues were locked away. The only other activity available was smoking, so everyone did, and cigarettes were the currency. An adjacent gym was locked and unused (no trained staff). There was no OT. Volunteers did OT with cancer patients in the next building every evening, but no one knew about this in the psychiatric wards.

My daughter reported that at night when she wanted just to talk to someone so she could unravel the real from the dream, the night nurse refused to listen (although the ward was quiet and the nurse was reading a book). When my daughter was on leave we spent many such nights, and she was able to sort things out for herself just by having me there as an interested listening ear. One night whilst an in-patient, my daughter disappeared with two men off the ward and later phoned a friend to pick them up from town as they had no money. They were all three drunk. So far as I am aware, no one had missed them from the ward. Clearly, there could have been more serious consequences too.

At one stage, my daughter suggested I should not visit every day, or bring her things (food, drawing materials, magazines and books, CDs, etc). She said the way to survive there was to become anonymous; most people had no visitors, and it was safer to be like them. I could see that visitors were not welcome and enquiries were met with the 'confidential' barrier.

The ward policy on making up prescriptions was to leave till last the people going on leave, so although you might have leave for two days you had to be back on the ward to collect medication between 5.00 pm and 6.00 pm. Effectively half the leave period seemed to be spent waiting around for medication or travelling back and forth collecting it (30–40 miles was not uncommon and with the hospital in a rural location with infrequent public transport). The senior consultant psychiatrist organised the ward round, and times were often delayed because of emergencies. So, if a patient was likely to get home leave, (s)he might be the last patient to be seen and carers might well spend 4–6 hours waiting. You were in no doubt that as a carer you were not even on the horizon for consideration.

These incidents and policies caused me to be angry, upset and frustrated. They confirmed my opinion that the ward nursing staff were sloppy, negligent and disinterested in their work and the patients, and that the ward as a whole operated on a hierarchical system valuing the consultants at its peak. The lack of information made me feel sad and helpless, but also gave me a determination to try to improve the system.

Commentaries

Susan Mitchell (Psychiatrist)

In 1990 Smith and Birchwood wrote, 'Considerable advances have been made in the family management of schizophrenia but there remains a major challenge for the psychiatric services to integrate these innovations into clinical practice.' These authors identified as a major issue 'the problem of engaging families in a therapeutic programme'. More recently in 2005, as part of the Partners in Care Campaign, a group of carers highlighted a number of key issues of unmet need during carers' assessments which included: lack of support, feeling excluded and that their caring role was not recognised, no sense of partnership with 'professionals', lack of information both about the illness and about services, and problems with access to services in a crisis.

All of these are well illustrated in this thought-provoking and at times uncomfortable account where Felicity describes her feelings leading up to her daughter's first admission and then gives a clear description of how alien the experience of admission can feel for the carer. For me the powerful impact of this is in its showing that if we do not fully understand the effects of the illness and of contact with mental health services on those nearest to the patient, we risk unwittingly making matters worse.

Of her feelings in the weeks prior to admission she writes movingly: 'nothing in my previous life had prepared me for this; I was as lost as my daughter'. The stigma and silence surrounding the illness further compound her sense of isolation. How often do we fully acknowledge this?

The nature of the illness itself may increase the sense of isolation and distrust. 'My girl had become a stranger to me and I was a stranger to her. I was no longer her loved and trusted mother, but often seen as "the enemy" (a view sometimes clearly shared by ward staff).' If we do not ask carers how they feel, try to understand their feelings and behaviour, how can we help? In my view it is important to understand the intention that leads to certain behaviour and not just the behaviour itself.

For Felicity, kindness, understanding and the kindling of hope are much valued when present; sadly for her they often seem to be absent in the impersonal 'ward staff'. Her perception of these staff as disinterested, uncaring, negligent, irritable and impatient is a sad reflection on the admission ward. Even if it is not strictly true, it is concerning that this impression can be created and it may have a negative effect on relationships between staff and carer and staff and patient. It is worth remembering that there is evidence that the negative effects of expressed emotion occur in care settings as well as in families. (Tattan and Tarrier 2000) The lack of consistent staff, changes in consultant and reliance on agency staff to cover shifts is a theme too often encountered in carers' accounts of services and one which cannot help in the building of trust.

This chapter suggests that we also need to look at the processes and systems in hospitals as well as the relationships. Those of us who work in mental health establishments may take these for granted; but we may not make sufficient allowance for how different they seem to those on the outside. We sometimes speak in jargon terms, set up meetings to suit our routines and not those of others; we may not be able to change them all to suit everyone but Felicity's account reminds us that at least we can give an explanation of why we do things as we do and seek to make changes where we can (Birchwood and Tarrier 1994, Kingdom and Turkington 1995). Engagement is a key part of this process, for without this no psychological understanding can develop. This includes making the ward as therapeutic as possible, in both physical and human environments. We need to pay more attention to the needs of carers to make them feel welcome and involved whilst respecting the patient's confidentiality appropriately (Royal College of Psychiatrists 2005). At the same time there is still a need to address the training of staff in psychological, social and family interventions.

The image of the admission ward as a lighthouse is a striking one. A beacon signalling danger – but not a refuge or safe harbour. Feeling helpless and angry is an understandable response to the onset of a psychotic illness in a close family member. Our job as doctors, nurses and other mental health professionals is to acknowledge this and help the person cope, not to add to these painful feelings.

Cliff Prior (CEO Rethink)

If only Felicity's experience was unusual. But it is exceptional only in its eloquence. Her account mirrors the stories of thousands of carers and shows how much further we need to go in making our mental health system human and caring at its most critical point.

Rethink is the national membership charity for people affected by severe mental illness – themselves or as carers. It also provides nearly 400 direct mental health services. As part of our work, Rethink regularly conducts surveys to collect service user and carer experiences and priorities, as well as more in-depth involvement to identify ways of improving services for the future. This commentary is drawn from such work.

Felicity documents the frightening and bewildering experience of first becoming a carer; the lack of knowledge about where to turn; the desperate need for information; the sense of 'living bereavement'; the lack of respect or even basic human courtesy towards carers; the impact of petty rules and procedures designed for staff convenience as though in-patients and their carers did not matter; the way confidentiality is used as a barrier rather than a benefit. All are commonplace.

Rethink surveys tell us that the in-patient care is one of the worst and most traumatic experiences for people. Some want it improved, some want it replaced. What can we learn for the future?

First on the improvement front: Felicity tells us that the psychiatrist involved was caring, helpful and respectful. Yet despite this the overall experience was appalling.

Wards are large institutions, hospitals larger and more institutionalised still. All history of large institutions shows that they can defeat even heroic champions of better practice. Staff get used to things and cease to see them – that's not a criticism, it's a reality of being there so many hours in the week. We must not carry on designing our mental health services in ways which require heroes in order to work well. If we are to make any headway, we have to recognise these as systemic problems and take a systematic approach to service improvement. This would include:

- a patient rights based approach, with advocacy built in as automatic
- a designated carer support advocate
- information services in the hospital, run by the advocacy service to be independent, with an information pack automatically given to every new patient and their carer that includes details of support groups and organisations
- an end to agency nurse staffing – which will entail significant improvements in pay and conditions, but no ward can offer sustained quality with constant staff change
- staff rooms too small to accommodate the team on duty at any one point – the only way to keep staff in the ward not in the team room
- changes to professional training, with user and carer trainers providing mandatory input, along with regular refreshers to sustain recognition; facts and figures stay in the head, but hearing first-hand from people who have been there changes the heart and the evidence is clear that that lasts longer
- changes to job design: listening must be a key part of the role; in surveys of Rethink service users, time to talk is the overwhelming priority

- extension of choice to mental health care – choice of hospital, choice of alternatives to hospital
- service users and carers employed in quality assurance roles by providers themselves and by inspectorates.

Frankly, these may only be sticking plasters. Lasting change may only come from a completely new approach.

As part of Rethink's Mental Health First work in 2005, we asked focus groups of users and carers what the future might look like without psychiatric hospitals. The first response was often fear: there is an overwhelming need for a place of safety in a mental health crisis, and the thought that hospitals might not be there was alarming particularly for carers.

Thinking beyond this, people recognised that the safe place did not need to be a hospital. There was a strong desire for small, purpose-built crisis houses with a therapeutic environment, individual en suite rooms, and people to talk to. Stays would be short to avoid institutionalisation.

The next consideration was prevention: investment in crisis prevention through self-management programmes, easy access early in a developing problem and intensive support in the home in an actual crisis.

Of course much of this is already policy and some is current practice. Rethink runs crisis help lines with linked crisis houses, and NHS trusts are required to have intensive home treatment services available for people in a crisis. But coverage is patchy and poorly developed, with much of the funding still tied up in buildings.

Helping more people to stay out of hospital requires changes in hospitals themselves. Those who do still need an in-patient stay are increasingly the most severely ill, people with additional problems such as drink or drug dependency, and those who are assessed as a risk to others, possibly diverted from the criminal justice system. Our current models for alternatives to hospital have still to address the needs for security, and further R&D effort is urgently needed to make sure the new approaches genuinely benefit all.

There are two other aspects of Felicity's account that stand out: the stigma around mental illness, and the view that professionals take about carers.

Stigma is at the heart of many of the problems facing mental health care. It means that people do not know about mental health problems, what to do about them or where to turn. It means services are separated, and too often of a lower standard – witness the Healthcare Commission (2005) report on dirty hospitals. Investment in services, research and information are lower. For staff, mental health is too often seen as the lower status career choice.

The prejudice, ignorance and fear, and the outright discrimination, which make up stigma must be tackled. And the programmes in New Zealand and Scotland show that a real impact can be made at an affordable cost.

Informal carers make up the majority of the mental health workforce. Nothing unusual in that, the same is true in dementia care and learning disabilities, for example. But only in mental health are carers still seen by some professionals as the enemy and by many as simply a nuisance. Forty years on from Laing's work we are still suffering a legacy of seeing families as the problem. It is something we must drive out of mental health training and culture. Practical tools such as carer psychosocial education and systematic approaches such as the Meriden initiative give staff tangible ways of engaging carers in a new and more helpful way.

Nothing can make a severe mental health crisis easy. Nothing can take away the pain of seeing someone you love in pain and so changed that they cannot see your love for them. But we can recognise the nature of the experience, the bewilderment, the pain and the fear, and respond to it with professional understanding and human warmth. Staff too often work in environments which undermine even the best efforts to do this. Let's change those environments, replace them altogether if we can, raise the status of mental health care, and make sure Felicity's account ceases to be familiar.

Questions and issues for your service

1   In what ways did the ward staff seem uncaring to this carer?
2   What role would a carer's advocate have on an acute ward?
3   If a patient sees his/her parents as the 'enemy' should the staff let this influence their own view of the parents?
4   Why do you think snooker could only be played until 6.00 pm? How do you think this could be changed?
5   Would reducing the size of the staff room be an effective way of stopping staff chatting together instead of being on the ward? Can you think of other ways?
6   What routines are you aware of in your service that are more convenient for staff than they are for patients/clients and their carers?
7   What are the advantages of a crisis house over a hospital ward? Are there any disadvantages?

Exercise

In your ward identify four ways in which carers' needs could be met better. Then clarify what would need to be done by whom in order to bring these changes about.

Chapter 13

Feeling grateful

Daniel and Jo Kirk

Our daughter Lorraine had suffered for years, with what it was difficult to establish – there was no label. She had a number of minor disabilities that compounded to become a major problem as she became a teenager. She was always unable to express herself, she always appeared content, very rarely showing delight or anger.

Lorraine had been under the care of a psychiatrist as an outpatient at the local general hospital since the age of 18. He appeared to have a really good grasp of Lorraine's problems and tried to provide the correct care, which worked for a while, the best his resources would allow. The counselling Lorraine received via him was very caring.

Then in September 1999 when she was 19, Lorraine tried to end her life.

The anxiety of living with someone in this frame of mind takes its toll on all members of the immediate family. We had to keep an eye open 24 hours of the day in case she tried to harm herself, making you tired, short tempered, jumpy and permanently on edge. It was like a bad dream that didn't go away when you woke up. Unknown territory, no apparent solution, what feels like a no hope situation all adds to the tension. We were very frightened.

After the suicide attempt the psychiatrist was very concerned as he felt the local hospital mental health wards were not appropriate for Lorraine. Finding alternatives, and the fight that ensued to gain her the help she so desperately needed, increased the incredible anxiety and pressure we were already under. Your shoulders rise and your chest tightens and there is no release. It is a very solitary place to be.

Lorraine was admitted to the Mental Health Unit. Once in the Unit she was heavily sedated and left, apart from routine checks to make sure everyone was safe, present and correct. Many of her fellow patients were alcoholics and drug addicts – the MH Unit was where the Casualty Dept. placed problem patients who could not be left on a normal ward. Her psychiatrist was very unhappy with this situation, as were we, as Lorraine is so vulnerable when functioning at her best, let alone with psychotic depression. The first time she was admitted to the MH Unit she had her own room that her psychiatrist had secured for her. At this juncture we were naively unaware of the sort of fellow patients she would be mixing with, but having her own room did shelter her from the majority of the scuffles, etc.

Subsequent admissions to the MH Unit were on shared wards of 4–6 beds. She was older at this stage and the staff felt she did not warrant her own room, so she had to witness a very different series of experiences which mostly left her further withdrawn and very nervous. She was left by staff pretty much to her own devices apart from being able to use the hospital gym 1–2 mornings a week under supervision. Apart from this the staff were uninterested in her and had nothing to offer her – no long-term care, daily monitoring, group meetings, cooking of meals, etc. – these appear not to have been considerations for the in-patient's return to health, just drugs. In fairness to them they were not just dealing with mental health patients, they were given patients who had nowhere else to go – at times a very unpleasant and violent environment.

When a decision to discharge Lorraine was made we were very surprised. She was far from well and we didn't know what to do with her. You feel helpless, there seems to be no solution. Her psychiatrist did arrange for Lorraine to continue at the hospital gym and continue her personal therapy, and he himself was always available to us as a family. Even so, we felt that Lorraine being at home would not help her become well, even with therapy and our love, because nothing changed. She was not being rehabilitated nor could be so, with such little professional care. He was convinced, as were we, that Lorraine needed residential rehabilitation.

We found an independent psychiatric hospital and had Lorraine admitted to the acute ward on our private healthcare insurance, as no funding decision had been taken. It was a huge relief for the whole family to have Lorraine admitted there as we were at the end of our tether, completely exhausted. We hoped some further light could be shed on Lorraine's problem. She was in a very caring environment and it felt alright to leave her there so far from our home.

Lorraine's first visit ended in success and she was returned to us for Christmas a very different young lady to the one who had arrived there. However, this slight sense of euphoria did not last long and within weeks all the old signs were back and we were on suicide watch. Although it does not seem possible, the shoulders rise another ¼ inch, the chest tightens yet again and you sink further into a state of anxiety and insomnia.

Lorraine had to be readmitted to the local hospital and her psychiatrist was very concerned for her well-being. She wanted to be back at the other hospital. If we paid again there was no way social services would fund her and it was in her best interests that we held out. She needed to be given a package of care, which was worth the wait as her care now is nigh on perfect, but at the time the battle was really something we could have done without. The psychiatrist's concerns over her decline and need for better care, and Lorraine's desperation spurred us on.

Finally, on threat of legal action, they relented and Lorraine returned to the other hospital's acute ward until she was well enough to join their rehabilitation ward, which was the care we were really looking for, guided rehabilitation. We felt safe, Lorraine felt safe, there was some hope again.

When Lorraine made it to the rehab. ward it was the first really positive move for many years. We felt looked after and part of her care. It was a joint venture to make Lorraine better and it was going to happen. Positives in what had been a very negative few years.

The structure of the ward and the communication with her carers, the contact with the psychiatrist and the regular meetings to which we were invited were all so professional, structured and had an objective – how can we help Lorraine become well and feel better about herself?

Both my wife and I welcomed the family therapy. It was such a help to air those pent-up emotions and understand them, although our other two daughters found it rather difficult. It perhaps touched too many raw ends for them. They had both taken Lorraine's serious suicide attempt and mental illness to heart; it had had a numbing effect on them. They too were very scared, but they came to therapy whenever they could and their contribution was welcomed and beneficial.

We visited too often initially. My wife wanted to be there every week, she wanted Lorraine to know that we were there for her, even though she was away from home. It became impossible, it just added to the strain on us and Lorraine. Once the staff suggested that we visit every few weeks, things progressed. Lorraine was able to start her development and recovery. She still telephoned when she wanted or texted, but when she wanted to.

Our visits in the early days were frustrating. Lorraine didn't have much to say and I felt we were making all that effort for no need. We were only adding to the pressure on ourselves. It took some time for my wife to come around to this way of thinking. She will always agree that she is a mother hen who needs to know her chicks are all fine.

We could always phone the staff at any time if we needed an update and likewise they would phone us with regular information. This accessibility helped us not to feel so isolated from our daughter. The information we were given was always just enough to get a feel of Lorraine's present situation and progress.

To begin with we found it a little distressing to access her ward via another ward, but we got used to that.

We did have a major blip, when Lorraine walked off the ward down to the nearby lake. This was just days before she was due home for a family Christmas with her sisters, and she was sectioned. We all visited Lorraine on Christmas Eve with her presents but emotionally we were back to being raw. That one phone call, around 10.30 pm, to report the incident took months off our recovery. Even now phone calls after 10.00 pm send a feeling of dread through our systems – the chest still tightens, things are, even now, only just under the surface.

After around eighteen months in the rehab. ward we began to feel even safer – we could see that Lorraine's situation was being monitored – a picture was forming – the regular meetings were gaining more purpose – a drug was prescribed that we hoped would make a difference.

The anxieties still rose and abated, particularly when funding by the local authority was discussed at the meetings. You never knew if they were going to say enough is enough.

We felt, and still do, that the staff at the hospital worked as a team, they had a goal, an aim, and resolved to achieve that aim in a professional, workable manner. We compared this to the state system, only experienced in our area, which appeared to prescribe drugs and contain the situation by keeping an eye on the patients within their ward. Does that count as a statistical tick in a box, claiming patients have been successfully treated? I shudder to think! We don't really know, we only know that in Lorraine's case the methods employed have worked; for this we are eternally grateful.

Commentaries

Glenn Roberts (Psychiatrist)

This family's experience has a ring of truth that is both sad and familiar. It carries important messages arising from their struggle to find an effective therapeutic response to their daughter's needs and poses a major challenge to those who commission, design, manage and pay for, and deliver services supporting the recovery of people with long-term conditions.

Suffering so often comes unlabelled and names when offered say so little about the deeper realities of experience. There is a frightening paradox in someone appearing inexpressive but content and being apparently well cared for, and yet trying to take their own life. Such mysteries are common, and they are commonly bewildering. This account is entitled, 'Feeling grateful', but for what? This family has been visited by tragedy, but, through their experience of alternatives, are grateful for receiving a style of care and treatment that should be a right for all in such circumstances.

These parents reflect the concerns and heartache of many who bring their loved ones for help only to have to leave them in the company of fellow patients with as many or more problems and the attendant fears of what being catapulted into such alarming company will do to their daughter. Current guidance (Department of Health 2001) suggests the need for alternative and dedicated in-patient resources for young people in first episodes of severe mental illness, but to date few exist.

They describe the complex and worrying experience of living on the edge of disaster and how these stresses changed family life for all its members. So often professionals meet families at a point of crisis and see the irritability and 'raised shoulders' and consider the possibility that this is a 'high expressed emotion family', as though that were a permanent structure and possibly the cause of the patient's problems, but fail to look beyond this immediate picture to see how high stresses and tensions can equally be a result of caring families feeling powerless and helpless in situations of great distress. Towards the end of their story they describe the benefits of working to reduce tensions and negotiate better patterns of interaction for all concerned. There is abundant evidence that this form of family work is of great benefit but is still little practised. Current guidelines (for example NICE 2002) are that such approaches should be routine.

In highly pressured in-patient settings where the focus is solely on the patient in front of us and our focus is to reduce risk and symptoms and cut duration of stay to a minimum, it is so easy to miss the complex sufferings within the families. These carers comment that after their daughter 'was sectioned' – 'we were back to being raw . . . a feeling of dread through our systems' – 'took months off *our* recovery' (emphasis added) – the Royal College of Psychiatrists Campaign, 'Partners in care' (2004) sought to bridge some of the unhelpful and unnecessary divisions between families and services – but this account importantly underlines that a severe illness in one family member affects them all, and all have recovery needs.

Boredom, inactivity, staff disinclined or incapable of engagement – these are the tragically repeated motifs of in-patient care: 'left', 'uninterested', 'nothing to offer', 'just drugs', 'nothing changed' – a perspective so far removed from being the pathway to recovery that anyone would hope for, and legitimately expect, from admission to what is probably the most expensive compartment of the whole service.

The comment, 'in fairness to them', helpfully links to the reality of in-patient staff frequently being as much hostage to the institution as the patients, and that clinical and general managers with responsibility for the morale, culture, atmosphere, case mix and resources of such units have a heavy responsibility. There is a great deal that shapes and constrains what is possible within an in-patient setting, apart from just the nurses on duty who also need to be valued and equipped in order to have something to give. These carers accurately sense that senior staff are also commonly caught between feeling responsible for someone continuing in an impoverished hospital setting or being discharged unwell, but at least 'out of hospital'. It is a sorry state of affairs that hospital is often seen as harmful to a significant number of in-patients, and the most important thing becomes how to get out.

The tussle these parents then had between the local unit and the charitable sector hospital, their entitlement to one and their preference for the other, is not untypical and holds within it the value of struggling and arguing for higher standards – indeed the whole of the national early intervention movement arose from the personal struggle of one couple of parents to get better care for their daughter (Shiers and Shiers 1998, Shiers 2004; see also Chapter 10). I was once told, 'you get the services that you fight for', and this from our then 'Regional Champion' (*circa* 2000) advising professionals on how to develop services described in the National Services Framework but which remain unfunded. Guidance without resource is like advising a blind man that what he seeks is the other side of a busy intersection but then failing to lend an arm to assist him across the road.

But this tussle also represents the reality of inequity. Of course non-NHS hospitals can provide better care, they have no open-ended responsibility to a population, they can choose whom they take, and every patient brings additional payment. But finding that this suicidal young woman absconded from even this unit and required detention under the Mental Health Act to ensure safety underlines just how difficult is the project of recovery at the deep end.

Their current service is described as, 'A team with a goal and an aim', a team that included the parents, but also one that takes time, 18 months and counting. If we are to develop or redevelop in-patient environments as places of restoration and healing they must clearly be hospitable, safe, friendly and with many stimulants to recovery readily to hand. You don't have to look far to see what people value, and as they say, it's not rocket science (Leibrich 1999). To my mind this is simply what rehabilitation and recovery services should be like. Committed, hopeful, purposeful, engaging and well paced. The time taken, the time needed, is a huge issue, but with it relationships become possible, and turbulence for everyone, including the ward, is reduced, and hope can be kindled with realism.

This account is a picture of contrasts: out-patient vs. in-patient, public vs. charitable sector, short term vs. long term, individual vs. family-focused. The writers are clear in what they have valued and what has helped both them and their family in an ongoing process of recovery; in doing so they pose a major challenge to public health services to respond.

Without being pessimistic this account pivots around appropriate care and treatment for someone experiencing a 'long-term condition'. Until recently the available guidance seemed blind to this reality, as though long-term conditions were an artefact of old-fashioned services. However, it seems that the forgotten need for rehabilitation is now being recognised (Holloway 2005, Department of Health 2005a) and we can only hope that this impacts on Trusts and Commissioners in order to protect, consolidate and extend high-quality rehabilitative care, such as this family found to be hopeful and helpful.

Simon Lawton-Smith (King's Fund)

In many respects Lorraine's story is sadly typical: a young woman who requires hospital admission for a severe psychiatric disorder but whose experience is by no means a satisfactory one, either for herself or her family.

Happily, Lorraine would seem to be receiving good-quality care and rehabilitation in her rehabilitation unit. Her family clearly feel at this stage that she needs this intensive level of care, but it is to be hoped that, in due course, Lorraine will be able to live more independently and play a full part in the life of her local community.

Three key issues come to the fore in reading Lorraine's story. First, the quality of care that Lorraine received on an NHS acute psychiatric ward; second, the quality of the rehabilitation service that she now receives from an independent sector provider; and third, the impact that Lorraine's mental disorder has had on her close family.

NHS acute care

Many concerns have been raised about deficits in NHS acute in-patient psychiatric care, including over-occupancy of beds, staff shortages and low levels of staff morale, a lack of activities for patients leading to high levels of boredom, poor physical environments and an increasing number of patients presenting with complex needs involving drug and/or alcohol abuse.

Lorraine's experience reflects many of these concerns. While the Department of Health recognises the problem and has issued guidance on adult acute in-patient care (Department of Health 2002b), services have often been struggling to respond.

There is evidence that small changes in practice – such as instituting protected engagement time between nursing staff and patients, and providing minimal funding for developing ward activities – can lead to significant improvements in patient and staff safety and satisfaction (London Development Centre 2006). Such initiatives need to become the norm across acute care and can be introduced despite the difficulties facing acute wards.

The rehabilitation service

Lorraine's family believe that her move to her present rehabilitation unit has been 'the first really positive move for many years'. It is worth reminding ourselves what rehabilitation is intended to do. It has been defined as 'A whole system approach to recovery from mental ill health which maximises an individual's quality of life and social inclusion by encouraging their skills, promoting independence and autonomy in order to give them hope for the future and which leads to successful community living through appropriate support' (Killaspy *et al.* 2005).

Such an approach means that staff work intensively with patients around improving daily living and social skills, such as buying food or going to the local pub, that patients have lost as a result of their mental disorder. It is therefore not strictly fair to compare the quality of care that Lorraine receives on her independent sector rehabilitation ward with that of the NHS acute ward that was so unsatisfactory.

The NHS does in fact have over 2,000 of its own rehabilitation beds providing multidisciplinary support, but in Lorraine's story the option of an NHS rehabilitation bed does not appear to have been considered. It has been argued (Holloway 2005) that many NHS rehabilitation services feel marginalised and under threat; that they are not a priority for mental health services required to meet targets in other areas; and their provision is patchy. This may be why Lorraine's family turned to a local independent sector service provider.

Lorraine's experience in her independent sector rehabilitation unit appears to be an extremely positive one. Staff, including the psychiatrist, keep in touch with the family and they are invited to regular meetings. Interestingly, the point is made that the staff team in the unit had an 'objective' and an 'aim' – which clearly the family found lacking on the NHS ward. These are all elements that the family value highly and that should not be beyond the capacity of NHS facilities to replicate at little or no cost.

Clearly, for patients with longer-term psychosis, intensive in-patient rehabilitation is a very necessary part of the spectrum of care that should be widely available. This may be through either NHS or independent providers subject to ensuring good value for money. Future commissioners of services need to bear this in mind.

The impact on Lorraine's family

This story is not just about Lorraine but about her family, and the distress and fear that mental illness can cause to families. The pressure on Lorraine's family has been considerable, and it has clearly affected not just her parents but her siblings as well. One phone call, to report an incident that led to Lorraine being sectioned, 'took months off our recovery'.

The pressure is heightened by the family's battle to ensure funding for Lorraine's care, and uncertainty about whether it will continue. This uncertainty is likely to continue as we move towards a new era of practice-based commissioning where decisions may be taken by GP-led consortiums who may, or may not, see rehabilitation services as a priority area.

The Department of Health has called on health and social services to assess the needs of carers of people with severe mental illness, and provide them with their own care plan and the care to meet their needs, and has issued guidance (Department of Health 2002c). However, with resource limitation in many local services, this aspiration has not yet translated into a comprehensive system of support for carers. More must be done to ensure that it does.

Questions and issues for discussion

1   How could the quality of care on the local Mental Health Unit have been improved?
2   Compare the action taken by these parents to get better care for their daughter with that described in Chapter 10 by David Shiers. Which approach would you have taken in their shoes?
3   What did the parents in this account value most about the hospital?
4   Good-quality rehabilitation and recovery services are not 'rocket science'. What would need to change for the quality of care provided by the hospital in this account to be provided routinely within the NHS for people with long-term severe mental health needs?
5   What is meant by the terms public sector, private sector, and charitable or voluntary sector?

Exercise

Identify the main elements of a good-quality rehabilitation and recovery service, from the perspective of the carer.

Summary of the main issues in Section 3

This section of the book brings us into contact with the distress and suffering of the carers – usually the parents or partner – of someone whose own mental distress is such that eventually, and sometimes in an unplanned way, they are admitted to a psychiatric ward.

Before the admission occurs there is often a rising tension and anxiety at home, as families struggle to cope with a member whose thoughts and feelings and behaviour have become increasingly bizarre, and which eventually threaten their own or other people's safety. Our commentators point out that the stresses during this phase are often increased by the high expectations carers have of themselves of being able to cope on their own. The sense of isolation that carers describe at this time is often made significantly worse by the stigma about mental illness and the lack of information available to the general public on where to seek help.

On the day of admission to hospital, especially if it is for the first time, there is a powerful mixture of feelings. There may be relief at having passed over responsibility to those better equipped to cope, but also a sense of failure at not having been able to cope any longer at home, however unrealistic that expectation may have been. And if the admission has been compulsory there are also feelings of guilt and of betrayal at having been party to a son or daughter being admitted against their will. As one of our contributors says, the hardest thing was helping to put handcuffs on his son.

The initial reaction on arriving on the ward is likely to be confusion, disorientation and helplessness. There is often a sense of complete isolation at a time when help and information have never been so desperately needed. Often no information is provided to carers of a newly admitted patient about what to expect, and little or no communication with busy staff who may seem even not to acknowledge the carer's presence.

In the days following admission new feelings begin to surface. The carers may feel a terrible sadness, almost a feeling of bereavement, at having lost the person they used to know and love, who has become as a stranger. There may be a sense of guilt at having abandoned a son or daughter, and fear for the vulnerability of a young person on an acute ward among adults with a range of problems including drug addiction, alcoholism, and personality disorder. And as the weeks and months go by there may be feelings of despair, hopelessness and exhaustion if it begins to look as though there is no hope of improvement.

We also hear of serious problems in the approach of the staff towards carers. There was puzzlement at the use of 'confidentiality' as a reason not to tell them what is going on. Carers were sometimes made to feel they were a nuisance, or were treated with suspicion by the staff if they showed too much interest or concern. If the person admitted saw their carer in a hostile way, it seemed that the staff sometimes adopted the same view. And the organisation of the ward seemed to show little consideration for the needs of carers, who may be expected to discuss their concerns in daunting ward rounds, or may be kept waiting for hours as the consultant and the team fit everything else in first.

The approach that ward staff take to carers was also a subject of our commentators' concerns. They too noted the distance and insularity of staff, the intimidating ward round, and the inappropriate use of the confidentiality barrier to stall enquiries from concerned relatives. They commented on the institutionalising effect of the ward setting and the tendency of some staff to see carers as 'the enemy'. One of the enduring stereotypes among mental health workers has been that families drive you mad, and that the parents of a newly admitted young person in a psychotic state are in some way to blame for this. While it's a truism to say that families are complex, and can be places of tension and conflict as well as love and support, the equation of this truism with families being the cause of someone's psychotic breakdown makes assumptions that are unwarranted and harmful. Even when this does not happen, staff can unwittingly make the situation worse for family members by ignoring their needs or feelings.

Another possible reason for the distance that staff may create between themselves and carers is the effect of intense distress staff are exposed to every day. This can produce in the staff a need to protect themselves from the potential suffering they might experience from the awareness of the deep aloneness and anxiety surrounding severe psychiatric disorders. One commentator stressed the importance of staying in touch with the need we all have for closeness, holding, intimacy, and attachment when things are falling apart.

This need, and its avoidance, was highlighted by the experience of Charlotte. The need for physical intimacy between sexual partners when one of them is admitted for a period of time was something that could not be mentioned, let alone discussed openly in an adult way – a no-go area for all concerned, patient, carer and staff. Of course there is a need for boundaries to protect vulnerable people from their own or others' sexual impulses, but the issue is whether there needs to be a fixed rule or if there can be a need-specific approach to the possibility of allowing a sexual relationship. Too often risk management is replaced with simple risk avoidance.

It wasn't all bad. Carers felt gratitude for kindness when it was received. They appreciated the efforts of caring staff, were relieved when they felt their family member was safe, and valued being included in planning meetings with key staff members and being able to meet as a family with a family worker. Some carers found the psychiatrist to be genuinely concerned but were struck by the contrast between this and the lack of interest or facilities on the ward.

Those carers who have contributed to this book are perhaps unusual – but perhaps not – in the efforts to which they have gone to improve things, for their own family member and in some cases for others too. They describe how their feelings of helplessness and despair at some point became a purposeful anger directed at challenging and improving the quality of care and the facilities available.

Taken together a number of possible improvements are suggested in the course of this section. As Glenn Roberts points out, what is needed is not rocket science, but is still very patchy. They include (and this is not intended to be comprehensive, rather a springboard for discussion):

- Being aware of when things are organised for the convenience of the staff – and explaining to carers and service users why things are as they are
- Developing strategies to counter the institutionalising effect on the staff of working in hospitals – e.g. built-in advocacy, small staff rooms (!), changes in job design
- Providing opportunities for 'dynamic reflection' to enable staff to reflect on the experiences of each patient, and on their own responses
- Acknowledging carers' feelings, including justified anger, and providing a proper complaints channel
- Organising training that includes input from carers.

Finally our commentators also noted wider systemic issues that need attention at Trust or national level if they are to change:

- The rigidity of service structures and boundaries between adolescent and adult services
- Lack of acceptance of long-term needs, as if the problems were an artefact of the system
- In-patient care as a low status career choice.

They also flagged up some alternatives to hospital that are beginning to replace the acute ward in the treatment and care of psychotic episodes:

- Crisis houses with a therapeutic environment
- Home-treatment services
- Crisis prevention through self-management programmes.

Section 4

Mental health staff experiences

In this section we hear the voices of the staff who work in in-patient services. They are the ones that feel the responsibility for creating an environment where users can benefit from their stay, but as we shall see they carry this responsibility sometimes with apprehension and frustration, sometimes with fear and confusion, and only sometimes with excitement and satisfaction. Taken as a whole, they offer a very representative perspective of the difficulties and occasional pleasures anyone associated with in-patient care has to face. To start off, we have selected contributions from professionals who have only recently started their careers in mental health, partly because these first impressions are likely to colour professional choices in the future. We will then present the views of those who feel either disenfranchised or marginal to the daily decision making, but who, as we shall see, can still play pivotal roles in transforming the ward into a humane, empathic and listening environment. We then hear the reflections of those who feel the burden of care, rightly or wrongly, falls predominantly on their shoulders, and the constraints this can have on their ability to be there for their patients or staff. Finally we will hear the poignant voice of the hospital chaplain, who to some degree encompasses in his account many of the central points raised previously by all the contributors. Do we walk alongside our patients?

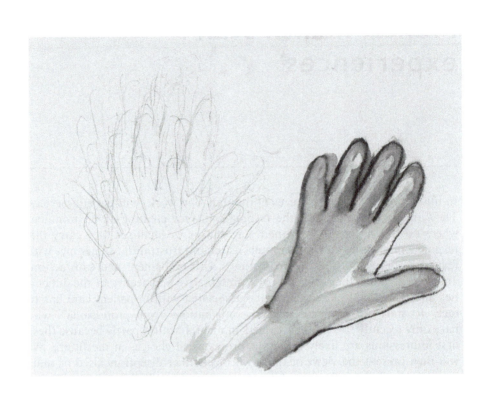

Chapter 14

Feeling helpless

Richard Duggins (Junior Doctor)

Arriving

I was enjoying my junior psychiatry training. I'd had luck with my placements, and had relished working as part of a team, getting to know my
patients, and trying to understand things. The majority of my experience
had been in the community. Acute wards seemed to be where our 'failures'
ended up. I had heard some horror stories from patients about their in-patient
admissions, and I had generally tried to minimise my time in such places.
However, my good fortune had finally run out, and I was instructed to start
my next six-month placement as a Senior House Officer on an acute in-patient
ward.

I found the in-patient ward hidden at the back of the University Teaching
Hospital next to the store-rooms. I wandered on to a scruffy unit, and introduced myself to a nurse. She was clearly not expecting me, and my arrival felt
like another chore for her. Almost immediately, an argument erupted between
an elderly male patient and another nurse. The nurse I was with rushed up to
the patient, stood face-to-face with him, and shouted, 'back down'. He did
so. I felt scared. The nurse then came back over to me, handed me the man's
drug card, and asked me to prescribe a sedative injection. I started to ask
about the patient, and what was troubling him. I received some curt answers
and the clear message I was wasting her time. I signed the card. She went
away. My heart sank.

Learning the rules

I had been on the ward for less than 15 minutes, and already I had sedated a
man without knowing anything about him. This was clearly expected of me,
and to my surprise I had fulfilled that expectation. Over the next few weeks I
quickly learnt what was expected from me, and what was not expected from
me. My role was to enforce decisions and to medicate patients.

However, I had my own mind. I resolved to stand firm and not blindly
follow these rules. I started to refuse to sedate angry and irritable patients.

Unfortunately, if I refused to prescribe sedation for a patient then I would be clearly informed I was putting staff at risk, because the patient would 'kick off'. Often this prediction came true, and the patient would 'kick off', leading to him, or her, being held down and injected. I then felt guilty that I had inflicted a worse fate on the patient. If the patient did not 'kick off', then he, or she, would often still be sedated because the nurses would just wait until I finished my shift, or went on my lunch, and then telephone the on-call doctor for a prescription. I felt helpless to find any other solution than to prescribe sedation, and the patients were helpless to discover any other solution than to behave or be sedated.

A role that was clearly not expected of me was spending time talking with patients. Such behaviour by a doctor appeared to be a sign that I was unfocused or had too little to do. Indeed, unfocused talking with patients appeared to be viewed as dangerous, because such behaviour did not demonstrate clear boundaries between staff and patients.

Another ward rule was attendance at the weekly Ward Reviews. In the Ward Reviews patients were invited to enter a room containing four or more multidisciplinary professionals, plus a few students. Before each patient was invited into the room, the professionals privately discussed the patient's progress and a plan was made. Each patient then had between five and ten minutes in the spotlight, during which time they were asked how they were feeling, told how we thought they were feeling, and what we would like the plan to be for the next week. A good patient at a Ward Review was politely deferential, and did not 'use up time' wanting to talk about their distress. Such patients usually progressed towards discharge. Patients who did not play the game in 'acting-out' by refusing to attend, expressing their anger, or by using the time telling you how upset they were, were usually not discharged.

Everyone hated Ward Reviews. The patients complained of feeling like 'a naughty school child' or 'a freak in a freak show', and the staff resented the amount of time they consumed. So why did Ward Reviews continue? The official reason given was that decisions needed to be multidisciplinary, but I found it hard to believe that something positive like multidisciplinary working could be the reason for such an outdated ritual. I think the Ward Review survived because it prevented any real contact with patients. The setting was so intimidating, and the time so short, that the focus could only be 'care plans' for managing patients, rather than a venue for understanding distress.

Becoming overwhelmed

As the weeks progressed I started becoming tired. I was determined despite the rules to talk to patients about their experiences and distress, and to try to think with them. Patients invited me into worlds that were often horrific and tortuous. One patient I got to know told me that he had the constant feeling that animal semen was ejaculated into his mouth and sloshed round. What could this experience mean to him? Such encounters with patients made me feel all sorts of emotions. How could I try to understand them?

I often felt intimidated and scared on the ward. It was a violent place. Frequently I witnessed verbal aggression, threats and even physical violence. Mostly this was between patients, but sometimes it was between patients and staff. I was also developing strong worries about my work: I was not sure I was doing my best by my patients, and at times I feared I might be breaking the golden rule of 'first, do no harm'.

It was clear that the ward did not wish to encourage patients to discuss their feelings, so what on earth could I, a member of staff, do with the intense feelings stirred up in me? I knew I needed to discuss my emotions, worries, fears and concerns, but I was helpless to find a suitable space.

Losing heart

I really started to struggle. I was low, exhausted and overwhelmed. I knew I needed to change my behaviour to survive. I took the easy option – I started following the rules. I stopped questioning some requests to sedate patients, and this made my life easier with the other staff. I stopped talking to patients outside the Ward Review, except to discuss medication or 'care plan' decisions. This made managing my own feelings simpler because I no longer had to try to understand the patients' distress.

In this politely deferential state I was able to withdraw into a protective shell. Life was much more tolerable; I said to myself things like, 'It's just a job' and, 'It pays the bills'. However, this subservient withdrawal only worked partially, and every now and then something painful would break through my protective shell. Certain encounters with patients would still touch something inside me. Teaching medical students on the ward would upset me, because I could see that their still idealistic souls knew this was not the way to help people.

In quiet moments my own questioning mind resurfaced. I was unable to reconcile the fact that we were teaching patients to be unthinking, dependent and subservient, when I knew out in the community they would have to be questioning, gutsy and assertive. I was also sad that I was learning nothing. In the community I felt I had grown as a person through my contact with my patients and colleagues, and yet on the ward the opposite seemed to be happening. The ward was a potential community of many people, all with different experiences and ways of coping, and yet nothing creative happened because all the staff and patients withdrew from contact with each other behind unthinking rules and personal protective shells.

Leaving

I noticed many of the ward staff left. One nurse left to be a lawyer, one to travel, and several applied for jobs in the community. The staff least able to shut down their emotions seemed to be the ones that left. I also chose to leave. The news of my departure was greeted unemotionally by the staff: 'They all leave' and, 'You've stayed longer than most'. I told the patients I was leaving. Some patients greeted the news with indifference, some told me how upset they were and how I had let them down, and some told me how grateful they felt that I had been interested in them and we had found times to talk.

On the day of my leaving I walked out through the door with excitement. I was never coming back! I understood what motivated a person to disengage with his or her care.

In hindsight I realise that this ward was really struggling, and thankfully may not be representative of all acute care. In fact, more recently I have worked on an acute ward in which certain robust members of staff did seem to retain a human touch despite the rules. However, I am convinced that numerous wards exist like the one I experienced, and many, many more wards are like it at times. One thing I did learn from my experience is that despite excellent community services, there are some people at some times who because of their distress or disturbance could potentially benefit from a period of in-patient care. This leaves me with a dilemma: how can I hope to work in a humane mental health system when such a crucial part of it as in-patient care can at times be so inhumane?

Commentaries

Leonard Fagin (Psychiatrist)

What a dispiriting and yet recognisable experience it was for me to read this account of a junior doctor that clearly was prepared to make connection with his patients in more meaningful ways than just simply giving them medication! I am of the view, like Richard, that in our current psychiatric wards his description is not unique, and that the harsh introduction to in-patient psychiatric services described here can put off future promising psychiatrists in the early part of their careers from making effective changes to a system of care that has lost its way.

Arriving

The arrival for the first time to an in-patient ward can be very distressing and confusing for all concerned, patients and staff. First impressions often determine and shape future attitudes. Perhaps in recent years we have been more aware of the need to welcome patients and their carers to the unit in ways which can reduce the fear and anticipated dread that is usually associated with an admission to a 'madhouse'. This role is usually passed on to nurses, sometimes the most junior ones, and it is questionable whether this is always done with the necessary empathy and understanding (Fagin 2001). Shouldn't this introduction and orientation be extended to all staff who arrive with their fearful preconceptions?

Learning the rules

Junior doctors are very much the go-betweens, in a position where they are inexperienced to exercise change, and yet hold a certain power by proxy, by the fact that they represent but really are not the ultimate medical authority. When it comes down to it, many junior doctors feel that they are either lackeys to their consultants or there just simply to fulfil nursing expectations to keep everything calm (Garelick and Fagin 2004). Their survival depends on toeing the line and distancing themselves from their own initial feelings and reactions, not only because their references and future career progression depend on this, but also because it becomes an emotional defence, a protective armour which starts to accrue progressively as time goes by.

Richard initially showed a spirit of resistance, an attempt to fight against what he felt was the wrong way to approach patients and his job. Doctors like this are often ostracised and get a reputation of being 'difficult and bloody-minded'. Whilst I was reading his piece I kept asking myself, why didn't anybody realise that here was somebody who could channel his views into making a positive contribution? Did he bring all this up in supervision with his consultant or discuss his reactions in staff meetings with the nursing staff? From what one could gather, there were many things left unsaid, and rather than come up with an agreed approach to the management of patients who would 'kick off', which could combine preventive measures, some understanding of what could lead to this behaviour, as well as the need for physical and chemical containment, staff were acting by short-cutting to medication as the only way to exercise control.

I was really puzzled as to why Richard experienced that it was not expected of him to spend time talking to his patients. Not expected by whom? And for what conceivable reason was this considered to be an unfocused and perhaps wasteful way of passing his time, crossing boundaries between staff and patients? It would be interesting to check out whether this was true or an impression he was getting from what was going on around him, in a ward that he described as dysfunctional but not unique. What is sadly true, however, is that junior doctors are having less and less time available to speak and to get to know their patients on the ward. As a result of the introduction of the European Working Time Directive, doctors are now more likely to be either on call or off work recovering from their night duties, effectively reducing the time that they are present during the day to talk with their patients and other staff, as well as attend supervision. The doctors who are available are possibly covering for others who are on duty, and therefore less likely to be disposed to spend time with patients who are not directly under their care. This problem does not have easy solutions, but over a six-month placement, I believe that it is important to anticipate this by discussing it with junior doctors and nurses, and at least set time aside when doctors will be available to spend uninterrupted 'quality time' with their patients.

Ward reviews

Ward reviews do present with dilemmas, because they exist to serve different functions, perhaps none of them being adequately accomplished in the traditional format. Ideally they offer an opportunity for the multidisciplinary team to discuss, clarify and decide the management of their patients in a collaborative effort, based on gathered information available and observation of the patient on the ward. The fact that they are often chaired by the consultant sometimes militates against this, because the feeling is very much that the consultant has the last word and that the medical model of care will prevail. With the suggested changes to the consultant role, ward reviews may soon be chaired and managed by the nurse in charge, and that may be an interesting development to observe in the future. When the ward review is handled in more creative ways, and becomes a safe sharing space, it can give staff an opportunity to disclose their feelings about the care of the patient concerned, and how this informs the team of what is going on in the internal world of their patients. Obviously this will depend on time available and pressure of work. Ward reviews can also be an opportunity to liaise with agencies and other professionals involved with patients in the community, tackling the artificial, but symbolically powerful boundary between the outside world and the ward. Junior doctors have also traditionally used the review to make a formal presentation of their patients to the consultant and the team, and this becomes a training opportunity where their skills at history taking, formulation and management are examined, preparing them for professional College examinations at a later stage. Finally, and perhaps most importantly, it has been used to get the patient seen by the consultant and the team. Richard is right to state that most patients find this experience intimidating at the least, and at the most, either traumatic or patronising and infantilising. Some patients, however, will request attendance as an opportunity to talk to their consultant, enquire about their condition, challenge the views of staff or simply make requests for leave or alterations to medication, but one wonders whether this is the most appropriate context in which to hold these meetings with patients. In the ward where I have worked I have seen the benefit of discussing this subject in general terms at the Ward Assembly meeting, a weekly group attended and chaired by patients, with staff participation. When patients have the support of others, they are more able to argue and suggest alternative ways of holding ward reviews. I have also found that consultant participation in therapy groups gives patients and consultants time for each other, and suits the crowded timetables of busy clinicians. Perhaps the time has arrived for a substantial re-think of ward reviews!

Becoming overwhelmed

I believe that any member of staff needs to be prepared and anticipate being overwhelmed by their experiences on an in-patient ward. After all, they are working with patients at heightened levels of distress, where violence is always around the corner, and where intolerable feelings are rife. In fact, if they were not overwhelmed, I would question how much in touch they are with their patients. Helping patients in these frames of mind is liable to make an inexperienced junior doctor confused and helpless, in a job where the tacit expectation is that they are there to offer solutions and relief. Feeling this way indicates that they have established an empathic bond with those in their charge, not an indication of weakness or incompetence. It is in supervision where junior doctors should be exploring these issues, because their future therapeutic style will depend greatly on the support and insight they receive from an experienced clinician that will help them to retain sensitivity whilst maintaining adequate boundaries that can allow them to think, and act clearly. It is a shame that Richard does not seem to have found someone to discuss the feelings that 'were stirred up in him', perfectly valid and informative feelings, so that he could make sense of them and progress his understanding.

Losing heart and leaving

I was even more concerned and disheartened to read the final paragraphs of Richard's piece, even though I was not entirely surprised. I have seen in my time many talented future clinicians who have been scarred by their in-patient ward experiences and chosen other areas to specialise in, or even leave psychiatry altogether. One of the observations that people have made to me is that the 'best clinicians are the ones that leave, not the ones that stay'. And yet it has also been my experience that in-patient admissions can be immensely rewarding and enriching experiences for junior doctors, if they are adequately supported and guided. The most important core skills of psychiatric practice can be gleaned during these placements. Bringing the 'humane' element to in-patient care is not only ethical, it makes common sense. We need, however, to address the issue that in-patient care requires highly specialised skills, that need to be acknowledged and valued. At the moment, however, those that work in in-patient settings feel as though they are second-class citizens compared with colleagues working in other 'trendier' fields.

Janey Antoniou (Service User)

I would like to thank this young doctor for trying to do his best for the patients on a difficult ward.

There is one thing that all the mental health service users I have talked to have in common, that is when they find someone that they feel they can talk to, they begin to start to be able to come to terms with their illness. I think it is important to say this at the beginning of a critique of a service that actively discourages talking to mental health service users.

Wards in general

I would imagine the ethos of a ward would come from a mixture of its architecture, the ward manager, the consultant(s), hospital policy, interpretation of guidelines, the staff and the patient mix. It would be difficult to compare them, but I would like to make some comments from a (my) user perspective about wards and the people in them.

Contrary to general belief, though a lot of people hate being in the hospital and are only there because it's compulsory, there are some service users who would prefer to be in hospital when acutely ill. They are not necessarily 'failures' but have made a choice based on how difficult it can be for their relatives and friends to live with someone who is hallucinating, deluded, very depressed or extremely frightened of the way their brain is working. A brief stay in a well-run acute ward can be asylum (with the word used in its true sense), a letting go of responsibilities for a short time and a space to become well again. And given that people get to know the other service users there, it also becomes part of the community – I visit my friends when I'm well, they visit me when they are.

It is true that psychiatric wards are generally scruffy but isn't it better that patients take out their frustrations and fears on the inert objects in the ward rather than on other human beings? Once when I was ill I destroyed a wash basin with my bare hands. I felt very guilty about this when I became well again but am glad it was the wash basin rather than another person. Also, although I have no problems with scruffy wards, they should at least be clean: a dirty ward does reflect the attitude that this group of patients don't matter so much.

The downside of the ward environment is that it is usually quite a cramped space for the number of people living and working in it. This in itself can lead to raised voices, individuals trying to wind others up, and fights. In addition, the people in the ward are in different stages of distress and are often from socially excluded groups of society and have little money, so anti-social behaviour such as begging and stealing can be fairly common. There can also be anger because people don't feel in charge of their destiny. I can remember how helpless I felt when I was expecting a specific drugs regime at medication time only to find that one of the tablets had been increased substantially without anyone having even talked to me, let alone discussed medication.

Ward reviews (or ward rounds)

It is always fascinating to hear the 'other side' of an experience I know very well. On reading this account, I had to smile at the description of a ward review, hated by staff as much, it seems, as by the patients. I don't know what the staff expect from the ward review. I don't even know what I'm expected to expect but I have always found it a profoundly dissatisfying experience – is the ward round there for the doctor to talk to the patient, or for the patient to talk to the doctor? In my experience the other professionals never do talk (at least not while the patient is in the room) so I don't understand how the review can be justified on the grounds of being multidisciplinary.

Most patients find the interval before they are invited in to a ward round completely agonising. They know they are being talked about, and possibly misunderstood, but there is absolutely nothing they can do about it. If the patient's illness has an element of paranoia in it, it is even worse.

The ward review is an area that could benefit from being completely restructured by all the stakeholders who attend them.

Stopping trouble before it starts

I can see how nursing staff could think that using threats, shouting and sedation would stop trouble in a ward before it started, especially if there had been serious incidents in the past where staff and/or patients had been hurt. (I was once threatened with seclusion just for kicking the ward door once in a moment's temper because I couldn't get hold of my care coordinator on the phone.) It may even be the easiest (or quickest) way to deal with things in the short term. But it could end up, as it has done here, in limiting the options in the way patients and staff communicate and frustrate patients into using aggressive actions to try and make any point and even to connect with each other. As far as I can see, in the longer term this is going to increase, rather than decrease, the 'risk' of someone 'kicking off'.

As the doctor clearly showed when he was saying goodbye to his patients, many people do respond over time to others who try to help them. But many psychiatric patients find change very difficult to deal with. Though leaving this ward may have been very good for the staff, it will have only had a negative effect on patients who were struggling with so many things.

Supervision of junior doctors

Finally, the thing that shocks me the most about this piece is the feeling of professional isolation I get from the writer. Is there no one to whom this young doctor could go to get supervision or even just advice about his working conditions? Where were the consultants and ward managers in this ward? In the end it sounds like he had to leave in part to maintain his sanity and humanity and that cannot be right in a system that is supposed to look after people's mental health.

Questions for your service

1   In what way could this young doctor's experience have been more fruitful and rewarding?
2   Was there a role for the consultant and senior nurse in helping new arrivals to an in-patient ward, and if so how would they go about it?
3   What 'rules' operate on in-patient units?
4   What can be done to encourage staff to spend more time talking to patients?
5   Should ward reviews be changed in order to become more sensitive and effective, or should they be replaced with something else?
6   What can be done to reduce the exodus of staff from in-patient care?

Exercise

Role play: a new doctor arrives on the unit. Busy staff are at the time attending to an emergency with a patient who needs to be restrained. The doctor is immediately recruited to help, and possibly recommend medication. The doctor is not happy to do this and the consultant and ward manager are asked for their advice. Explore the issues and feelings that this situation provokes.

Chapter 15

First experience

Anna Chickwama (Acute Ward Nurse)

Working on an acute ward for a year has been an experience that I will value as a foundation for my future career in psychiatry. The last year has taught me how to communicate with patients, the medical team and other agencies. It has also enabled me to understand the view other professionals and patients have of acute nursing.

I have found that the medical model is the most influential perspective that informs patient care. Although attempts are made to involve patients in decision making about their own care it is ultimately, in most cases, the doctor's view that has the final say. As a result communication tends to be top-down, with nurses on the receiving end.

There are a lot of consultants based on my ward and at times one finds that information can be lost as there is too much to pass on. There is always a need to follow up issues and because nurses do not work in teams but cover all consultants, there are occasions when this is not done. I have, however, witnessed some doctors who try to work more collaboratively with patients and nursing staff.

Admissions to the ward are mainly based on risk assessments rather than a fuller understanding of the nature of the crisis the patient is in. Probably this is due to the need to cover oneself in case of an untoward incident. I am not saying that it is not important to consider risk assessments but I think that admissions need to be more focused, with clear goals either to offer short respite or to deal with the specific health needs of the patient.

Turnover may be improved by using resources such as the Crisis Resolution Teams to gate-keep appropriately so that acutely unwell patients are only admitted when it is required. In my experience patients are often admitted as a result of an inappropriate referral. I think they could have benefited more from the input of community teams without the need to come in. I also feel that patients that require detoxification should be worked with in the community.

There are occasions when patients with neurological problems are imposed on the ward and it takes a while to move these patients to appropriate units as funding for placements takes a while to sort out. Such situations affect the morale of the ward, as it is frequently short staffed. At times we have to rely on agency staff. I think situations like these leave staff feeling vulnerable and some patients can pick up the strain on the ward and may act out.

The caseload on the ward at times is overwhelming. Patients may feel neglected because of the paperwork that is involved in the admission process and it is difficult to give patients the daily quality time that they require. In the end, patients view nursing staff as controllers and are therefore more likely to rebel against them. Their reaction to other professionals who do not see them 24–7 may be different and they may be more open to their suggestions.

Not all is bad on acute wards. We get the occasional 'thank you' from the medical team or from patients who are happy with the treatment they have received. The team also get support from psychologists and nursing management, especially when the staff carry out good work under the pressure of a huge caseload. Nurses also get clinical supervision and are offered professional development opportunities.

To conclude, working on the acute ward has given me a starting point in learning good communication skills with various teams and patients, which hopefully will benefit patients I work with in the future. This should also be helpful to me when I assess risks and seek appropriate interventions for acute patients in the community.

Commentaries

Keith Coupland (Nurse)

I have sympathy with the problems encountered by the acute in-patient care nurse and I believe that acute wards are an essential education for all psychiatric nurses.

The dominance of the medical model, as in this case, may lead to passivity among nurses rather than action-orientated advocacy for the patients' recovery. However, I have worked with in-patient teams where the ward round, the most powerful expression of the medical model, has either been abandoned or where the nurse has led the meeting. In the case of nurse-led meetings, the medical consultants appeared relieved that the administrative effort had been lifted from their shoulders and they were free to be consulted about physical and medication-related issues, rather than every aspect of patients' *care*.

Care, after all, is the responsibility of nursing and medical, psychological and occupational professionals; all are *parts* of the holistic view of care. I believe that this is an issue of responsibility-taking rather than a simple power struggle between disciplines for control of the patient. Where nurses are confident about their abilities *and their underlying philosophy* they seem able to take on the role of ward leaders without a struggle. They should show *leadership in caring*, not in displays of power over other disciplines or patients. I believe that holistic care means that no part of the care is demeaned, least of all the importance of high-quality interactions by nurses to understand the experiences of patients on the ward.

It is a lazy ward staff group that contains patients until medication takes its toll. An active ward feels they know where medication is helpful and where the limits of medication are. We know that at least 30 per cent of patients continue to experience symptoms no matter how much medication they are given. We also know that side effects remain a major and sometimes deadly issue. We also know that a judicious dose of medication can have a great impact in reducing distress.

Communication is complex on acute wards and patients are often the least informed of all, although many carers feel left out altogether. Communication can be improved by a strong, cohesive team of nurses who work as key workers and co-workers for a service user. This means there is usually some-body with considerable information about their assigned service user and can inform the patient and their carers of what is happening *and* take the lead in moving situations towards recovery, including finding out what further information is required. The information sharing and exchange is done through a good working relationship with all who help in care as well as with the patients receiving care.

Care can extend to distinct therapies offered on the wards by nurses as well as sports therapists, physiotherapists, occupational therapists and psychologists. A support and recovery worker who has considerable knowledge of all the patients, through frequent meetings and outings, leads the recovery group. A nurse consultant, a paid service user and a team who join the group occasionally, including a psychiatrist, chaplain, nurse specialist and a carer, support this worker. The group effort is about sharing the experiences of recovery from mental illness.

However, patients' care is sometimes led by risk assessments. Patients leave when the risk is minimised. It is an understandable approach in situations where ward staff feel they must protect themselves from criticism. However, this is clearly defensive treatment and not always in the patients' interest. The reality is that we need to manage risks.

Crisis teams can be helpful in preventing admissions but sometimes admission is the most appropriate action. So often in research documents the criterion for a failure is a relapse that led to hospital admission. This is directly opposed to the idea of the hospital as a part of positive planning for recovery. Experienced community staff help ward staff and crisis staff bringing about respite admission *before* a major relapse occurs. I have worked with a patient who was very unpopular with ward staff because his admission was always forced by a section of the Mental Health Act 1983 and involved him being highly resentful, violent and abusive. The same person brought to the ward for a respite admission was a delight to staff as he was friendly, curious and interested in his care and was discharged after a weekend, whereas before, his average admission was six months. The ward staff were able to like him and respect his courageous struggle because they saw *the person* behind the 'patient' presenting with 'illness'.

The issue of control of patients on wards is complex *and* interesting. Staff who take a dialogical approach, that is they actively engage with patients to attempt to understand their experiences rather than simply attempt to extinguish the experiences, by physical or medical methods, are often able to prevent violence and suicidal actions through their empathic actions.

In conclusion, acute in-patient wards could be the places where the most proficient nurses work and where they illustrate the highest level of skills in co-ordinating holistic care. They will be enthusiastic practitioners who are able to engage patients in therapeutic interactions, based on empathic understanding and focused on long-term recovery. They will take responsibility for their actions because they are well informed and well supported by clinical supervision. This process could be aided by clear goals that are mutually agreed and prompted by high-quality patient-focused pathways. Their job will be hindered if there are power struggles, poor staffing, too many temporary staff or defensive attitudes to care. It will be further aided by good-quality supportive managers who lead by their example of focusing the ward towards the needs of the patients, in their diverse and gendered needs and recognise the needs of their carers rather than the defence of the psychiatric hospital as a system.

Leonard Fagin (Psychiatrist)

I was left quite disturbed on reading this contribution, from an obviously inexperienced nurse who was reporting on her first experience of in-patient psychiatry in this country.

My principal discomfort was not in response to her observation of power relationships on the ward. She confirmed in many ways that the traditional hierarchical structures continue to be alive and well, at least where she has worked, with the notion that 'what the doctor says, goes'. Nurses in this approach are no more than hand-maidens in the medical model of care, with what she calls 'communication' (in my book this looks more like orders) coming from the top and expected to be responded to by overworked nurses, who have to relate to a number of consultants and teams, and who are thus unable to keep track of what is going on. Despite a great deal of lip-service being paid to the equalisation of roles and responsibilities between different professionals in the mental health care field, and especially between doctors and nurses, the in-patient ward continues to be the area where we still seem to be living in the nineteenth century (see Fagin and Garelick 2004).

I think my main concern was about the theme running behind her comments and examples, the notion that in-patients are dumped on nurses, often on spurious grounds. In her experience, patients are presented to the ward as a result of inadequate assessments, or with inappropriate conditions, in order to cover 'somebody else's' back, or simply because community teams are not doing their jobs properly. She is aware that this causes negative reactions in ward staff. I would go further than that on the basis of her account. This feeling of being imposed upon, closely linked with being overworked in what appears to be a very confusing and unnecessarily bureaucratic environment, creates major obstacles which militate against the possibility of nurses establishing significant human interactive contact at times when patients are distressed and vulnerable, and most likely to benefit from understanding and time spent with them. Patients in this situation become burdens, which need to be disposed of as quickly as possible in order to free up a bed. The reaction of nurses in this predicament is predictable. They need to feel in charge, and expect that patients will do what they are told, take their medication, get better and agree to their care plan. If they don't, and we know that this is more often the case than not, patients are considered to be 'rebelling'. Is it surprising that patients report that they are not heard, that they receive unsympathetic responses from overstretched nurses, who spend most of their time enclosed in the office involved in paperwork? What appears to be totally missing in this account are examples of how her work with patients has enriched her experience, and I found this especially worrying.

Even though she dedicates a few words to the 'positive' thanks the nursing staff occasionally receive from other professionals, I had the distinct feeling that she couldn't wait until she found another job in the community, where perhaps for her the job is likely to be more satisfying, where her expertise may be rewarded, and where she can feel she can relate more meaningfully with those in her care.

It is this last comment that made me feel profoundly sad. I do believe that 'good-enough' in-patient care is one of the most difficult things to achieve and to sustain in the field of psychiatric nursing, and yet it remains undervalued and exploited. It is no wonder that nurses seek alternative careers when this branch of highly specialised care, that makes so many personal demands, is not given the status it deserves. In-patient psychiatric nursing requires considerable expertise in the assessment and treatment of severe forms of psychiatric illness, with psychodiagnostic and psychopharmacological skills, psychotherapeutic insights, knowledge of group and family dynamics, psychosocial and cultural awareness and an ability to relate to other professionals and relevant outside agencies. And this list is not exhaustive. It deserves to be seen as an equal to other nursing specialties, and until it is recognised as such, we will continue to offer sub-standard care to our patients.

Questions for your service

1   Are there alternative modes of working to the traditional 'medical model'? If so, how would you go about changing it?
2   When there is more than one consultant on the ward, how do you organise communication with nurses?
3   Should risk be the prominent defining feature of an in-patient's assessment?
4   Is there anything that can be done to reduce the administrative paperwork for nurses so that they can be released for clinical activities?

Exercise

Role play: two nurses, a recently arrived young new recruit, and a more experienced staff nurse, are having a cup of coffee in the staff room, where they are gossiping about the patients, their ward manager and the doctors. The young nurse feels uncomfortable in her new role, in particular not having an opportunity to have her say during the ward rounds and feeling angry at having to perform menial tasks. What are the feelings that are raised in the discussion by both nurses?

Chapter 16

Feeling unprepared

'Louisa' (Hotel Services Assistant)

I have been working in a rehabilitation unit for adults with mental health problems for two years. This is my first experience of working in mental health. When I applied for the job I thought I was going to be working in hotel services because of the job title and not in mental health. I did not realise until my first day at work that I was actually going to be working in a mental health service but I thought this was okay.

I feel I am fine working within the rehab service. I enjoy the work because it's different every day. When I am on my regular ward I feel I know the client group and I know what to expect from them. I like my role, I have always had cleaning jobs but I find this job a challenge in a positive way. I like working directly with the clients and helping them clean their flats but sometimes I feel this is a contradiction – if people are in rehabilitation why aren't they cleaning their own areas? I enjoy talking to the clients and they talk to me quite a lot. I spend time on my break talking to them and I feel I know people here and I can relate to them. They talk to me about their lives. Sometimes perhaps they may tell me too much. They say things that make me feel my job is worthwhile, such as people saying they have missed me when I have been away, also people thanking me for cleaning their rooms.

At times I feel frustrated by the students who spend long periods of time here on the wards, reading clients' notes, and not talking directly to the patients. How can they get to know the patients if they don't spend time with them?

Sometimes I am moved for short periods of time to acute admission areas. I find this very stressful. I feel very frightened there when people are distressed and I find this difficult to cope with. When I first went to work on the acute admission ward I felt very frightened and wanted to run away. I feel scared of people when they're aggressive. I don't know any of these people and I don't know how to respond to them. Only being in an area for a short period of time to cover doesn't allow me time to get to know people and I don't know how to respond to their difficult behaviour.

I find the male acute admission wards very difficult because you work hard and clean an area and shortly afterwards people may have a drink for example and make a mess and it doesn't look as if it's been cleaned. They can't help it though but it is difficult.

Sometimes when I am moved to other areas for short time periods I work with fellow domestics and they point out people who I need to be aware of but when I am on my own I don't know any of the clients and the nursing staff do not tell you about any of them. They probably have discussions with the regular domestic staff but not with people covering. This makes it very difficult for me to know how to respond to people.

I was moved around on a regular basis for the first two months and it was very difficult for me to settle in. I feel that it is very useful for patients to have a regular person in this role as a domestic because they get to know you and you get to know the client group and what they want. I have discussed this with my colleagues and we all share the same view that we need to work in regular areas. My manager wanted to rotate the cleaning staff on a regular basis but we raised concerns because of the effects this would have on the clients. There was then a meeting between the Trust and the contractors and it was decided that this would have a detrimental effect on clients and so it was decided that we would not be moved on a regular basis but would stay in our own areas.

I feel that there should be more preparation for new staff to enable them to work with a client group. Some of the people I am aware of have taken up post and then left after a couple of months. When I first started working here I found it very difficult on the acute admission areas but I thought I would give it a try. I needed to talk to myself each day. I needed to remind myself that I had to go to work. It took me two months to decide that I really wanted to do this job. I did not feel that I had had any preparation for working in an environment where there were people with mental health issues. At interview people should be clear about their role. I was interviewed by a contract company and did not realise this was connected to the hospital. I did not realise I was going to be working in mental health until my first day.

I feel very valued in my current role. I get thanked by other staff, by the nursing staff and the service users, and this makes me feel that what I am doing is very worthwhile.

Commentaries

Jenny McAleese (Independent Hospital CEO)

How someone's role is described by others tells you something about their relative position in the pecking order of an organisation. In our hospital the staff who clean wards are known simply as 'domestics', which has always struck me as a singularly anonymous and even dismissive term. I admit that up until now, though, I've done nothing about it. This omission has been brought home to me even more clearly after reading the account of the 'hotel services assistant' (HSA).

I will use their self-description because I find it a more helpful one than 'domestics' in characterising their contribution to the daily life of the organisation. I'm also attracted to it because it allows me to draw parallels outside mental health settings, which I find valuable. I do want to think that our patients are staying in accommodation which is well maintained and serviced by our staff, and somehow the term 'hotel services' conveys that more clearly. I would be surprised if hotel and leisure organisations used a term like 'domestics' to describe their staff servicing accommodation, so why do we continue to, I wonder? I suspect the term has its roots in the days of the large mental health institutions, and continues out of habit.

The HSA is obviously someone who is committed to the work she does and who finds it extremely rewarding. For me, the most powerful issue raised by the article is that of the key role played by HSAs in the multi-disciplinary team on a ward. Very importantly, their relationship with patients is one of equals, because HSAs spend time talking with patients as people rather than carrying out clinical interventions. They often do not know about the patient's illness so can, as does this person, just talk about 'their lives' without this being limited or cluttered in any way by knowledge of the patient's clinical history.

For this important role to be fulfilled to the benefit of both patient and HSA alike, it is vital that hotel services staff work on one ward area and get to know the patients and become seen by everyone as part of the team. This HSA talks honestly about how stressful she finds it when she is moved for short periods of time to the acute admission area. She admits to finding it difficult to cope with people who are distressed and to feeling scared, not least because she doesn't know the patients or how to respond to them. This prevents her from being able to make the important and beneficial contribution she does on her rehabilitation service area, where she seems to enjoy a quality relationship with patients, extending to their expressing how much they have missed her when she has been off duty.

I suspect that the contracting out of hotel services throughout hospital settings has meant that HSAs become much less a part of the regular ward teams and much more a moveable commodity and part of an anonymous community of casual workers. It is therefore encouraging to read that in this particular hospital it has been recognised that hotel services staff should not be moved but attached to a specific area.

Like all organisations, however, there do seem to be some communication issues which need addressing by the hospital where this HSA works. It started at interview when she thought she was going to be working in hotel services (one of the obvious drawbacks of using the term in preference to 'domestic'!) and only discovered that she was working in a mental health setting on her first day. She states that she was not even told that the contract cleaning company that interviewed her was connected to the hospital.

It also looks as if communication between nursing and hotel services staff could be improved. We are told that when she moves to new areas it is her fellow HSAs who point out people she needs to be aware of and that 'the nursing staff do not tell you about any of them'. I suspect this is one of the consequences of outsourcing, with nurses not seeing hotel services staff as part of the team. It may also have something to do with nurse education and a sense that domestic work on the ward is increasingly done by others. It may also be a reflection of the nursing hierarchy and I wonder whether nursing support workers would have similar complaints about the lack of communication from qualified nursing staff?

By the sound of it, this particular HSA had a tough couple of months settling in to her role, particularly as she was new to mental health services, had not been prepared for it and was moved around at first. Thankfully she did settle in but mentions others who did not and who simply left the organisation. This suggests that retention rates for outsourced services may be worryingly low, with all the waste and loss of potential that that implies. It would be worth considering some induction training to enable those new to mental health services to learn more about the environment in which they will be working and to gain a general understanding of mental illness. This would help address the issue of improving retention.

In a mental health setting it is inevitably the clinical staff who oversee and are responsible for the care regimes. However, others in the team such as HSAs can have a refreshingly different perspective. For example, this HSA rightly asks why people in rehabilitation are not cleaning their own rooms. Similarly she queries how the students (presumably student nurses?) can get to know the patients if they don't spend time with them and just read their notes. These questions serve to illustrate the important role that hotel services and other support staff play in the overall provision and quality of care and how they so very often see things the rest of us somehow manage to miss. Sadly, their voice gets lost all too often.

Claire Ockwell (Service User)

Until reading this it had never occurred to me to wonder how hotel services staff were recruited to posts on psychiatric wards. However, it comes as little surprise that when the author applied for her job no mention was made of where she would be working. It is most likely the employer's belief that the stigma attached to people with mental health problems would make it harder to attract staff. Probably some people would be discouraged from applying but surely then it is better that they should know what they are letting themselves in for? No one would expect other ward staff to apply for a post without some

idea of the client group they will be working with and it should be no different for hotel services staff. It is not surprising that she was left 'feeling
unprepared'.

The point raised about rehab is a good one. Rehab should be about helping
people return to living as independently as possible and no doubt some services do that brilliantly. However, there are also rehab services which keep
people on their books for several years, yo-yoing in and out of the ward on a
regular basis and so promoting institutionalisation. Doing chores alongside
someone in rehab is not necessarily a problem as long as it is done in a way
that educates and encourages us to carry out chores independently. Otherwise
we are stuck in a dependency culture which does nothing to promote
recovery.

People who have been in-patients on any kind of mental health unit often
relate how the most helpful and easiest people to talk to were the ones doing
the cleaning. This aspect of their role is often ignored and greatly undervalued. There are frequently occasions when even the best care staff are too
busy with administration and the day-to-day running of the ward to be available just to talk to us. At these times a chat with one of the domestic staff can
be invaluable. It is a role that deserves recognition. No one takes on a cleaning
job expecting to give informal support to a ward full of people who are
experiencing mental distress. It makes sense for people to have fore-knowledge
and some kind of preparation for this as well as the opportunity to access
supervision if needed. Although many prove themselves naturally gifted at
supporting people, safeguards should be in place to ensure this is not to the
detriment of their own mental health.

The stress the author experiences when working occasionally on an
acute ward demonstrates this need to prepare people properly. The fear she
experiences also raises the question that if she as a well person feels this way
then how will someone in acute distress react to this environment? More
steps need to be taken to make acute wards places that alleviate rather than
add to our distress, providing a safe rather than a frightening environment.
Although single rooms and modern facilities help in some ways towards this
they can also leave people even more isolated and in need of those friendly
faces to talk to. Further cutbacks in bed numbers have also meant that people
have to be in ever greater extremities of distress before being admitted. This
means that it is more likely that they will be exhibiting disruptive behaviour
which will contribute to the disturbance in the therapeutic environment.
Despite this, we may need active encouragement to help by clearing up after
ourselves rather than a resigned acceptance that we are too unwell to contribute at all. If we are to recover, expectations have to be raised. Not to do so
does us a great disservice.

For many people who experience mental distress, feeling able to trust
people can take a long time, so as much continuity as possible is crucial. Staff
should not be moved around unnecessarily as familiar faces are reassuring,

particularly in wards where for various reasons a high proportion of the nursing staff come from agencies and are here today and somewhere else tomorrow. It is so much easier to feel safe with people you see on a regular basis. This safety aspect works both ways too. I am sure that hotel services staff will feel safer working where there is a client base they know just as much as we will feel safer with them.

Staff retention is another facet of providing continuity. I have referred elsewhere to the need to prepare people for some of the less conventional aspects of domestic work on a psychiatric ward. Over the years countless domestic staff have demonstrated that it does not take specialist skills to help people with mental health problems but it does take a special kind of person. It is unfair to hurl anyone into this kind of situation without any kind of preparation or opportunity for debriefing. It is unsurprising that in these circumstances some people choose to leave after a couple of months. With more information probably some of them would have decided the post was not for them but others would feel better able to settle into their posts. Proper preparation is the key.

For people staying on a ward the person doing the cleaning is often *the* most valued member of staff. It is good that the author feels what she is doing is worthwhile because it most certainly is. Long may she carry on!

Questions for your service

1   Should non-clinical staff also receive appropriate induction to the functioning and aims of the ward? If these staff are employed by contract companies, should it be a requirement to impart necessary information to help staff when they are first employed in in-patient services?
2   Is the clinical role of non-clinical staff adequately acknowledged, and should they receive some support and supervision in this regard? Should they join multidisciplinary discussions when appropriate?
3   Is there something that can be done to reduce moving non-clinical staff too frequently?
4   Should users be encouraged to take more responsibility over the cleanliness on the ward, or just leave it for hotel service assistants?

Exercise

Role play: a hotel assistant complains that patients are not taking responsibility for cleaning after themselves in the kitchen, bedrooms and dining area, expecting her to do everything. The matter is taken up at the patients' meeting. Assume roles of patients, nurses, occupational therapists and hotel assistant in the meeting and argue your case.

Chapter 17

Mixed feelings

Paul Scally (Nursing Assistant)

I started working in the mental health service in 1980. I knew people who had been in and out of hospital and I'd met a person in a pub who was talking about his nurse training and I thought this would be an interesting area to work in. I also had an uncle with mental health problems and I didn't like the way he was treated at times, by the service and people in general. I saw adults and children ridicule him and when he went into hospital I heard people talk down to him. This did not seem right and I wanted an opportunity to do something about this.

My first job in mental health was working on night duty on an elderly ward. To say it was an eye-opener is an understatement. The first night was frightening. To see people who could have been my grandmother or grandfather lying in bed crying or shouting at each other was difficult. Seeing an old person crying and no one doing anything about it was very difficult. I was not sure I could stay for the night. It was an enrolled nurse who helped me. She sat me down and explained why these people were behaving like they were. I felt nothing was being done for them, but she explained what people were trying and this helped but I still felt uneasy.

Then I moved on to a long-stay ward, which was also quite a shock but I felt I could make a difference there. The shock was the noise and general mayhem, and the fact that people's clothes did not fit properly and they had to go out into the street looking like this. It's no wonder that the public stare. I felt we had a duty to make sure people were dressed appropriately to maintain their dignity.

After three years I went to work on an acute admission ward. I felt very distressed at seeing people being forced into hospital, handcuffed. I felt angry and wanted to know why this could not be done in another way. Although this may have been done for safety reasons it appeared inhumane, especially when people were very unwell. I remember one night a young man in handcuffs being escorted to the ward by the police accompanied by his parents. He seemed very preoccupied and was praying to God but otherwise seemed settled. I went with the nurse in charge to admit him to the unit and I asked the police to take away his handcuffs but they seemed very reluctant to do so. When I asked why, they said he might become angry. Although he had not done so they seemed reluctant to take the handcuffs away. About two years later I bumped into the man in town. He said hello and actually referred to that incident. He said that when he came on to the ward in handcuffs and saw me he saw a very big man and felt very vulnerable because he was in handcuffs and he felt I was going to hit him so he was praying to God for protection. He was clearly feeling very vulnerable and frightened.

There was a period when staff believed that clients' swearing was totally inappropriate and would not accept this type of behaviour. I do not feel that staff should judge others' morals. If clients want to swear in the confines of their own flat or home they should not be judged. I have seen people having cigarettes withheld because they swore. Staff set rules by their own standards that cause patients unnecessarily to become agitated. I don't think we spend enough time asking patients what they want.

I have enjoyed seeing the change over the past twenty years from people being restrained and medicated to seeing staff trying to talk people down and intervene in other ways. I enjoy my job now and get a great deal of satisfaction knowing I can help and make a difference for clients. There have been times when clients have said thank you for the support I have offered and this has been worth a great deal more than the wages I earn. I really enjoy it when I can help people do things when they are unmotivated. I also enjoy it when I see people after they have been discharged and they are moving forward. It is great to feel that you have played a part in this. I am inspired by seeing someone who's very unwell get better. It makes me think that if they can achieve this, then what can I achieve and what can others achieve? When people leave hospital and get work it makes me want to continue in the job I do and come to work.

I find it frustrating when clients are moved into our unit who are not suitable to be there and the unit becomes disturbed and this affects other clients. Or when staff are moved to cover shortages in other areas and this results in activities that we had planned being cancelled. It's very difficult when we have to explain this to clients. It's also difficult when clients are moved because there are no beds and no consideration appears to be given to the needs of the clients. I feel that some decisions are driven by budgets and targets and not by the needs of the clients. I heard someone say recently that we must be loyal to the Trust, and I said no, you must be loyal to the clients. For a few years I felt very disillusioned because there was no investment within mental health services. Things have changed now and more agencies are working together to move people on.

In the past I felt that when I came to work I was just told what to do and given instructions and people were too busy to listen to my ideas and views. However, in the last three years I feel that I have been asked for my views and been able to use my own initiative to do things for clients. I have been actively encouraged to attend clients' reviews and write in clients' notes and I feel that this is valued by other staff and I am thanked for my role.

I have thought about completing nurse training and I have been encouraged by some staff to do this. I have seen people who had started their training and spent a lot of time reading books in the ward office and spending less time with the clients. Once people qualify they do not appear to get the time to do the things I enjoy doing, such as going for a walk with a client, or spending half an hour talking with someone. I wonder if people are being trained for the benefit of the clients or just to answer questions. They can say what particular course of action needs to be taken for a particular client, they can say what it is, but when asked if they are implementing it they answer, not yet, because they have not had time.

Commentaries

Bill McGowan (Nurse Educationalist)

This interesting narrative begins with reference to a chance encounter; a meeting in a pub with a stranger which resonated with something deep in the author's mind and which motivated him to work with individuals with mental health problems. It continues with reflections on further encounters within the mental health system; his initial experience of working with individuals with dementia; the institutional atmosphere on a long-stay ward, the institutional dress code and its impact on the individual's demeanour; a chance meeting two years later with a patient whom he had admitted under difficult circumstances and the dialogue which followed illuminating the unique personal perceptions and vulnerability felt by the patient at the time.

Although it is difficult to place the narrative events as they unfold within a precise time frame, I do get a clear sense of the author's experience as he moves through the mental health system over a twenty-five-year period – from the tail end of the asylum era to the emergence of community care. Most importantly I note the emotional responses – the confusion, perplexity, anxiety and unease experienced in the elderly care ward; the dismay and shock experienced in the long-stay ward; the distress and anger felt in the acute admission ward.

With these snapshots in time, we get a picture of a 'culture of care' which is dominated by social standards and behavioural norms set by the staff group. This can result in a disregard for the patient voice with consequent tensions leading to 'acting out' by patients. I note also the more positive tone generated by changes in the system over the last few years as conditions appear to get better. However, this optimism is tempered by a concern with the familiar and recurring problems of an unsuitable in-patient population mix, the 'booking out' of staff to cover shortages elsewhere in the system. New concerns emerge, such as the premature transfer and discharge of patients because of the need to meet targets, release beds or stay within budget and the conflicts felt around split loyalties.

As an educationalist, a number of issues arise for me from this narrative. Whilst this is a very personal account I am reminded that the closer one gets to the 'individual experience' the closer one gets to understanding the 'universal', since in an uncanny way, these highly personal 'snapshots across time' mirror the experiences and concerns of our mental health nursing students during their three-year educational programme.

Significant 'prior experience' is a feature of many of our students who, like the author, appear to have been genuinely motivated to enter the profession through their own personal experience of mental health problems and those of family members, relatives, friends and neighbours. These 'prior experiences' provide the seed bed for their professional values, which infuse and strengthen their sense of professional identity and integrity and provide a 'moral compass' which helps guide them in developing and sustaining good practice.

I note also the importance to the author of a 'significant person' who helped him understand what was happening during his first frightening exposure to people with dementia. I suspect that there were many other 'significant others' along the way who in other settings continued to help him contain his emotionality and make sense of his new experiences.

Engaging in a series of random encounters with clients is a central feature of mental health nursing work in day care or in-patient/residential settings. Stepping back from such experiences and creating the space to reflect on what has happened does require access to more experienced 'significant others' in order that experience can be converted into learning.

One of those issues which recurs as a central theme in our discussions with students is the tendency towards 'avoidance' of patient contact. We do know that there is a strong 'gravitational pull', drawing staff away from socio-emotional work with patients by 'taking flight' into the nursing office and into other non-direct patient care activities. Whilst many students are aware of this tendency there is also a conscious awareness of a genuine need to escape from over-exposure to highly emotionally charged interactions, albeit for short periods of time. It may be that the author's reference to students in the office represents a snapshot of this dynamic 'respite process' in progress. It is, however, true that this may not be a time-limited respite phenomenon as some teams can at times create semi-permanent ritual patterns of defence where avoidance of patient contact can become the norm – unfortunately, students can become drawn into this.

My view is that if the socio-emotional component of nursing work is to be seriously developed and sustained, it will require a radical shift in culture and resource provision whereby structures are created which will free up space for reflection in practice settings. Mainstream services up until now seem unable or unwilling to provide 'good enough' clinical supervisory structures for their nursing staff. In the absence of adequate support one cannot but expect a strong valency towards withdrawal and the unconscious creation of protective rituals of the sort described by the author.

The random series of experiences over time has clearly served the author well in enabling him to remain inspired and committed to his work. In my experience individuals do matter and I hope that the author will take his extensive experience and commitment into a formal educational programme where he will be able to enhance his expertise and harness his experience to help make a difference where it also matters – from a position of responsibility and authority. If not, I am sure he will continue his search for inspiration and still make a difference along the way.

Jen Kilyon (Carer)

In many ways this account by a nursing assistant echoes the experiences of many family members who are usually thrust unprepared into the mental health system. When first confronted by the mental distress of our family member we may be frightened and confused. We, too, often feel anger, frustration and despair when we see our loved ones and others apparently not treated with enough humanity and respect when they are at their most vulnerable.

It is heartening to read that this nursing assistant went into the service for good reasons and is, after twenty-five years, still very much viewing his work from the user's perspective. My initial reactions when I read the account from his early career of a young man being admitted handcuffed to hospital followed by his parents was, 'Who spoke to them and what must have been going through their minds?' The trauma of watching someone you love undergoing such frightening experiences needs very sensitive and thoughtful handling. Were there any members of staff whose role it was to provide such support? The young man's recollection of these events two years later is very illuminating and shows how crucial it is to hear directly from those who have had psychotic experiences. I wonder if the psychiatrist or ward manager had the opportunity to get this valuable feedback. Later in the account the writer describes the motivation he receives from learning of patients' recovery stories. This demonstrates how important it is for all staff to hear about service users moving on and leading successful lives. This sense of hope and belief in recovery should be integral to working in an acute ward so that this message can be conveyed to service users and their families.

My experience of reading recent Care Programme Approach notes shows that value judgements are still being made about people's behaviour and appearance and that rules made for the benefit of staff can often make life very difficult for clients and their families. The statement 'I don't think staff spend enough time asking patients what they want' sums up much of what needs to change about the running of acute wards. The writer's observations towards the end that he is disinclined to train as a qualified nurse because '[they] spend a lot of time reading books . . . and . . . less time with clients' is a view commonly held by most service users and their families. Visitors to wards regularly describe arriving to find most of the staff in the office and our family member's experience of being hospitalised is that it is still very much a 'them and us' mentality. The nursing assistant's view that, if qualified, there would be little time to 'do the things I enjoy doing, such as going for a walk with a client', is very telling. It is being engaged in these kinds of activities, often away from the ward, that staff have the opportunity to really get to know patients and can most effectively help them through their distress.

The frustrations and difficulties the writer notes about sudden changes through inappropriate admissions, staff shortages and clients being moved are very much reflected by families. Too often I hear of carers being unable to visit because of travel time and costs when their family members are placed outside their local area when beds are not available. It can be very difficult to maintain contact and to have input into the patient's care when they are at a distance. This can cause great distress for all and be detrimental to patient recovery. Where wards have staffing problems meetings are often cancelled at short notice because staff are not available or may take place without key staff being present. Carers may not even be invited, leaving them feeling more powerless and excluded. Named nurses may not be given time to sit and talk with families to gather vital information about the patient in their care or answer questions about their treatment and therapeutic activities.

When it is clear that nursing assistants can and do play such an important role on acute wards, management must ensure that they receive appropriate professional development and supervision. Each client could additionally be given a named nursing assistant who could provide a valuable role in liaising with families, helping them to feel welcome on the ward and supporting them in finding out what they need to know. I do know of one psychiatric hospital that has carer liaison workers on each ward. These are carers who volunteer their time to support families and raise awareness of their needs for all staff. Where service users and carers are actively involved in training, selection and recruitment they can ensure that attitudes and behaviour meet everyone's needs. Experience of services from a personal perspective should be regarded as at least desirable for all staff wanting to work on acute wards. Time spent with individual users should be regarded as the crucial part of all staff's work – all too often paperwork seems to take precedence. In my experience of being with our family member it can often be more productive to discuss things if you are involved in an activity that the person enjoys. Mental health nurses need to be able to talk to patients about what is distressing them rather than being afraid to uncover something they cannot deal with. It should be a core part of their training to develop these skills and to be able to work effectively as a team with psychiatrists, psychologists, therapists, nursing assistants and others, including the family, to find the appropriate support and recovery plan for the patient who should be at the heart of their work.

Questions for your service

1   How best can your service induct new nursing assistants to the in-patient ward? Who should take responsibility for this?
2   How can the team benefit from the first impressions of new staff to the unit?
3   How do we help staff integrate and take advantage of their 'previous life experiences' which are likely to motivate them to join the profession?
4   How do we promote reflective clinical practice in a setting which feels safe and confidential?
5   How can the team benefit from new members of staff who question embedded staff culture?
6   What can be done to prevent excessive movements of users and staff for non-clinical purposes?
7   What can be done to hear more from users about their 'recovery stories'?

Exercise

Role play: a nursing assistant is discussing his difficulties in supervision with a senior nurse. He confesses that he finds it difficult to relax after work, and that he takes many of the problems of his patients back home. How does the supervisor react to this? The observing group then comments on the interaction.

Chapter 18

Feeling marginal

Catherine Allen (Clinical Psychologist)

The recent Sainsbury Centre review of in-patient wards noted that only a quarter of them have access to a clinical psychologist. Why is this? On the Thursday that I read this, after six years working wholly in an acute in-patient environment, I think, 'But how silly! It's so interesting, so varied, so much camaraderie, such an obvious need.' And the following Monday, I'm thinking, 'But of course, who would want to, it's impossible, psychological ideas just aren't wanted here, no one's got time.'

The thing is, psychologists aren't really much help in an emergency. There are very few situations that call for 'let me through, I'm a clinical psychologist!' And acute in-patient services are a kind of chronic emergency. Psychology, with its emphasis on reflection and analysis, prioritising meaning and understanding, can seem self-indulgent and precious.

James had an appointment with me yesterday but chose instead to go on home leave; his daughter was up from London and he wanted to see his grandson. (No one told me, but organising that leave for James required such a lot of jobs to be done.) The Ward Manager had a meeting with me to discuss involving families and carers more but the alarms went off; a patient had hit a member of staff. We had a case discussion planned for someone whose distress is affecting the team badly, but someone had phoned in sick and the nurse in charge was struggling to find someone to cover the night shift. Of course these are priorities, but if all three happen in a week, it's easy to think, 'Why am I here?'

The wider psychology service is glad that I'm here, someone in an unusual post, consistent with government guidance, but they think I'm a bit barmy. I'm a bit marginal there too. They tell me that when I start carrying my keys on my belt, they'll come and arrange my discharge! But I need my keys all the time. In my first week, I leave them in the ward office, the loo, an interview room, a patient's bedroom. And the locked doors aren't just some piece of control-freakery, it's an old building full of nooks and crannies and there are real worries that someone will self-harm in a rarely used room and not be found in time, that someone will stash drugs for dealing to their fellow-patients, that a disinhibited or predatory patient will find the privacy to molest someone. Policing the wards is so important and time-consuming, though the nurses say sadly, 'I didn't come into this job to be a policeman.' My role is to support the other side of the coin, the therapeutic function, but it's not hard to see why it so often comes second.

Not that being marginal is necessarily always a bad thing. I can control my diary: no one needs me urgently enough to want me to carry a bleep. One psychology post in a team of a hundred won't be able to provide everything a psychologist could theoretically do, so I have to choose. And neither in-patient nor psychology managers have a blueprint for this job, so I choose things I like: therapy, supervision, training, audit, developing ways to support families and carers (and avoid: research, psychometric testing, meetings, but that's another story). And people are happy with the little bits of success, happier than I am, sometimes, but no one minds if I fail (and usually no one dies). Marginal, after all.

Even the direct clinical work can feel marginal. The psychology service is drafting some guidance about 'suitability for psychological therapy' that would exclude nearly everyone I see! They don't seem unsuitable to me, and from my semi-outsider position I can tackle the issues that the medical and nursing teams, however competent and caring, don't: the sense of a relapse or a breakdown, a suicide attempt or a hospital stay as an existential crisis, an ordeal in the proper sense, a disaster and a potential turning point. But I suppose it doesn't look like 'proper' therapy, with a clear plan and a contract and a time-scale. People's circumstances can change so rapidly in hospital, or they can get unexpectedly 'stuck', so I sometimes can't tell if this contact will be for a week or a year. I've got very good at prioritising what we can cover in the session we've got. And sometimes it's magic, and sometimes it's frustrating and inconclusive.

James sticks in my mind as an example of the magic. A middle-aged man with a long history of admissions with psychosis and mild learning difficulties, he starts to hint to a student nurse about 'something bad in his childhood'. She asks me to meet him with her and he says he would like to talk about it 'but not on my own'. We ask who he would like with him and he says he would like to include his sisters, so we invite them. He tells them about years of being molested by a local man on his way to and from school. They tell him it wasn't his fault and everyone cries. Then, just as they are about to get into their taxi, one of them says: 'You know, Jimmy, if you'd told mum she would have stopped it.' Devastated, he falls to his knees and they send the taxi away. We all sit down again and discuss the reasons why children don't tell, and the particular issues for a boy going to a special school. An hour later, he is a changed man, smiling and relaxed. Within a few days he is home from hospital and four years later he has not been back.

But my contact with Marilyn is maybe more typical. She is preoccupied with being under a curse, and her psychiatrist has a vague sense that this is somehow connected with her family situation and history and that it might be worth exploring the meaning of it. Nursing staff are nervous, worried that I'll upset her. I don't try to persuade them; I've learned to wait until the discussion reaches a conclusion before saying anything. They conclude that she is so upset anyway that it would be perverse to try and stop her discussing it. She tells me she is under a curse. I ask her who has cursed her and she says it is her ex-husband. He was violent to her and sexually abused her daughters until she left him, was successful in having him prosecuted, and threatened him with a knife when he broke into their house. However, the daughters now have a very good relationship with him, and blame and reject her for breaking up the marriage. 'Yup,' I think, 'that sounds pretty much like a curse to me.' She says it has been hard to talk about it but that she is glad she has. I comment on her resilience and the extent to which she has built up a life for herself and she smiles. I ask if she wants to see me again and she says she does. The next day she discharges herself from hospital. The nurses are quick to reassure me that it was nothing to do with our discussion: 'It's just what Marilyn does.'

But because I can control my diary, and because I don't have to: detail compliance with medication, ensure a robust risk-management plan, cover the wards, explain patients' legal rights, deprive people of their freedom or give them their tablets, answer the phone, fill in the endless forms, liaise with everyone involved in complex care plans about everything, I can afford to just be there and I can try and put the emotional side on the map. And that's the bit that endless service user surveys say is so often missing from an in-patient stay. Long after she had moved to another ward, an experienced nurse said to me in a meeting: 'What I learned from you is that it's OK to have negative feelings about patients, to get angry and frustrated, that what makes you a good nurse isn't about not having human feelings, it's about what you do with them.' And if that's the message my team associate with me, well, maybe it's not so marginal after all.

Commentaries

Nigel Short (Service User)

The first thing that strikes me about this account is the psychologist's ability to reflect upon her role and to consider what benefit, if any, she might be able to offer the people she works with. These include clinical colleagues, managers and the people who are admitted to the ward where she works.

I warmed to her as a person early on in her commentary and her attitude suggested a desire to try and help. The difficulty for her seems to be in knowing how to help and measuring if she has helped. There is much call for evidence-based practice in mental health, which, although an applaudable goal, is often highlighted at the expense of what people really need, a need that has been identified in numerous user publications: a sense that people are being human with them and treating them with dignity and respect. This is born out in Catherine's comment about the organisation's standard approach to therapeutic tasks, as opposed to her more informal style.

Many of us who have used mental health services want to try and understand why our distress is happening. Is it our upbringing? Have I got something wrong with my brain? Am I weak because I am unable to manage myself? Our experiences are changing regularly and this poses a difficulty for us and, as a consequence, for the people trying to help us. What I desperately wanted was for someone to normalise my experiences. I often thought that there was something the matter with me, that I was wrong or had some 'abnormal' experiences. There were many occasions when there was nobody around to help me with these types of enquiries of myself. Most of the staff seemed to be busy just keeping the place going. I think that Catherine has a wonderful opportunity to offer people time. Again Catherine identifies that this is something she can offer people.

When I was experiencing my difficulties the staff asked many different disciplines to come and see me and give their opinions. The people who entered my side room ranged from the art therapist to a neuropsychiatrist. There was very little involvement or discussion with me and I don't remember anybody suggesting that another person sit with me, a relative for example. The person who had the biggest impact with me was a psychologist who had experience in cognitive behaviour therapy. He offered me an explanation that made sense to me. He had taken the time to get to know me. I used to go off the ward to see him. Interestingly the person on the ward who thought this approach might help was a bank nurse. She spent most of her time 'sitting with people'. She played chess with me and we chatted about the content of the daily newspapers. This seems to reflect the semi-outsider position that Catherine discusses.

Perhaps that is one of the advantages of being on the semi-outside. It is very easy to be seduced into joining the messy swamp and losing any objectivity. Staff working in in-patient settings need to change their attitude and develop the formal and informal skills needed to respond properly to people who are experiencing distress. Most ordinary people expect that when they are in any sort of crisis the first thing they should be offered is a chance to talk to someone. In reality unfortunately this is often the last thing that happens on hard-pressed wards. The only word of caution is to bear in mind that just talking isn't a panacea and some kinds of talking may be unhelpful, e.g. blaming or pathologising. Workers need to free themselves from being experts and explore the assumptions they have about people. I like the honesty that Catherine demonstrates and the acknowledgement of her limitations and would encourage her to continue to just be there and . . . try and put the emotional side on the map.

David Kennard (Clinical Psychologist)

Catherine Allen's account reminds me of so much that I experienced working as a clinical psychologist on busy psychiatric wards. I think the issue of marginality is central in a number of ways, and, as Catherine points out, has both its negative and positive aspects. Clinical psychologists are marginal in that they are not necessarily required for the key decisions (no pun intended) – about admission, medication, observation levels, use of the Mental Health Act, home leave and discharge. They may also be marginal if their contribution is experienced as puzzling and difficult to understand, in particular by staff who are not psychologically minded – of which there are quite a few. For them a sudden eruption of anger or an impulsive move, like walking out or taking your own discharge, comes out of the blue, or is the result of some unknowable internal prompting, or, even worse, attributed to an insatiable desire for attention. The attempt to see the behaviour as understandable in terms of what was going on for the patient, internally and externally, currently and in the past, is viewed at best as a long shot and as irrelevant to the immediate situation. In the example Catherine gives near the end of her account, one plausible explanation would be that the patient felt sufficiently relieved by her conversation with Catherine that she didn't feel the need to hang around to see her again – even though she said she would. This may be frustrating for the psychologist, and possibly unwise for the patient, but not 'nothing to do with our discussion'.

Given the risk that the clinical psychologist's concerns may seem 'self-indulgent and precious', one important strategy I found was to offer practical help where possible – helping to design a behaviour rating scale for a particular patient, finding a relevant questionnaire, evaluating an intervention or enabling ward staff to do this, etc. From her comment about the cancelled meetings I guess Catherine was actually doing quite a bit of this.

The marginality of not being involved in emergencies and in meetings (where planning decisions are presumably taken) is probably something that Catherine has traded for the freedom to follow her own likes. From the outcomes she describes – both for patients and the nurse at the end of the piece – I think this has worked to her and the ward's advantage. But there are other ways. Psychologists in secure settings are often key players in decisions about maintaining someone in seclusion. In some places clinical psychologists are beginning to have admitting rights for specific therapies. And proposals being batted around for a new Mental Health Act include provisions for clinical psychologists to have legal powers to detain patients. There is an issue here of clinical freedom versus responsibility, and it is quite a hard one to call. Is it more in the interest of the patients on Catherine's ward that she is free to follow her sense of what is helpful and on some occasion for this to pay handsome dividends, as in the case of James and his sisters, or to get more involved in time-consuming meetings that might bring her closer to the information loop and decision-making processes?

I think perhaps one of the key issues for a psychologist in an in-patient team is how far they are able to gain the trust of the 24/7 ward staff. Even non-psychologically minded staff want the best for their patients, and will value the contribution of a psychologist if the patient feels better for it. But the mantra of 'a good shift is a quiet shift' runs deep in many nurses, who do not welcome the prospect of a psychologist (or a psychiatrist or any other therapist for that matter) prodding a patient with penetrating questions that lead to increased agitation that the nurses will have to cope with after the therapist has left the ward. I was impressed by Catherine's wisdom of waiting for the nursing staff to decide it would be okay for her to see a distressed patient. I know I have sometimes found it particularly difficult when a patient has been secluded following a violent outburst, and I'm thinking they need to talk about it while it is fresh but the staff see this as re-enforcing undesirable behaviour. This raises a key question for all non-nursing staff on in-patient units: is it more important to address the immediate needs of the patient or to maintain a good working relationship with ward staff?

Catherine also mentions the attitude of her clinical psychology colleagues who joke about the keys she has to carry, and draft therapy protocols that exclude her model of a single session time frame. These psychologists seem to lead protected lives where no one is ever in physical danger (just wait till one of their psychotherapy clients tells them they are planning to kill their neighbour) and clients duly turn up for their allocated ten sessions or are removed from the waiting list. As with many protocols, including the NICE guidelines for schizophrenia (2002), the intention of evidence-based practice is worthy but the reality often demands something for which there is as yet no systematic evidence. Yalom (1983) once wrote some very helpful guidelines for a one-session approach to running groups on acute wards, but I don't know of an equivalent for individual psychological therapy, other than the basic principles of assessment and treatment planning.

Like Catherine, I was also drawn to the uncertainty and challenge of in-patient work where what is at stake – the complete dislocation of someone's life and its wider impact – is profound and bewildering. However, the potential to make a difference if you can find the way is enormous – as in the case of James. The challenge Catherine faces every day is how to maintain her own sense of being valued in the face of repeated frustrations and letdowns. What Catherine brings to the ward is her capacity to keep on thinking and being interested in peoples' experience as they experience it, such as the lady who felt cursed and the nurse who learnt it was okay to have negative feelings depending on what you did with them. This is very close to the basic containing function of a mother with a distressed infant – to give back to the infant a more manageable version of their experience when he or she is ready to take it in. It is a job calling, in addition to the professional skills of a psychologist, for flexibility, consistency and love. And just as the mother needs a supportive partner, someone in Catherine's role needs the understanding support of a few close colleagues, which I like to think she has cultivated for her own well-being, although not telling us directly about them.

Questions for your service

1   Is there a role for a clinical psychologist on the ward?
2   Can psychologists and ward-based staff work together?
3   How can psychological insights about patients be best imparted to all clinical staff?
4   Can psychological input help staff examine their assumptions about the patients they are asked to look after?
5   Are most in-patients in acute crisis and receiving short admission stays unsuitable for psychological help? If not, how can therapeutic opportunities be maximised?
6   Should psychologists see patients on their own, with staff, or be involved in group therapeutic activities?

Exercise

A patient who is under treatment by a clinical psychologist in the community mental health team has been admitted in a suicidal crisis to the ward. The clinical psychologist comes to the ward round and requests that she continues offering the patient sessions during the admission. At the ward review staff had different opinions. Discuss the issues raised by this situation and a possible solution.

Chapter 19

Feeling apprehensive

William Travers (Psychiatrist)

On Monday morning the anticipation of walking through the doors of our in-patient Unit fills me with anxiety and apprehension. I usually get an immediate sense of the atmosphere, whether tense or relatively relaxed. There may be new arrivals of patients admitted over the course of the weekend. Often they are familiar, sometimes new; and invariably they prompt immediate questions in my mind about how the individuals concerned came to be admitted. Had they been brought to the hospital by the police; admitted under section; and in what circumstances of distress for them, their families and any others who just happen to have been involved?

For those patients known to me, the question arises of possible deficiencies in the arrangements for their regular treatment and support; had there been any indication that a crisis was imminent; had reasonable steps been taken to monitor and intervene appropriately and in time?

I am always amazed at how calm and steady the nursing staff seem. Their orderly and pragmatic approach to the usually hectic atmosphere is on the one hand soothing, but on the other, liable to trigger a surge of increased alarm. If they are so calm then surely somebody needs to worry! Our patients are often at the centre of disturbing circumstances and events, and I usually feel unable to relax until I feel confident that we have 'got to the bottom' of the situation.

This particular Monday morning we discuss Stuart. Stuart is a 24-year-old single black man who as a child was brought to the UK from Nigeria by his family, who then returned to their country leaving Stuart in the care of social services. He has been admitted several times in the past with psychotic episodes, invariably associated with the use of cannabis and sometimes crack cocaine. He has previously presented in traumatic circumstances, including jumping from the window of his first-floor flat with no clothes on.

On this occasion, I learn that he had been admitted the day before having been found by the police outside his home, naked, shouting at the top of his voice and behaving in an aggressive manner. I learn, also, that the police had picked him up a couple of days before that, exposing himself, and he had been charged with indecent assault. This time the police brought him to the

Unit on a Section 136, but already he has absconded. In quick succession I feel first a sense of apprehension: meeting him again is likely to be a very unpredictable encounter, followed by immediate relief that he is not there at that moment, followed by further fevered speculation about what might be happening whilst he is not in the hospital when he is supposed to be.

I am not in suspense for long. In less than an hour, the police have phoned the Unit to say that they have picked Stuart up again. Within a few minutes, they've brought him back and I am hearing from the police officers about how they found him. He was lying, arms and legs outstretched in the middle of a road with the traffic driving around him. He was completely naked, his clothing having been scattered in the nearby vicinity. Once approached, he was aggressive and agitated and had to be handcuffed.

By the time I tentatively walk into the 'safe' room to see Stuart he is wearing boxer shorts only and has been given some oral medication ('10 and 2') by the nursing staff. Stuart is surprisingly welcoming to me, remarking with some apparent humour that he recognised he had come back to a familiar place. His account of why he was found in the road with no clothes on was quite straightforward; he had needed to get the sun onto his skin and it was quite alright really because the traffic would just have to drive around him.

He started to talk about his sister. She was no longer his sister. She had put 'shit . . . mud' over his body and this somehow meant that he had needed to put himself in the sun. He shows me the skin on his legs which looks quite dry and cracked. Halfway through the conversation, it becomes clear to me that Stuart is not talking to me but to some invisible presence. 'Leave me alone, get away Ann.' I quickly realise he is hearing the voice or feeling the presence of his sister Ann and so there is more going on in the room than initially seems to be the case.

As Stuart is sitting, leaning against the wall, I have decided to squat, though at a distance of about 10 feet, so as to be able to try to establish some sort of rapport, but without putting pressure on him, or placing myself at risk. I'm nearer the door than Stuart, but the ward doctor, Dr Saffu, is standing at the door as are one or two nurses; I'm pleased my colleagues are there but if I suddenly need to get out of the room, they are actually standing in my route! Throughout this time, I am wondering how wise it is for me to be in the room at all but initially figure that Stuart seems relatively relaxed with me. Quite soon, and for no apparent reason he is asking Dr Saffu, 'What have you got in your trousers?'

Is he really asking what I think he's asking? Simultaneously he is casually exposing himself. What do you say when someone asks you a question like that? Should I intervene on behalf of Dr Saffu; should I wait and see how Dr Saffu responds? When a quick and straightforward answer isn't forthcoming from Dr Saffu, Stuart explicitly demands to know whether he has 'a penis in there', exhorting him to 'be a man and say whether you've got one whether it's big or small'.

Dr Saffu's response to Stuart that such questions are 'inappropriate' seems inadequate to the situation but I don't know that I could have come up with a better one. I feel intuitively that this turn in the conversation is related to Stuart's need to assert himself and test out how powerfully he can behave in a situation of some helplessness. Much of the content of his presentation over the preceding days had been of a similar theme. Telling him that his question was inappropriate cuts off a potential avenue for further exploration of what is going on in Stuart's head. But do I really wish to explore this idea in more depth right now?

After about 10 minutes, I figure I've gone far enough in talking with Stuart; he is clearly getting a little tired of the conversation and progressively more tense and irritable. Having initially felt a little calmer, my tension levels and heart rate are telling me that it's best to quit while I'm ahead. I've established that Stuart does not think that he is ill and would not agree to stay in hospital. I retreat to the office and pull out the piece of pink paper on which to make the recommendation for ongoing compulsory detention under Section 3 of the Mental Health Act. I discuss with Dr Saffu and the nursing staff that Stuart requires 'Level 3 observations', i.e. 1:1 nursing in order to attempt to prevent his absconding again and to manage any potential changes in his immediate situation and behaviour. We also discuss and decide on the medication he is likely to require and I suggest that he should be referred, immediately the Section 3 paperwork is complete, to the Psychiatric Intensive Care Unit (PICU). This will provide a 'locked ward setting' with a higher ratio of staff to patients, and a more structured ward environment and routine. Stuart will be unlikely to be able to abscond from there.

As I leave the Unit, I feel satisfied that it's been possible to complete a reasonable assessment of Stuart's immediate circumstances and to institute an initial plan to manage and treat him. On the other hand, I feel full of misgivings that I've got to know only a small part of the picture of what's going on for him and that over the course of the next 24 hours I may have little control over how quickly the formalities for the completion of his detention under Section 3 will be done. It will be difficult to predict exactly when staff from the PICU will visit to assess, and even more difficult to know whether they will accept his transfer to their Unit. In the meantime, the risks of further absconsion or of challenging behaviour which may put him and others at risk are high.

The next day, and things have not settled down with Stuart. The process for completing his 'sectioning' hasn't been completed, which in turn means that the staff from the PICU will not yet consider whether he will come to their unit.

Stuart has been intermittently confrontational, argumentative, demanding food allocated for other patients and generally intimidating. Just after I had seen him the day before, and despite being nursed on a one-to-one basis, he had again absconded, eventually getting brought back by the police for causing a disturbance in the block where he lives, causing the neighbours to feel scared.

Things go on like this for the next few days. He is placed on Section 3. The staff from the PICU come to assess him. They say we should carry on trying to manage him but to let them know if he absconds again, which of course he promptly does, this time bringing himself back a couple of hours later. To speak of exasperation is an understatement. Now, the PICU doesn't have a bed, and it then takes several more days to identify an alternative PICU unit in a private hospital. This has to be funded from local NHS funds.

As the process gradually and inexorably unfolds, I go through a rollercoaster of emotional responses. On readying myself to hear the latest about Stuart, there is the rush of adrenaline, heightened on one occasion when he says he wants to fight and raises his fists. There is immediate relief when the meeting is over, followed by continued unease in knowing that the crisis is not yet dealt with. I feel further relief on leaving the ward, but such feelings are tinged with guilt about walking away from such a tense and overwhelming situation to leave nursing staff in the thick of it, not to mention the other patients.

I often carry a strong sense of being observed as I go about my work; a kind of feeling that one is, or is about to be, judged for any unfavourable outcome that may befall our patients. Things don't go wrong in a major way that often, but when they do, for example when a patient kills himself, harms or otherwise traumatises others, the post-incident review of events can be very painful. Keeping a perspective in which a balance is achieved between an acceptance that the unpredictable will happen and destructive self-reproach is invariably difficult. The ability to be able to continue to think about what is happening to the patient, their family, the staff, the other patients and oneself has to be constantly under surveillance and be struggled for.

Eight days after he was admitted, Stuart is continuing to behave in an angry, obstreperous way. The options to allow any relaxation of his confinement in the unit remain very limited; he is so irritable and resentful about his incarceration.

Then all of a sudden he is transferred to a PICU. Our unit is relatively peaceful. I relax; the staff appear to relax somewhat too. But that feeling is followed almost immediately by a sense of anticlimax. We haven't been able to contain Stuart; another hospital unit and its staff have now taken that on, albeit temporarily. It's not that there's a sense of failure, more a sense of the loss of the thread of the saga with Stuart.

When he is returned to our unit, having been 'stabilised', I wonder whether we'll be left with any opportunity to talk it through with him; for Stuart and us to place this period of florid disturbance in his mental health into any kind of meaningful context. Will there be a possibility to recover some sort of spirit of collaboration and make plans with Stuart to understand his situation, to help him stay out of difficulty and avoid yet another repetition of the same cycle of events?

Commentaries

Sheila Grandison (Art Psychotherapist)

What struck me about this account of a difficult-to-contain young man admitted to an in-patient unit, and the decision of the ward staff to transfer him to the locked ward environment of a Psychiatric Intensive Care Unit, was not so much the vividly described unpredictable, high-risk and bizarre behaviours of the patient, but the thoughts William had once the transfer had happened.

We are invited to picture the following scenario. Eight days into his admission, the young man, Stuart, has absconded from the ward on several occasions, raised the anxiety levels of the staff sufficiently to be placed on Section 3, and then: 'all of a sudden he is transferred to a PICU'. Afterwards, William reflects: 'When he is returned to our unit, having been "stabilised", I wonder whether we'll be left with any opportunity to talk it through with him; for Stuart and us to place this period of florid disturbance in his mental health into any kind of meaningful context.'

As an art psychotherapist, my question is two-fold. Why is meaningful communication with Stuart only identified as verbal and why is meaningful communication thought only to be possible after he is stabilised (whatever that may mean)? Stuart communicated emphatically and non-verbally through his acting out behaviours whilst on the ward. How might these behaviours be understood? What might Stuart be 'saying' through his behaviours? An art psychotherapy intervention offers the opportunity of establishing a predominantly non-verbal channel for communication and expression and as such is a therapeutic intervention that is available to patients when actively psychotic.

William confirms that the open in-patient ward had not been able to contain Stuart, leaving the option of the more secure setting of a locked ward identified as the only way forward for the ward staff in their treatment of him. Perhaps rather defensively, he adds: 'It's not that there's a sense of failure, more a sense of the loss of the thread of the saga with Stuart.' But it may be a failure of a profound kind. It is a failure, in my view, to not provide the therapeutic option of the arts therapies when working with patients in acute states of mind. The task of establishing and maintaining communication, especially where there are severe blocks to verbalisation, needs to continue in order to meet more fully the overall remit of 'duty of care'.

On a ward in the UK, when the first language of a patient is not English, the skills of an interpreter are immediately called on to enhance the possibility of meaningful dialogue. I would like to think that when a patient expresses themselves in a predominantly non-verbal way through their behaviours, then the specialist skills of the arts therapists are identified as the resource most needed. Not to interpret, but to extend the possibility of building sufficient therapeutic rapport with difficult-to-reach patients through acknowledging that, for whatever reason, not everything can be expressed in words. First, you have to find them. Imagistic forms precede the capacity to put experience into thought and understanding.

The central use of arts media – be it art, music, drama or dance – for working between non-verbal, sensory and verbal levels of communication, within the safety of a clearly defined psychotherapeutic relationship, is a unique resource of the arts therapies. Yet, so often, the arts in the arts therapies, and their usefulness, are identified as leisure pursuits. Imagine the change in mental health economics if it were to be clearly established that the arts therapists were able to hold the anxiety levels of highly aroused patients sufficiently for them to be able to be contained more satisfactorily on open admission wards, thereby reducing transfer to Psychiatric Intensive Care Units.

The art psychotherapist can also help the rest of the ward team to better understand patients such as Stuart, who are so often identified as difficult to manage, rather than difficult to reach. What, after all, were the underlying team dynamics on the ward Stuart was admitted to? Ward staff often express surprise when their most difficult patients have engaged with art therapy, in a whoever-would-have-thought-it type of way. The fact that they can, and do, brings with it a restorative, humanising space to the ward, through which ward staff also gain a reflective opportunity to think about patients in a different way, enabling them to better deal with the challenges and limitations to treatment posed by patients presenting with high levels of disturbance.

My surprise as an art psychotherapist is with the urgency with which those same patients engage with simple art materials, to connect, for example felt-tips, pastels, paints, pencils, charcoal or crayons, with paper. For those with severe communication problems, the connection to another through the intermediary of a mark-making object with a piece of paper of a clearly defined shape and size, can be experienced as less threatening than attempts at one-to-one verbal conversation.

How might an art psychotherapist, together with the ward team, think about Stuart? Look at what gets repeated during his admission. Stuart is described as a 24-year-old single black man who as a child was brought to the UK from Nigeria by his family, then left, and taken into care by social services. These circumstances come to be repeated in hospital where William feels the sense of anticlimax when Stuart is transferred to the PICU and has 'a sense of the loss of the thread of the saga'. For Stuart, his life's thread was suddenly interrupted. The suddenness of what happened as a child – being abandoned by his family – gets mirrored in the suddenness of the move to the PICU and the team is left to feel the loss. Diagrammatically, Stuart's loss and emptiness – his nothingness, his nakedness perhaps – can be imagined as a space that came to be filled with the bizarre behaviours associated with his psychotic episodes. An emptiness so big perhaps that it becomes solid, an obstacle that is in the way, just as he was found before admission, lying naked in the middle of the road, in the way, arms and legs outstretched, an obstacle the traffic had to drive around.

Beginning to understand empathically and connect symbolically with that loss, with the therapeutic aim of beginning to recover lost feeling states, might well have been the contribution of an art psychotherapist whilst Stuart was in hospital. Every acute ward should have one.

We cannot tell if Stuart would have engaged positively with an arts therapies intervention as it wasn't made available to him. Had it been, a route for the recovery of a communicative channel might have been found, and a severely contact-impaired service user reached.

Ann Beales (Director of Service User Involvement, Together: Working for Well-being)

When William describes feelings of 'anxiety and apprehension', 'tension', a 'rollercoaster of emotional responses' and 'exasperation' followed by 'anticlimax' we have to wonder if this work setting is positively contributing to individual workers' well-being?

William also acknowledged uncomfortable feelings of being observed himself as he goes about his work. 'A kind of feeling that one is, or is about to be, judged for any unfavourable outcome.' One can only conclude this environment is not healthy.

People who access services, at times of crisis, need to be supported by staff who have the space and realistic resources that will meet our needs.

By understanding our distress within the context of recovery and well-being, it becomes apparent that many agencies such as housing, police, social care services, places where we worship, cultural centres, health services, drug and alcohol support services, our families and friends, etc. need to work together with us and our distress to find a way forward.

It would appear from William's commentary that this holistic approach cannot be achieved working within the system that exists at present, which further adds stress and frustration to individuals whether they are psychiatrists or not. Therefore, I see no short-term solution to the stress the system places upon professionals whilst still having expectations that they will 'deliver'.

This conundrum has been visited again and again by those who wish to find a solution and create environments of hope where people's recovery can be truly supported.

The commentary still leaves many questions that need answering which the system has yet to address. 'The admission rates are three times the national average for black men and twice the national average for black women. Detention rates are between 25%–38% higher than average for black men and between 56%–62% higher for black women' (Census by the Health Care Commission NIMHE/CSIP 2005).

The system William describes functions within our society where it is still the case that people are stereotyped, a fact which is further reinforced by the media. We need to expose the myths, e.g. that people who experience mental distress are violent. In the description, it was clear Stuart's actions posed the most danger to himself. One also has to wonder, given that the police had taken him into hospital before, where he had been sectioned (alongside facing charges of indecent assault by the police), if shouting at the top of his voice was in fact an appropriate reaction when they came to pick him up.

We have to ask the question, are the police generally known as being sympathetic and well trained when supporting/escorting people experiencing mental distress to hospital? If this is not the case, has the distress escalated before people even reach services (William and the staff team)?

With the stress levels William describes, there will inevitably be huge difficulties in creating consistent situations and opportunities where individuals can be engaged sympathetically, with empathy and understanding. The commentary does not outline a positive environment where staff have the space or time to address needs such as housing, physical care, exploring relationships people have with others, etc. The staff appear not to have the time to explore Stuart's angst and where it comes from, but clearly the clues were alluded to. Who would have the appropriate insight to understand the trauma of being brought over from Nigeria and, whilst still young, being placed into the care of social services? What clues can be found from Stuart's history that could clarify Stuart's drug use? One can only imagine the trauma this young man had experienced and, unfortunately, given today's society, the types of racism he would have been subjected to in his life.

The weight of evidence suggests that it is at the point of crisis that interventions can be effective, preventing escalation and speeding the process for people to become better equipped, at an earlier point, to move towards feelings of hope and empowerment about their recovery.

The 'New ways of working' (DoH 2005b), which looks at teams taking increasing responsibility, with the psychiatrist taking on more of a consultancy role, may foster the discussion and debate around collective approaches to support for individuals.

We know there is an understanding that things need to change and healthier environments must be created. This will benefit everybody, both those employed to provide services/support and the people who access services.

International experience suggests that people who have experienced distress are well placed to support others in their recovery process, so we must be innovative in how we include service users directly in service provision. Service users must be enabled to work in partnership with individuals who provide support to us. We need reassurance that all agencies share agreed values and will work with carers, family members and friends, and that all staff are committed to partnership working with us.

We need to be creating environments and support where psychiatrists and staff do not 'retreat to the office'. What we do need are environments where everyone 'retreats' to the lounge/dining room looking forward to engaging with interesting people who have huge potential and talents, some of whom experience periods of distress. A place where people from the very onset of their distress gain advice from others who have experienced similar issues. Partners, friends, carers and family members need to be informed about their potential role in supporting the person experiencing distress. Settings where staff and service users are enabled to work in healthy partnerships enjoying mutual respect and equality of input to problem solving and seeking solutions that will support individuals towards recovery. These partnerships need to be well resourced and have wide and diverse networks that can deal with a myriad of social issues, from child care to combating racism, from the effects of poor housing to lack of job opportunities. Most importantly a space needs to be found where everybody gains from the process of recovery so that everyone's well-being is maintained.

If or when I need to access services again, it is important to me that those who work with me are happy and hopeful.

Questions for your service

1 How does your service manage potentially risky situations without jeopardising relationships with patients?
2 How can staff management of challenging behaviour by black patients incorporate a culturally sensitive approach?
3 Does the unit need 'safe areas' to assess potentially violent users?
4 After an incident where a patient has to be forcefully restrained, does the team meet to discuss how it was done, and whether it could have been managed differently or prevented?
5 How can one-to-one observations become not only a means of control but an opportunity to engage meaningfully with a patient?
6 How do staff help each other when they inevitably experience stress as a result of their work?

Exercise

Role play: a consultant psychiatrist has referred a black psychotic patient with a history of serious, unprovoked violence. The consultant states that at the moment he is not expressing any violent behaviour, and wishes to keep him on the ward, but the staff are understandably anxious. Taking the roles of consultant, junior and ward manager, outline what measures you will take to reduce risk and establish a relationship with the patient.

Chapter 20

Taking control

Geoff Brennan (Nurse)

I have been in a state of some trepidation since I agreed to write this commentary. I find I am concerned about being honest whilst capturing the complexity that comes with the in-patient nurse role. It would be easy to focus on negative events and emotions as these are the ones that immediately spring to mind – the difficult times with what seems an overwhelming tide of need and little felt in the way of resources, when my friends and colleagues would ask why I was 'still on the wards', as if it was some sort of failure of will or ability. Yet to say only this would detract from the nurturing team cohesion you can get on wards, or the immediate, buzzy high from dramatically helping someone, or the intimate ward 'banter', which usually consists of dark humour, or the real positive human presence that 'patients' can have and the warm relationships you can develop.

So I have decided to talk about my time with a lady called Janet (which is not her real name), and how I came to have to intervene/interfere in her life. I find that, although this all happened years ago, I remember the following events very clearly, in most parts. My feelings, although also remembered, are complex.

Janet was admitted to the ward where I was a charge nurse in what one could only call a 'terrible state'. I can't remember who brought her in, whether it was a professional or her family taking her to A&E, but I do remember her coming onto the ward. She was crying. She was dehydrated. She was acting as if we were all going to attack her, and was the instant receiver of pity and concern. She was also incoherent and could not finish an understandable sentence, saying 'don't' a lot, as in:

Where do you want me to sit? Ah don't. Come on, please don't!

I'm not sure what you mean Janet. What don't you want me to do?

Oh yes. I'm sorry about this. Please. Please don't. I will do anything, just don't, please.

There was a history of mental health problems and admissions in her past, but Janet had effectively been out of hospital for three years, which is a healthy period between relapses. She did have 'community involvement', but looked at closely, this had been at a minimal level. Janet had been effectively well and surviving, having a job, adolescent children and a partner. Later we were able to ascertain with Janet that there were tensions in her family and her work that contributed significantly to her relapse, but when she was admitted we were in no position to explore these with her and she was in no position to tell us.

The core issue of everything was the intense agitation Janet exhibited. It is hard to describe how this made the ward team and indeed the other patients feel. Initially, the other female patients were just gathering her in. The ward layout meant that the women's area was one six-bedded dormitory and one four-bedded dormitory. Janet was in the smaller four-bedded dorm and the women in there took her in tow, all bar one having been in before and all being basically decent caring people. In this, and within a few hours, they tried to talk to her, helped make her bed up and were trying to help her settle along with the nurses. It was clear, though, that Janet was finding it difficult to settle.

In-patient wards can be frightening for everyone. They are strange places full of strange people and strange rules. People are normally frightened because they perceive they are under some form of threat. Mostly this is reduced to a direct physical threat, that a person will be punched or sworn at. Both patients and staff can feel the threat. But there are other forms of threat. In this case the staff felt the threat was that Janet, in her state of extreme agitation, would 'die at our feet', as one of our health care assistants put it, and we had not done enough to stop it.

She had not slept for many days prior to admission, we discovered. Indeed, she had taken to sitting outside her children's room at home, frightened of some unmentionable 'thing' that would cause them harm. When she came onto the ward she showed the results of this insomnia in that her hair was greasy and lank and she had a patina of sweat on her pale face. Add to this, she had stopped eating or drinking some days before and constantly seemed startled, frightened: you can see why she aroused strong emotions in both staff and patients.

Whilst the vast majority of these emotions were sympathetic, there was also a touch of irritation. Being with Janet made you feel as if you were doing something wrong. The incessant distress began to make you feel overwhelmed and reluctant to be with her, as if you wanted to remove yourself to somewhere cheerful, somewhere you felt it was OK to be happy.

I am always interested when people talk about in-patients as some homogenous mass, sitting pitifully waiting for professionals to interact with them and 'give them therapy'. They are anything but standardised. A patient can be a nineteen-year-old, street-wise man who wants to be as far away from an in-patient ward as he can get and will tell you where to go in no uncertain terms if you insinuate that he might even have an inkling of a problem. The emotions that can be stirred up are not standardised either. The street-wise boy can generate sympathy and be charming, kind and fun while Janet's distress could cause a guilty irritation because you knew she was in real and evident distress.

In truth, being irritated is not a bad thing – emotions are just there. It is our interpretation of the emotion and how we deal with them that is often the problem. While I must admit there were times, in trying to build a rapport with Janet, where I would find myself strangely annoyed by the flinching and cowering, these would be followed by a feeling of shame. How did I deal with this? I would like to say I took it to supervision or to some sympathetic forum, but in truth I guess I just suppressed it and felt uncomfortable.

Janet's distress (not Janet herself, you understand, but the distress she radiated) made the whole ward on edge. Witnessing her distress was painful for everyone. Her distress became so powerful that within a day she was the first to be handed over at each change of shift. Everyone had an opinion as to how we should proceed. The female patients were beginning to talk about the negative effects of witnessing Janet's distress in their own care meetings. Another patient had absconded and the general atmosphere was subdued, niggled, and tense. The opinion crystallised into the general feeling: 'We have to do something, this can't go on.'

In a situation like this, there is one intervention which is identified as the 'answer'. That intervention is medication. Hence, 'we have to do something' quickly became 'we have to medicate Janet'.

I remember an account by George Orwell of being a policeman in Burma when he was told he had to shoot an elephant. In the account Orwell described how he doesn't want to shoot the elephant, but his position in the culture and the collective will of the villagers who want the elephant shot make it virtually impossible for him to refuse. He is the policeman with the gun. It is his role. When the intensity of the distress Janet was experiencing spread to others and became public, I was Orwell with the gun. I was the most senior nurse at the time. I couldn't give my opinion to someone else and leave it as their responsibility. It was I who should persuade the doctors to allow us to medicate, as it would be us, the nurses, who carried out the act.

As it happened I thought I also believed that we should medicate. But was this purely my decision? I was finding Janet's distress difficult, I was feeling that we should alleviate the stress for the community, but was I truly considering Janet's needs as well? Make no bones, I could make a convincing argument that this is *absolutely* what was needed, but the fact is that once a decision such as the one to medicate is suggested, it affects the possibility of using other alternatives and will have definitely different outcomes.

Janet was adamant that the medication was poison. 'You are trying to kill me', she screamed when one of our skilled female nurses approached her with a prescribed sedative. Now that scream had to be heard to be appreciated. It came from the solar plexus and was full of a base fear, as if all the 'don'ts' had finally come to home to roost. It only stopped when the medication was taken away. Janet was now more distressed than ever.

The staff reconvened in the nursing office and we began to plan how to force medication into Janet. Events were moving at speed. The junior doctor on the ward asked for one last attempt at persuading Janet to take the medication orally, and we all agreed. Janet went with the doctor into his room. He sat with the medication on the desk. She sat opposite him. They sat like this, talking for over forty minutes.

While they were in the office, I took one of the nursing assistants to one side, a woman whom I had tremendous respect for, who I felt would give me an honest opinion. I asked her what she thought we should do. She looked me in the eye and said, 'Let's get it over with. This is no good for anyone.'

I went into the office and apologised for interrupting. I remember saying to Janet that we had come to a decision point. She needed to tell us how she was going to take the medication. She screamed again. We escorted her to her bed area and she didn't struggle, but let us lead her, screaming. She lay on the bed and refused to take the oral medication which was a liquid. She did compliantly roll to one side and allowed a female nurse to inject her. She screamed all the way through. When it was done, and as I moved away from her bed, she looked at me and said I was an evil bastard. We left a nurse with her and, a short time later, she slept.

How did it turn out? Well, Janet did recover and returned to the community. The junior doctor, whom I greatly respected, was furious and focused his anger on me. I didn't blame him and we got over it, eventually. He was genuinely one of the most caring doctors I ever met.

I tried to talk to Janet about the whole incident much later, when she could communicate. She said she couldn't remember the event properly and didn't hold any bad feelings towards me.

Do I hold bad feelings towards myself? This is more complicated to answer. I chose and continue to choose to work as a nurse in acute care because I believe we can make a difference in a positive sense, but it does come at a price. Sometimes that price is making a decision in the grey areas of life and living with it afterwards.

Commentaries

Dee Fagin (Nurse and Psychotherapist)

Here is a wonderful account of a clinician who has listened to his feelings rather than depend on the somewhat sterile format that can all too often determine decision making in impossible circumstances.

Geoff describes a passion for his work; he is aware that colleagues are unable to understand quite what the attraction is. The account details Geoff's sense of being part of something focused and intense, staying with it and living with the consequences.

Janet, a distressed and regressed female patient on the ward, mother, wife and employee in her life outside the hospital, has effectively monopolised the ward as her state of mind is unbearable to others. There is a challenge as to who can bear it and who wants to put a stop to it. One might deduce that the one who least enjoys the experience is Janet herself whose torment becomes known to all those she has contact with. The dilemma for Geoff and his team is whether to intervene or hope that the situation will resolve/dissolve. The overriding anxiety concerns Janet's survival, both physically and emotionally. The responsibility for keeping patients alive is given without question to the doctors and nurses supposedly attributed with those necessary skills. Such is the burden called duty of care.

Years after the event that Geoff describes, Janet has been kept in mind, his feelings still readily available for further consideration; as Geoff says, he remembers them and they are complex. Why we might ask would any clinician want to be reminded of the difficulties incurred in such an interaction and what can be learnt from this? For those able to give of themselves and remain alert and aware of their own reactions and responses, much can be gained. Hence the question about what makes the work attractive, but it is a fine balance and depends on being able to think with necessary freedom from defensive strategies.

Janet's communication is immediate and impacting: 'Look after me. I am vulnerable and helpless and cannot do this for myself.' There is a question about what Janet wants to be heard and responded to as she also directs us to her 'don't's, so the message becomes: 'Come here, go away.'

As described, Janet's behaviour might be understood as a defence, not to get too near or too close but also to take the unbearable away; a bit like having a really painful splinter but not allowing anyone to get near enough to pull it out.

The management of this intractable situation is being delegated to the ward team. The 'Do something!' is felt by those too close to the pain. The 'Take it away' feeling is carried by those who want removal of the responsibility, even if this means temporarily handing it over to the next shift, or by the attempted negotiation by the doctor who was trying to give it back to Janet, who clearly did not want it. 'It' was agony, an unbearable torture that provoked an equal persecution of discomforting and troubling responses in others.

The unanimous voice of reason was that the situation could not go on as it was. This was what provoked Janet's admission for intervention of one sort or another; it could not have gone on in her home or indeed anywhere else. 'It' had to be taken charge of by something stronger than the disturbance inhabiting Janet. Seemingly this was the communication Geoff responded to in activating an executive decision, thus drawing a line under the paralysing ambivalence that reigned over this very sensitive situation.

The immediacy of Geoff's intervention, although carefully considered and in consultation with a trusted colleague, had not been harmonised with the ward doctor who is deprived of his part in the less attractive act that followed. The possibility of splitting being laid open as the ultimatum is delivered to both Janet and her appointed ally, the ward doctor, I wondered how Janet might have perceived this doctor who had not persuaded her to accept medication and who had been publicly overruled by Geoff taking charge. Would she have felt responsible for the doctor's possible humiliation, or perhaps felt relief that Geoff stopped the fruitless efforts to gain her compliance? Furthermore, there is no mention of the ward consultant sharing this burden or taking up authority for the inevitable need to make a decision one way or another. Presumably a decision had already been made when the prescription was written up. Although not stated, I assume that Janet had formal status and responsibility had in part been removed from her already. Certainly Janet verbalised a refusal to be medicated but was this refusal to actually have it or a refusal to accept responsibility for agreeing to it being given to her (this being carried mainly by Geoff)?

In Geoff's reflections he asks, 'Do I hold bad feelings towards myself?' He also relates to suppressing what he felt and being uncomfortable with it. Brief reference to supervision and sympathetic forums begs the question: what more would make a difference for staff working in these settings to avoid residual feelings of discomfort?

When working with emotionally distressed and disturbed people, staff necessarily need to protect themselves. Janet's communication is complex and contradictory; not surprisingly therefore, responses in team members, notably the ward doctor and Geoff, had varied. The need for a response to care for a vulnerable and helpless patient was obvious. Less available for understanding is the investment made by the ward doctor in his 'last chance' or the complicated feeling of irritation that Geoff experienced. There is, at the beginning, reference to Janet's fear of some 'unmentionable "thing" that can cause harm'. This might be understood as a projection from Janet. Perhaps what is more pertinent here though is how to deal with these issues, both as an individual and as a member of the staff team. Examining one's own difficult/ unmentionable feelings seems to be one of the least explored areas of acute work despite the frequency of encounters with patients most likely to evoke these responses. And yet the only relief and indeed the learning is to share these thoughts, ideas and feelings and to check them out with colleagues in order not to be inhabited by an 'unmentionable'. To be receptive inevitably requires an openness of the self and without the safety of ward structures, supervision and talking to each other, there is, as Geoff so rightly suggests, a price to pay. The saying, when you sup with the devil, take a long spoon, is perhaps a useful reminder that as well as being receptive we need sometimes to stand back. Geoff is called 'an evil bastard' in the peak of Janet's projections; later she denies any memory of this but Geoff remembers it very well.

The staff involved in this incident are depicted as mindful and careful in their interventions. We cannot expect that everyone will be receptive in the same way and to the same communications from patients in their care. A 'united front' may seem like an impenetrable fortress for someone like Janet; it may also offer the strength of containment lacking in Janet's internal world.

Richard Duggins (Junior Doctor)

I painfully identify with the junior doctor in the above account. I have on several occasions begged the staff team to give me 'one last attempt' at speaking to a patient before they were medicated against their will. Mostly, as in the account above, such attempts with patients fail, and like the junior doctor here, I am left feeling guilty that I could not do more, and angry with the staff for enforcing the medication.

In this commentary, I would like to explore some reasons why patients, especially patients with psychotic experiences such as Janet, arouse such strong feelings in in-patient staff. I would also like to examine why particularly strong and polarised feelings are provoked in staff when patients are given medication against their will. Finally, I would like to consider ways in which staff effectively manage their strong feelings so they are more likely to be able to act in their patients' best interests.

Strong feelings in staff

In reading the account of Janet's care, I wonder if there may be three main reasons why she aroused such strong feelings in the ward staff. These reasons are shared distress, the repeating of past relationships, and the projection of responsibility.

Shared distress

If you have ever been with a person in physical pain (such as someone who has broken a bone), then you know how hard it is to be with them while they are in pain. You are so distressed by the pain they are in, it is almost as if you are in pain yourself. It is such a relief when the person is finally given a painkilling injection – it not only helps their distress, it also relieves yours.

It is the same when you are with someone in severe mental pain. Janet is in so much mental pain that the whole ward feels her distress. Her agitation is so intense that the staff become agitated and worry she will 'die at their feet'. The other patients too feel the distress, and the ward becomes niggled and tense. The author tells us that 'the incessant distress began to make you feel overwhelmed'.

Staff in in-patient settings have to regularly share their patients' severe mental pain. This can feel unbearable for staff, and can lead to a desire in the staff to sedate distressed patients. It could be argued that the real priority of sedating such patients is not to treat them, but to calm the staff members' mind. Main (1957), in his famous paper 'The Ailment', discussed a study on an in-patient ward in which nurses discovered that they tended to give sedation when they, rather than their patients, could not take any more. This study showed that better psychological support for the nurses reduced the amount of sedation given to the patients.

Repeating past relationships

In 'The Ailment', Main also describes certain patients, whom he called 'special patients', whose management seemed to evoke particularly strong feelings in staff. He found that staff often fell out with each other around the management of such patients, and that this could lead to splits in the team. Main felt that the strong and polarised feelings in the staff were related to the way such patients unconsciously related to the staff. Such a patient treats staff members not as people in their own right, but as aspects of people from the patient's past. For example, some staff members may be related to as frightening fathers, whilst others may be related to as idealised mothers. Strangely staff members who were treated in this way often tended to take up the roles unconsciously given to them by the patients. Thus staff members may, for example, find themselves feeling more strict, or more indulgent, than they would usually be with such a patient.

If I find myself having strong feelings aroused in me by a patient, and especially if I find myself saying or doing something that is out of character, I find it very helpful to wonder if I am unconsciously playing out an unresolved relationship from the patient's past.

Projection of responsibility

Hinshelwood (2004), in his helpful book *Suffering Insanity*, describes how patients with psychotic experiences project responsibility onto the staff. Janet does not seem to care that she is so distressed that she is endangering her physical health due to her lack of water, food and sleep. Instead she is solely preoccupied with some unmentionable thing that might harm her children. Janet has therefore effectively projected (or handed over) all responsibility for her own health to the staff. She has no concern for herself, and therefore the staff have to hold all the concern. This is a heavy burden for staff to bear.

The staff now have all the responsibility, and this responsibility evokes strong feelings – the staff rightly know that they have to make the decision for

Janet about how much mental suffering she should be allowed to take, and how much more physically unwell she can be allowed to become.

Feelings around medication given against a patient's will

In Janet's management, the strong feelings really come to a head around the decision to give Janet medication against her will. The fact that the staff share Janet's feelings of distress, and may be feeling overwhelmed by her psychosis, is likely to make many of them wish to sedate her. However, some staff members may react to this wish to sedate Janet in an unusual way. Such staff will feel guilty at having such a wish, and to protect themselves from feeling this guilt, will promote the opposite and refuse to sedate Janet in any circumstance. Thus emotionally the staff group may be split, with some members wishing for Janet to be sedated, but others unable to contemplate sedation under any circumstance.

If we add to this the experience that some staff members may have because Janet is reacting to them as people from her past relationships, and also the fact that Janet is requiring the staff to take full responsibility for her health, we can see that making the decision to medicate starts to feel highly complex.

Managing strong feelings

It is a real challenge for the staff to make a rational decision on whether, or not, Janet would benefit from medication. The staff are full of powerful emotions around the idea of medication. Some wish it to happen quickly, and some wish to avoid it at all cost. The staff group can only come to a decision that is likely to be in Janet's best interests if these strong feelings can be effectively managed. Janet's case illustrates some good examples of the way the author manages his emotions. He is able to tolerate his feelings long enough not to be rushed into making a quick decision. He does not take an easy option and avoid the decision by leaving it for other people (such as the night-staff) to sort out. He consults widely with other people, including other staff and patients, and so he is able to balance his own feelings by weighing up alternative feelings and opinions. He is also aware consultation in other arenas such as supervision might have been helpful. (If a weekly staff sensitivity group existed on the ward this could have been another useful forum. When I worked on a ward with an externally facilitated staff sensitivity group, I found such a group invaluable in these situations.)

A key aspect of the care, in my mind, is that the author was able to reflect on his actions with Janet after she had recovered. This discussion allowed Janet to feed back on the experience, and offered both parties a chance to learn from it. The discussion may also have been an opportunity for Janet to express a preference for the way the staff should proceed if a similar situation arose again in the future.

Summary

Patients such as Janet evoke powerful emotions in the staff in in-patient settings. These emotions are painful to bear, and often threaten to dominate decision making around key issues such as medication. I, like Janet's doctor, have found myself overwhelmed by emotions on such occasions, and I have as a result acted unhelpfully and taken my feelings out on the other staff. It is often much harder to manage such powerful feelings than it is to act on them. However, it is crucial that staff are able to manage the powerful feelings that patients evoke in them, because this is necessary to allow the staff to make the thought-through decisions that are most likely to be in their patients' best interests.

Questions for your service

1   How do staff deal with strong emotions generated by patients, such as irritation, threat, overwhelming concern, disaffection, repulsion or rejection?
2   Do you think Janet should have been given medication against her will? What do you think the reasons for, and against, giving medication in this situation are?
3   How do staff try and help other patients deal with uncomfortable feelings generated by one of them?
4   Have you ever had the experience that a patient was sedated because the staff were feeling overwhelmed? What could have helped prevent this?
5   How are decisions to medicate agitated patients taken on the unit, and whose responsibility is it?
6   Is it reasonable to forcibly medicate a patient in order to safeguard other patients or staff, the ward atmosphere or to calm unpleasant feelings he or she may generate in others?
7   Have you been a member of a staff sensitivity group, and if so how did you find it?
8   Do you think advance directives (living wills in which patients express their preferences for future treatment) are helpful?

Exercise

Role play: in a sensitivity support group taken by a psychotherapist, staff express views that a patient with borderline personality disorder, who is disturbed and suicidal and attention-seeking at times, has been observed laughing and boasting to other patients about the way in which she is provoking the nurses. They have suggested discharging her immediately. Discuss what could be going on with the feelings of the patient and the staff in these circumstances.

Chapter 21

Feeling frustrated

Kate Hughes (Occupational Therapist)

I am the Occupational Therapist (OT) for an in-patient rehabilitation hostel-ward for 'treatment resistant' schizophrenic clients, who have come to us from high dependency, forensic or acute psychiatric services within our Trust. Our service is the step between hospital living and a return to community life. Our job, which can take a number of years if the client has been in hospital for long periods, is to re-equip them with the skills they have either lost through long years of hospitalisation or not had the opportunity to develop if their illness struck them down when still quite young.

Often I begin the day with having to counsel or encourage clients to enable them to feel positive enough to participate in therapies. Sometimes there are negative voices or thoughts to combat, disabling anxiety, or simply lack of sleep due to other patients' night-time distress and/or early morning feelings of over-medication, which can make it difficult to engage in therapies. Sometimes planned activities get cancelled in favour of something easier to manage. Sometimes a supportive social chat is what turns out to be most needed.

This is a frustrating situation for clients, for whom progress towards being discharged into a non-hospital setting where they can get on with their interrupted lives must often seem very slow, taking two steps forward and then one back. It can be particularly frustrating for clients who at the beginning of their stay with us lack the insight to see how far they are from having the necessary skills and daily practice to manage life outside.

It can also be frustrating for me when I schedule time to take someone out into the locality in order to practise skills, or arrange community work placements, and then find that the client in question is finding it too much to cope with it all and will not be able to participate in the programme. It is frustrating to spend a couple of hours preparing and gathering equipment for one of my groups, such as Stress Management, Life Skills, Social Outreach, Communication Group or Coping with Symptoms, to find that only one client is willing to attend or that one or two are so disturbed in their mental states that they disrupt the group for others and nothing useful can be achieved.

It is also frustrating when I have worked for a long time with a client to enable him to move on – he may have been attending a college or work placement for some time, may have learned how to cook a range of menus and be on self-catering status, may have been shopping for and preparing his own meals, managing his own laundry, etc. – and it may then be almost impossible to find him the right place to live in the community where he can use those skills, as nobody really wants a guy with a mental problem living next door.

Stigma is alive and thriving in suburban England and stigmatising reactions occur and re-occur. In recent months we have had more and more trouble moving our clients on, as these are people who have problems that are not going to go away and so some social support network is needed to sustain them. Often it seems that community placements prefer to select easier clients to work with and/or the client's healthcare purchasers are not prepared to pay enough for the care package we have assessed that our client needs. Thus I have repeatedly had to watch someone that I have worked hard with lose their skills again due to the combination of hopelessness, loss of confidence and increasing low self-worth that this situation creates.

Mine was a hard-fought-for position. I was brought into a team of nursing and medical staff in order to improve our clients' chances in life through daily living and social skills training. The nursing staff had been managing with our multi-disabled clients without Occupational Therapy input for quite some time by the time of my eventual arrival. Initially it was hard work getting other professionals who had been doing things their own way to understand the change of emphasis.

It is extremely frustrating to discover that a member of our own team, while I have been trying to build skills and enable a client, is inadvertently de-skilling and making the client more dependent through the understandable, but misguided desire to look after them. I have had many times to explain patiently, for instance, that doing someone's ironing for them may be a caring act, but that it is not enabling the client to develop necessary daily living skills.

In the first few years, I'm afraid to say that I precipitated some conflict over a range of these kind of issues. There were hurt feelings all round because I and the nurses both felt that we were trying to do the best for our clients. As time has gone on, however, because I guess we knew we were all in it for the long haul, issues have been resolved. I am happy to say that we have tried as a team to jointly create our own ward philosophy, and the outcome is that these arguments happen less often.

However, I do have to spend time with new staff explaining why at our hostel I and the nursing staff do family visits, write care-plans, Major Review reports and goal planning together, rather than me being expected/permitted only to contribute to the Occupational Therapy sections on the CPA form – which the nursing staff in other parts of our service leave blank. I see this attitude as foolish, as clearly nursing staff in a home-like situation witness some activities of daily living which I am not around to observe or practise with clients.

Some nursing staff on coming to our hostel have an attitude of non-co-operation with other occupational therapists but I am not a person who gives up easily. I have always believed that nurses and occupational therapists bring to collaborative work different but equally valuable skills. It seems to me that many nursing staff have low self-esteem regarding their skills in rehabilitative areas and also regarding group-work, and I have had to do much encouragement; I feel that now I can work with the majority of my nursing colleagues co-operatively.

In the early days it was particularly difficult to get nursing involvement in groups. After I sat down with the senior nurse who kept the off-duty sheets and we allocated a member of staff to each group, sometimes I would find that on the day (despite myself and the nursing assistant concerned having made plans together) the nurse in charge of the shift could have different priorities and would reallocate the nursing assistant to a different task. Sometimes this happened without their even letting me know, which left me trying to manage on my own a group of up to eight clients with differing mental states.

This was extremely frustrating as I'd sometimes have to cancel the group if we were supposed to be leaving the unit, or at the very least I'd have to scale down the activities planned and/or tell clients that they couldn't attend, which they might take as a reason to stop attending groups at all! This was an issue I took to our staff meeting to get resolved and so it happens much more rarely now.

Overall I feel that, hard going as it has been, major progress has been made in teamwork. Possibly this has been helped by being the only occupational therapist in the team and the fact that we are in a home-based situation where group-work takes place in the sitting room rather than away from the nursing areas. In my 30 years of practice I have worked in many situations where the nursing team is based on the ward and the Occupational Therapy Department is elsewhere, and as the priorities are often very different, there seems to be little impetus to support each other.

The reason I have remained where I am is that our team today is not like that (though I think it is pretty rare). In the five years I have worked there I have done much staff training and co-therapist work (with the support of the hospital's nurse specialists in family work and psycho-social interventions) in order to raise and maintain staff skills. I have also supported nursing staff to carry out individual and group interventions and am now proud to say that we are an excellent team who understand our clients' needs and work well with them to maximise their capabilities.

Our efforts, however, can so easily be undermined by lack of support from other services or agencies. Our intensive assessments and skills training programmes can be to little avail if, after working hard to show a client that he can manage to look after himself, can train for some form of employment, and has the confidence to envisage establishing a social and working life out of the hospital, everything we have worked for together is proved to be a sham for the client when he reaches the point of capability and no placement is offered thereafter.

Commentaries

Mark Hardcastle (Nurse)

I am, I confess, a fully paid up member of the Occupational Therapists' Fan Club (OTFC). I am particularly impressed by the profession's expertise in effectively addressing practically and meaningfully issues of disability. Gary Kielhofner's Model of Human Occupation known as MOHO (Kielhofner *et al.* 2002) offers an academic framework for practice which should be widely recognised and practised beyond the occupational therapy profession itself. So when it was suggested that I offered a commentary on Kate's occupational therapy contribution I was already favourably primed, expecting it to reflect the values and practices which would enable people to find pathways to recovery (Anthony 1993) in a mental health rehabilitation in-patient setting. Unfortunately, my somewhat biased and idealistic assumptions were quickly run down by Kate's steamroller of an account of her experience.

I'm particularly struck by the pessimism and paternalism of the account and a sense of a service which is having difficulties adopting values and practices which would allow users to define new ways of living after their acute illness through a process of recovery.

The Recovery movement has been championed by service user interest groups for nearly two decades and what started as a near radical civil rights lobby group has now been incorporated into mainstream mental health policy (NIMHE 2005). This statement of intent urges mental health services to adopt the following value-based principles as a basis for action:

- Working in partnership with service users (and/or carers) to identify realistic life goals and enabling them to achieve them
- Stressing the value of social inclusion
- Stressing the need for professionals to be optimistic about the possibility of positive individual change.

As to how much these principles reflect the original intention of the service user movements of the 1980s is debatable. There must be a concern that there is cynical interpretation of these principles resulting from a wish to be seen to adopt and succeed in meeting governmental targets, for example the mere re-badging of mental rehabilitation services as a recovery service with very little real change for the service user experience.

Kate's account reflects a rather more honest portrayal of the values and practices of a 'rehabilitation hostel-ward for treatment resistant schizophrenic clients' and does not attempt to disguise the fact that the service she describes is not quite what a modern needs-led, evidence-based and recovery-focused service should be or is expected to be like. Kate describes how her clients are struck down, fail to have insight into how unskilled they are, struggle to gain acceptance when *moving on* due to stigma and have the temerity not to attend the groups that she has worked hard to set up. Hardly the stuff of optimism, strengths-based collaborative working and inclusion.

Kate's work is entitled 'Feeling frustrated' and her piece reflects this emotion. She plans activities, runs groups such as stress management and helps clients gain life skills in laundry and cookery, all good pursuits within the canon of occupational therapy. Unfortunately, she is let down by her clients when they feel too negative to participate or other aspects of their mental state intervene. Kate describes client-based programmes but the therapy appears not to match need or is presented in a way that does not enable people with motivation issues to find a way of participating without stress. She acknowledges that a supportive chat is what is most needed, but it is a pity then that this rather low technology and low expressed emotional approach is not valued to a greater extent. Such befriending interventions are becoming increasingly recognised as important. The development of Support, Time and Recovery (STR) workers would seem to support such a principle.

A further source of Kate's frustrations is in the relationships she has with the wider multi-disciplinary team and in particular her nursing colleagues. Although joint working has improved over her time in the hostel it is clear that there do appear to be professional tensions and demarcations that do little to help the client. Kate has tried hard to engage her nursing colleagues in some of the groups she has run and, despite working with the charge nurse to ensure that a nurse is allocated to working with her, these arrangements frequently fail to materialise as other priorities intervene. I can resonate with Kate's frustration with this. Kate feels that the reluctance of staff to be involved may stem from low self-esteem. This may be so, but it might also be due to nursing staff not wanting to be involved in such activities as they can't see the point (perhaps like the clients themselves).They may also judge that clients have different needs or they may have very narrow perspectives on what their job entails and see themselves as agents to control safety rather than provide therapy, or maybe a little of all these possible reasons. It is encouraging to note that Kate perceives that nurses are now obtaining a greater sense of being therapists through psycho-social interventions and that as a result the nurses won't be leaving 'therapy' to other professionals.

The encouragement for nurses to take on wider therapy roles is supported by the recent Chief Nursing Officer's Review of Mental Health Nursing (Department of Health 2006). The review also identifies the adoption of a framework of values based on the recovery model as one of its main recommendations. With this important document in mind I would like to conclude and reflect upon the fact that like nursing, occupational therapy will need to move from the value base of professional paternalism described by Kate as an OT in order to take on approaches which are far more emancipatory in outlook if recovery is to be achieved.

David Kennard (Clinical Psychologist)

In her account of her work as an OT in a rehabilitation service Kate Hughes lists a number of frustrations that will be familiar to anyone who has worked in such settings. There are frustrations that have to do with the lack of motivation, confidence, or realistic appraisal of their own limitations that can often occur in people who have had a long-term schizophrenic psychosis and have been in hospital for a long time. These frustrations may be experienced differently by the client or service user and by the enthusiastic but single-handed OT who sees a carefully worked out programme of activities halted because the client is not up to it. Of course this doesn't only happen to OTs, but is perhaps most keenly felt by staff whose *raison d'être* on the ward is a specific programme or therapeutic activity (clinical psychology and art therapy also come to mind). For the client the predominating feeling may be one of terror at being exposed to what are experienced as intolerable threats to his/her safety, or there may be a kind of 'magical' thinking that all this activity is beside the point because you can make things happen by thinking them. For the staff member who has devised a range of rehabilitative activities on and off the ward (or hostel-ward in this case) the difficulty is having the flexibility in being able to move from Plan A to Plan B and even Plan C according to the fluctuating capacities, motivation and tolerances of the clients. As Kate herself says, sometimes a supportive chat (Plan B) is what is most needed. What hinders this flexibility may be partly the frustration of seeing a carefully prepared activity abandoned, partly a feeling of having to justify your presence to the rest of the team (having a hard-fought-for position might be a bit of an albatross at times) and partly the external pressure to achieve agreed goal plans.

We can see from Kate's account both the pros and cons of not being the kind of person who gives up easily! The same attribute can help you win through the initial reluctance of colleagues to change their practice or attitudes, but can also make it hard to adapt to the moment-by-moment fluctuations in clients' mental states.

The two other main sources of frustration highlighted in this account are to do with colleagues and with the wider system that eventually provides the service user with a place in the community.

The wish, indeed the urge, to help someone who is struggling by doing it for them is probably one of the strongest impulses that bring people into the caring professions – perhaps nursing in particular. To be told that this is the wrong thing to do can initially seem an affront on both a professional and personal level. (Elsewhere I have contrasted the impulse to care in a 'protective but controlling way' with the 'therapeutic community impulse' [Kennard 1998].) It is heartening that Kate's efforts paid off and entirely believable that there were hurt feelings all round in the process. It is important in this situation to have a model of care that focuses on the clients' needs rather than on a competition between professions. One useful model in this respect has been developed in the book *A therapeutic community approach to care in the community* (Tucker 2000), where the emphasis is on 'being with' rather than 'doing to', facilitating engagement by 'being alongside' the individual being cared for.

Another very common source of frustration in a staff team is when competing priorities lead to staff being reallocated at the last moment. The same issue is raised elsewhere in this book in Allen's account of being the only clinical psychologist on the ward. A nurse goes off sick or levels of observation are raised, and the nurse in charge makes an instant reallocation by taking someone off a group they had planned to co-lead. The lesson here is 'take it to the staff meeting', let everyone know what is happening. In my experience it can be helpful to audit the situation, showing how many groups have been cancelled or curtailed in, say, a month. Again, this takes it out of the realm of one dissident member of the team complaining and puts it in the realm of meeting clients' needs.

The source of frustration mentioned that is the hardest to deal with is the one Kate returns to at the end of her account – the lack of somewhere to move to for the client who is ready to move on. Kate highlights both the problem of stigma – people objecting to having someone with a history of mental illness as a neighbour – and the reluctance of health care purchasers to fund the necessary support. While there is no getting away from the huge obstacles these represent, the issue this raises for me is the need for rehabilitation services to work closely with the move-on providers from the moment of a client's arrival. In my experience it can take months if not years of meetings and negotiations with community placement services, starting with the identification of a care co-ordinator for the client. Kate is rightly concerned that the Care Programme Approach should be a joint undertaking among staff, but this needs also to include those responsible for finding and funding the necessary support and accommodation once the client is ready to leave. In effect, the concept of the 'team' needs to include ward staff, health care purchasers and community-based workers. This in turn requires skilled and committed leadership within the rehabilitation service that links the efforts of the hostel-ward staff and the wider system requirements, using the CPA from the outset to structure this process. Otherwise the risk is just as Kate portrays it, with the feeling of a 'them and us' transferring from an internal split between clients and staff or OTs and nurses to a sense of 'us' being the hard-working staff and clients, and the 'them' (in the community) being carica-tured as unhelpful, prejudiced and mean. When we work with and alongside the 'them' in joint meetings, the situation can change towards a shared appreciation of the goals, obstacles and possibilities and joint planning that includes the client.

Questions for your service

1   How do we deal with the frustration involved in working with patients who show poor motivation or who progress at a very slow pace?
2   If patients have to wait a long time for community placements, can some-thing be done whilst they remain in hospital which can be to their benefit?
3   How can nurses and occupational therapists resolve conflicts of responsibilities over the unit's daily programme of activities?
4   How can conflicting priorities be resolved in order that pre-arranged activities are disturbed to a minimum?

Exercise

Role play: an occupational therapist and experienced nurse are planning a group to help patients overcome their concerns over stigma in the com-munity, but they are disagreeing about the emphasis of the group. The OT wishes to discuss practical ways in which patients can overcome stigma, whilst the nurse wishes to explore the emotions patients have when they feel ostracised by their communities. How do they resolve this?

Chapter 22

Taking it personally

Jenny McAleese (Independent Hospital CEO)

I'm a chartered accountant by profession with a general and fairly superficial knowledge of psychiatry. My role as Chief Executive of a psychiatric hospital means that I do not routinely have access to patients' records and I therefore only know what the individual chooses to tell me. As a result I think that I have the advantage of seeing the person rather than the illness, which is a good thing and something to which all psychiatric services aspire.

However, my non-clinical background can also work against me. It means that I have had limited contact with other in-patient psychiatric services and so my benchmark for the quality of life we offer our patients is normal, everyday life, rather than that offered by other psychiatric hospitals. Using this as a comparison, our hospital, which is said to be better than many, falls a long way short in my view and that often leaves me feeling guilty and inadequate.

I am fascinated by this whole issue of what we call the people who use our services: I know that it is a matter of personal preference but *client*, *service user* and even *resident* all imply a large degree of choice. I don't believe many people choose to be in hospital so let's be honest and call them patients, which I shall for the remainder of this article. Interestingly enough, I once spent time with a very angry individual who found it deeply patronising to be called a client and wanted to be recognised as a patient.

The acid test for me is that if I wouldn't sleep on it, sit on it, eat it, wipe my bottom on it or have it in my home, why should any of our patients? Despite our best intentions, we would be misleading ourselves if we thought that the hospital environment was anywhere near the standard of the homes of those of us who live beyond the hospital walls. Most uncomfortable of all is the way we find ourselves somehow justifying this on the basis that it would be a waste to improve the environment significantly as it would only get ruined by the patients.

But it's not just the physical environment that is lacking. Whilst I am very proud of the increase in social programmes that have taken place over the past few years, there is still a deficiency in one-to-one activities and there is very little going on at the weekend. I feel particularly guilty when I drive off on a Friday afternoon, full of my plans for the weekend, knowing that it will in all likelihood be very quiet and unstimulating for the majority of our patients.

As in many psychiatric hospitals, most of our patients smoke. Many might choose to smoke anyway, but I cannot help but think that the reason they smoke so much is the lack of any meaningful alternative activity or other sources of pleasure. My dream would be that we could make available enough choices of alternative activity that smoking would decrease. I do also worry about the physical harm that they are doing to themselves and the risk of passive smoking to other patients and staff.

I am conscious that many of our patients have been at the hospital for a long time so it is their home and I am respectful of that. This and a desire to compensate for our failings means that I operate an open door policy for patients as well as for staff, and I am surprised and encouraged by the number of patients who do come in to see me. Just as my relationship with them is uncluttered by any therapeutic relationship, theirs with me is free of line management complications and they are the only people in the organisation who actually see me as a person rather than a role. I find that a refreshingly straightforward and even comforting reality check sometimes. Some patients just come for a chat and others come to complain, usually about the problems of living in a community with a number of others, not all of whom they get on with. I listen, offer help and advice where I can and make a point of always having a word with someone if I am asked to do so by them. The other day a patient asked me to explain to her our Statement of Purpose and Values as she didn't understand it: doing so made me realise that, whilst the sentiments it expresses are solid, the document needs completely re-writing so that everyone understands it, not just the staff who wrote it.

A few years ago I became very friendly with Abigail, a woman who had spent much of her life in various psychiatric hospitals. She would come and see me most days, often for a coffee and a chat but sometimes just to sit in my room whilst I worked, something I found most reassuring and comforting. One day she asked me if I wanted to know what she really wanted. When I said yes, she told me that she wanted a nice man to come and take her away from this dump of a hospital and look after her. This really brought home to me that, however hard I tried with the small things, I could never make the big things all right. When she died I felt real grief and missed her dreadfully, but really hoped that heaven turned out to be how she and I had imagined it when we talked together. It was only after she died that I learned from her family what had happened to cause the onset of her illness: I was glad I hadn't known it all before but very touched to realise that she had chosen to confide in me quite a lot about it anyway.

I must admit that I am wary of getting that close again but I believe you sometimes just meet people and find there's a special bond between the two of you. I always try and find time just to be with patients and to listen to them and their stories, and feel bad if they come along and it's just not possible because of work pressures. Then I make a point of trying to go and seek them out later.

Whilst I feel that there are many good things happening in psychiatry, particularly around 'service user involvement' and initiatives to keep people out of hospital and in their own home, I think that the service is deluding itself in terms of the accepted quality of in-patient care. In my view hospitals are by and large run for the benefit of the staff rather than the patients. Maybe it's because I'm not a clinician and I do not appreciate the complexities, but I still do not understand why nursing shift systems seem to operate in such an apparently inflexible way. I am concerned about the shortage of psychiatric nurses generally and the rapid expansion of the agency nursing business sector, all of which is adversely affecting the quality of care throughout psychiatric services. Until we can guarantee continuity of staff and eliminate the excessive use of bank and agency staff who are inevitably strangers to the patients and the environment, I don't believe we are even on the starting blocks.

I've tried really hard over the past few years to reduce our use of bank staff to an absolute minimum, with no success at all: bank shifts are higher than ever and I am now facing a request from senior colleagues to create a Bank Co-ordinator post. I think that will just make the situation worse. The lack of success makes me feel frustrated and demoralised. I am encouraged to continue with my quest by our recent Staff Stress Survey that showed that working with bank staff was a major source of stress. And that's before we take the patients' views into account!

When I first arrived here I was struck by the lack of respect staff showed for one another. I've tried hard to change that, mostly by setting an example myself and things do seem to be a bit better. However, there is still very much a sense of 'clinicians are good, managers are bad' and I find some of the very personal comments addressed to 'senior management' by staff extremely hurtful. It feels unfair that staff feel they can say what they like about managers but if managers challenge staff at all (let alone in relation to performance) then they are accused of being unreasonable.

A couple of years ago it all became too much for me, I became very depressed and was off work for a few months. Part of the problem was that I had taken it all much too personally and that, coupled with working too hard and trying to do it all myself, eventually took its toll. I am certainly wiser since that experience and now look after myself much better, working from home on a regular basis and also having six-weekly coaching sessions. I also try not to take it all too personally but have to admit that I still sometimes struggle with that.

Maybe we'll never be able to get it right because the challenges are just so large and apparently costly. For me the main issues are around choice and freedom. If I choose to stay in a hotel for a holiday I am likely to enjoy it so long as the accommodation and food are good. That is very different from how I feel if I have to spend a week staying in a hotel because I am working away from home. It can be the most luxurious hotel in the world but I still won't be able to wait until the end of the week when I can go home, eat what I want, where I want, when I want and with whom I want. We'd do well to remember how it must feel to constantly be somewhere you don't want to be and often with people you would rather not be with.

As for me, I'll continue to do my best and no doubt to feel inadequate. I guess that the day I stop feeling that will be the day to move on and do something else.

Commentaries

Judy Wilson (CEO)

This is a refreshingly honest perspective from a Chief Executive and certainly provides significant food for thought. I have always tried to keep in mind the fact that our services should be ones where I or my family would be happy to receive help but it is often easy for this to slip as a priority in the context of the NHS policy agenda. It was interesting to see that some of the same frustrations about the inability to change things are also evident in the private sector.

Although the drive for healthcare provision in the NHS to become more business-like is overwhelming, we need to be mindful in particular of the fact that people are at their most vulnerable when they need mental health services. It was interesting to read the intense personal awareness of the author of the plight of people in her care. However, I think it is a difficult balance to strike between care and concern and a level of involvement which may hinder the manager/CE in implementing the kind of changes that need to be made to transform care.

As a chief executive I realise that changes need to be made on a corporate scale and in relation to the culture of the organisation as a whole. Keeping a particular patient in mind can be helpful in acting as a reality check and I can vividly remember that I used to apply the 'Jimmy test' to the plans for implementing the National Health Service Framework for Mental Health when I worked in the north-east of England. Jimmy was a real character who was often to be seen in all weathers walking around the hospital grounds and passed my office window several times a day. He was keen to talk to staff, fellow patients and dog walkers alike. A number of eloquently worded plans bit the dust when they failed the 'Jimmy test'!

I was somewhat dismayed by the author's apparent frustration at her inability to change things, although I have found that being a chief executive has enabled me to make changes that I could not have made as a middle manager or even as an operational director. My background is in mental health nursing and for all my frustrations about how much there is still to do, I am only too well aware of the significant strides that have been made over the last thirty years. Perhaps this makes it easier for me to understand and influence what is happening clinically as I am familiar with the language used by clinical staff and can engage in some of the more detailed debates. However, I am also aware that it can potentially become a drawback as there is no doubt that I probably tolerate things that the author would rightly question, because inevitably I suppose I have become somewhat institutionalised.

Within the NHS, Chief Executives are ultimately judged on their ability to deliver against national targets and rather less on whether or not they relate well to their service users and their carers. However, the Chief Executive is key to setting the tone of the organisation and the way in which it conducts its business. I believe it is possible to strike a balance between getting the job done and delivering on the performance targets and ensuring that this is done in a way which is as sensitive and caring as possible. It is a tough job and we get paid a lot of money, by most people's standards, to make difficult choices and decisions. We have to balance risks, public expectation and the political agenda – and these may well be in conflict! You get a sense from this piece about how lonely it can be as a Chief Executive and I very much appreciate the extensive support network I have available to me. I find it helpful to have friends and peers for less formal support but it is invaluable also to have access to a mentor and possible executive coaching. If the only challenges come from those to whom you are answerable or yourself, then objectivity and constructive action may prove to be more elusive. I actively encourage senior staff to identify a mentor and ensure that they have appropriate personal development plans. There have been occasions when I have been quite ruthless in protecting my time with my coach.

I have been described at times as a 'terminal optimist', and it is fair to say that I have a 'cup that is half full'! It is important when someone has been so open and passionate in their writing that I don't jump to conclusions from relatively little information, but I did pick up a sense of frustration at the author's inability to progress much-needed changes. I have difficulty empathising with this apparent frustration as I always assume that change can and will be made. I endeavour to generate a 'can do' culture in those around me and while it is vital to listen to the different views and opinions in framing the course of action, once it has been agreed, we need to get on with it! Every organisation will have people who want to see change and are bursting with ideas; the trick is to harness that energy and then support them so that they can deliver. The Chief Executive on his or her own will not make those changes happen, but can make sure that doors are unlocked and bureaucracy and red tape minimised so that people can get on with the job in hand.

There are now many senior people in health care, myself included, who are increasingly comfortable with admitting that they have experienced mental health problems. The author addresses this in a heartfelt and quite poignant way. I would endorse the need to ensure that there is support available and that there is some flexibility over working arrangements – without such support and flexibility, there are times when I would struggle with the demands of the job. I did not rush to become a Chief Executive and was all too well aware of the stresses and strains involved. However, I have no regrets to date and can honestly say I love the job and believe that I can make a difference for our staff, the people who use our services and their carers.

The NHS always seems to be under pressure to perform better and deliver an increasingly political agenda. I believe that we have raised the expectations of the public such that they tend to run ahead of the pace at which the NHS can deliver service change and improvement. Much of what is proposed makes sense at a simple system level – for example, if there is more community infrastructure in place there will be shorter lengths of stay and demand for beds will decrease. However, the reality is that we end up doing everything at once, often because the financial envelope is such that it is not possible to fund the double running costs that would allow us to develop and embed the new service model before reducing the bed base.

Because system reform is so rapid, often with largely quantitative targets, we sometimes struggle to take the hearts and minds of our staff and services users with us! There is an incentive to get the 'tick in the box' for the performance target in relation to the Trust's overall performance. This can mean that corners inevitably will be cut as the viability of the organisation and the continuing careers of the executive team may well depend on it. I support the direction of travel but would value more time to implement and then consolidate change.

The most obvious example of the impact of the scale and pace of change is in relation to bed reductions. It is actually quite easy to physically close beds but if the rest of the system is not geared up to cope, then we end up with patients being treated in services away from their local area. This is obviously a significant challenge and we need to find a better way of managing this across the service as a whole. We need to think more creatively about the way we use our smaller bed base – should we still be admitting all acute episodes to the same unit/ward regardless of diagnosis or need? If we want to change the models of care we need to find more effective ways of engaging with and supporting clinical colleagues in relation to the management of risk in particular. At a time when public safety is high on the agenda, clinicians are often having to take very difficult decisions within a system in which they may well feel that some of their options have been reduced or even closed off.

Mental health care delivery is increasingly dependent on the various elements of the system working effectively. There are still key gaps around move-on facilities and supported accommodation which cause pressures in the service as well as discharge delays. The system is a very different one from the one I entered almost thirty years ago as a student nurse. At that time the numbers of community psychiatric nurses across the country could be counted on the fingers of one hand! We have made huge strides in many areas but there is much still to do and we need to try to harness the energies of our staff to help us deliver safe, effective services, while continuing to fight to maintain a focus on mental health at a national level with the resources we need. Our part of the bargain as mental health service providers is to give the assurance that we are using our existing resources in the most effective way.

Paul Scally (Nursing Assistant)

As someone who actually works with clients I was very glad to hear that the Chief Executive has an open door policy for clients, but was dismayed by her comment regarding staff who voice their opinions to managers, although I agree that in no circumstances should staff make derogatory or disrespectful comments about each other. We should at all times remain professional.

We all have a duty to deliver the best care possible to our clients and at times this does not happen. Very often senior managers are more concerned with budgets and client care gets pushed to the rear. We are all aware that there is not a bottomless pit of money in the Trust, but I get angry when money is spent on technology and not on patient care.

Far too often clients are not being given choices as to what they want but are told 'there are not funds to do this and that' – mainly when it comes to funding for living in the community. At times decisions are made about care without managers talking to staff and this causes friction. Maybe a way round this would be for senior managers to meet with elected staff from the units (and I don't mean union representatives) twice monthly to discuss what they envisage for the future and how this can be achieved.

I found the comment that 'by and large hospitals are run for the benefit of the staff rather than the patients' particularly offensive. I am annoyed when we are frequently told the wards are short of money, we can't get enough staff, you will just have to cope. Whilst I appreciate that they work hard, most senior managers have gone home by five o'clock, and don't work weekends, bank holidays or nights. They do not realise the pressure this puts on staff and clients. They forget that the majority of ward staff have to work unsociable shifts, for example working a 'late' from 13.15 to 21.15 and then having to be back on duty at 7.15 the next morning. By the time you have got home it's time for bed. You don't have much time for your family, especially at weekends. I know that 24-hour care needs to be provided, but we also need to care for staff and maybe look at revamping the present shift system.

Many senior managers never have any contact with clients and do not see what is best for the client; we have a better understanding of their needs. Maybe if some of them had the same approach as the Chief Executive their priorities might change. Her approach should be sent to all staff: 'we are here to listen'. I think senior managers should meet staff and should also meet clients on a regular basis to hear what they have to say first-hand and not get a sanitised version from someone else.

We must at all times remember that 'the client's needs come first'. If the old saying 'treat others as you would like to be treated' was put on every Trust publication, it might make more people think about what we are here for – the client.

I believe most people working in the Trust do want what is best for the clients but have different ways of achieving this. We need to pull together otherwise everyone suffers, clients and staff. I hope this will be of help.

Questions for your service

1 How can you keep your CEO informed of day-to-day issues on your unit?
2 If standards fall or are in danger of falling, how can management be appraised of the situation and act swiftly to remedy the problem(s)?
3 How does the CEO communicate his/her standards of care to ward staff?
4 If desired change cannot happen immediately as a result of financial, bureaucratic or other obstacles, how can staff and the CEO work together to make the best of it?

Exercise

Role play: the CEO is concerned after hearing about a serious untoward incident in which a patient attacked a member of staff. In a letter to the manager of the ward, the CEO points out that this is the third time this has happened over the past three months, and wants to know if the attitude of staff has anything to do with these attacks. The staff feel under pressure and unsupported by these remarks. Explore in discussion the feelings expressed and held by all parties.

Chapter 23

Finding meaning

Mike Pritchard (Hospital Chaplain)

In an address which I gave during a Service of Thanksgiving at the closure of a large Victorian psychiatric hospital some years ago, I suggested that there was much that should be left behind as we closed the doors on the institution; much that represented the failings and shortcomings of those old asylums. One of the issues very much in my mind as I prepared for that event was a piece of work that a consultant psychiatrist, a manager and I were doing with some patients to help the staff who would be moving out to work in smaller units in the community to better understand how patients felt about the quality of their care.

This small group of very bright and articulate patients didn't feel that they had the confidence to participate face to face in the staff training programmes, but they were willing to make a video for the purpose. That video was to prove so uncomfortable to the few staff who watched it that the facilitator, wrongly in my view, decided to withdraw it, rather than use it with subsequent groups of staff. The service users, in the video, had very simply portrayed a couple of staff sitting at a table idly glancing through magazines; when they were approached in turn by patients who were distressed and in need of no more than a little support and some TLC, they were sent away and told not to be a nuisance.

Later in that Service of Thanksgiving, items which had been seen as significant symbols of that era of care were brought forward. One of those items was a bunch of keys which, for many of the patients who had devised the service with me, represented the perceived indignities of power and control which the system exercised over them. In the current mental health in-patient environment there is a new symbol of authority which is despised by many of the patients – it is the clipboard – signed at the required intervals to state that the patient has been 'observed', but not necessarily spoken to by the member of the 'caring' team assigned to the task. Sometimes, even when patients are on continuous observation, they are barely spoken to, and tell me of staff talking to each other or on mobile phones, often in a language which the patient doesn't understand!

Perhaps the raising of 'spiritual awareness' among mental health professionals would assist the process of making patients feel of some worth, if, by spiritual awareness, we understand this to be primarily about the person's inner self –

- What helps them to keep their spirits up?
- What makes life feel worthwhile for them?
- What is it that gives life some meaning and purpose?
- What do they live for?
- What are their hopes and their dreams?

The above are all questions which in-patients discuss with me, and more often with each other, sometimes at a very profound level, and they are the very essence of spirituality. Patients do have a huge measure of understanding and compassion and frequently, albeit inadvertently, demonstrate enormous spiritual awareness.

At that same Service of Thanksgiving a large candle was lit to represent all that had been good within the institution, all that had embodied that depth of spirituality, and at the end of the service very many smaller candles were lit from it and taken to the community units.

If I had just one pound for every time over my twenty years of working in mental health that in-patients have told me that few of the staff really talk to them, I would be a very wealthy man indeed, and the gratitude expressed to me for time spent simply listening to their stories has been wholly disproportionate to any effort or skill on my part. So a question I've asked myself time and again is: 'Why might it be that so many members of staff, who to me seem to be able and caring, manage to make patients who already, because of the circumstances associated with their illness, feel of little or no value, feel even worse?'

Could it be that simply coming alongside the patient with no motive other than to make her or him feel that she or he matters does not fit into any medical or therapeutic model? Could it be that some of the staff are just not adequately equipped to deal with emotional pain?

It is frequently stated by patients that the staff team seems to come into its own when there appears to be a threat of some physical disturbance, but that there is less inclination to make any attempt to deal with emotional disturbance.

As a chaplain, for me, even more worrying in some respects than not talking to the patients are those members of staff from across the multi-disciplinary team who openly parade a religious conviction but fail to translate this into any form of spirituality which values people! Worse even than this are those who embark upon a process of proselytism. There should be no place, to my mind, within a mental health setting for those who believe that their religious belief system and theirs alone contains absolute truth to the exclusion of all others. It never ceases to amaze me that mental health 'professionals', people who have undergone a rigorous training programme, can emerge at the other end believing that it is OK to make judgements about the patient based upon their own religious convictions. It is, of course, possible to truly but naively (in my view) believe that whatever the issue the answer is Jesus, but the problem with such a belief is that it leaves the believers in a position where they have no alternative but to impart this fact to others. I have seen this do untold damage to service users over the years – it can be quite brutal and harmful in its presentation:

• hearing those who have attempted suicide tell of the way they have been lectured about their evil and selfish behaviour;
• witnessing patients who have no religious belief have the Bible read to them 'for their own good'!
• listening to so many patients who have been told that they need to pray if they are ever to get well;
• being told on numerous occasions that it has been suggested that their illness/behaviour is akin to demon possession.

These incidents have all reinforced my opinion that an essential role of a healthcare chaplain is to protect patients from any form of religious excess, and it is extremely worrying that it is becoming more, rather than less necessary to exercise that role today!

The other side of this coin, and of equal importance, is the fact that for some patients, of course, their spirituality does find its expression in a specific belief system, and for many of these, it is their faith which helps them to get through their illness. However, they frequently tell me that they are not able to talk to their psychiatrist about aspects of their faith for fear that this will be seen as part of their illness. The biological and medical model doesn't always allow the professional to work with the patient's 'reality', so that patients fear that if they are open about their deeply held religious convictions these are likely to be pathologised. If issues of meaning, purpose, hope and value don't sit easily within the realms of science, risk management or community safety, what possible chance is there for prayer, the sacraments or meditation?

Chaplaincy in a mental health setting has long entailed exploring the spiritual reality that underpins the dogma of the belief system in which one has grown up and to which one is committed, and this spirituality is, for me, at its very simplest, *the well-being of all others; believing and imparting to them that they matter*. Love, understanding, forgiveness and compassion are the watchwords of such spirituality. So many of the people with whom we work feel of little or no value; their illness or their life circumstance, or frequently both, have led them to believe that they are utterly worthless, leading to despair, anger and hopelessness.

One of the things that we can do, even when all else seems to be failing (and perhaps within psychiatry there will be an element of failure which as a discipline it will not share with other branches of medicine), is to let people know that they matter to us. This will inevitably be time-consuming, and will mean perhaps that many of the other tasks which mental health professionals are required to undertake from increased amounts of paperwork to finding beds will have to be reviewed. It is, however, holistic care at its best, it moves us away from a cure and control culture to one which is genuinely concerned with restoring wholeness and could lead to a re-lighting of the candle in our current in-patient units.

Commentaries

Cris Allen (Nurse)

It is interesting that Mike begins his piece with a reflection on the closure of a large Victorian psychiatric hospital, explaining that a service of 'thanksgiving' was held to mark the leaving behind of the failings and shortcomings of the mental health care system that many of us were involved with.

I often feel sad, however, that in our haste to escape such places for the promised land of the community we may not have found time to celebrate some of the better things that the old institutions provided. And there were some, honest.

In my work I visit the sites of three former asylums – where some modern facilities, including in-patient units, have sprung up – which still provide office accommodation for Trust staff, among the decaying buildings, overgrown sports fields and crumbling chapels. I am not sure why, but the dormant chapels have a particular resonance, like the often beautiful, but now redundant churches that pepper rural areas of the UK. Symbolic of societal change or a transfer of religious, or spiritual, affiliation towards other faiths or interests – or perhaps towards the out-of-town temples erected for the new god, shopping.

Maybe it's because I grew up in vicarages. My father is an Anglican priest, and whilst I was never especially 'religious' I liked churches, the comings and goings of parish life and the 'spirituality' that was somehow intrinsic to people and things around me.

As a nurse I liked the chapels of the old bins. On the asylum sites I visit, two of the chapels now only have pigeons as their congregations whilst the third is being refurbished to provide a day nursery for the offspring of the well-heeled residents of the expensive apartments, shaped from the gentrified wards of the former hospital.

My rose-tinted spectacles cause a recollection of the chapel as a significant place for some patients and staff. Many found some religious, or spiritual, succour in them, through music, prayer, words, and the essence of community that the coming together of patients, staff, chaplains and others fostered for them. Some found the chapel, at quiet times, a place for peaceful reflection, a shifty shag with a fellow patient or a refuge to which one could bunk off from institutionalised 'therapeutic' activities.

But of course Mike prods consciences and, rightly, reminds us of the poor practices of some asylum staff – those infected by all that was bad about bin life who absorbed the habits of the sloppy, the cruel, the bullying, the uncaring and the burnt out. He also observes accurately the symbols of power and authority and the meanings that were attached to the ward keys – the emblems of the 'nurse in charge'.

Mike suggests that the clipboard has now replaced these emblems, as part of what he implies is a mechanistic process of 'observing' patients. He could have listed other accoutrements – bleeps, alarms and those lanyards, with keys attached that can be seen swinging from staff member's hips, in some settings.

Clipboard observation conducted by numbskulls lacking in communication skills and emotional intelligence does prevail among some staff, in some settings, but not all nurses practise in this way. Many have forsaken the *Sun*-reading, ignore-the-patient school of observation and have embraced the notion of therapeutic engagement and use their time – and their 'self' – with the patient constructively, empathically and compassionately. We all need to do more, however, to ensure bad practice is eradicated from contemporary care arenas.

What interests me is Mike's thesis that raising 'spiritual awareness' among mental health professionals would assist the process of making patients feel of some worth. In this context he proposes a taxonomy that might help us to better understand the person's inner self – what helps keep their spirits up, what makes life feel worthwhile, and so on. A taxonomy that few would disagree with.

However, I believe that this, if embraced by policy-makers, practitioners and patients, would address some of the other issues that he goes on to raise. For example, staff not talking to patients, not spending time with them and not listening to them: coming alongside the patient may not fit with any, contemporary, medical or therapeutic model. Furthermore, it would help us all recognise that many people in the mental health system feel of little value, believe they are utterly worthless and as a result experience anger, despair and hopelessness. And that, as the old joke goes, is just the staff! He goes on to suggest that a shift towards care that lets people know that they matter to us will require a reduction in the bureaucratic and bed-finding burden on staff. Nurses' hats will be flung heavenwards if that comes to pass!

All these things are perhaps the nub of the problem and the source of some of the solutions. Nursing staff and others could be imbued with some sense of hope, value and worth, within a culture that takes a reasoned view of risk and values, in fact the basics of skilled care, in the true sense of the word. If this was practised rather than the buzz definition of *care* apparently put about by some patients: **C**over **A**rse **R**etain **E**mployment, with an emphasis on therapeutic engagement and relationship-building, then this would have an effect on their ability to work better with, and understand the spiritual aspects of those in their care. This will happen if coupled with better support, supervision, leadership, time for the job, development opportunities, improved physical environments and some respite from the plethora of reports that continually slam in-patient mental health staff, whatever they do, or don't do. Staff who are spiritually impoverished are in no position, arguably, to spiritually nourish impoverished patients – and, God knows, it is high time this equation was acknowledged.

It is good to see that Mike explicitly uncouples spirituality from religion, and many people need to recognise this distinction. Inquiring into a patient's 'spirituality' on assessment means much more than scribbling 'C of E' or 'Muslim' on a pro-forma. Of course he is right too that leaking one's own religious convictions all over the place is unhelpful, inappropriate and highly unbecoming in any professional. And using such convictions in the ways that he illustrates is a wake-up call to those, very few, staff who mistakenly think that such approaches are acceptable or helpful. As is any assumption that religious conviction in a patient is synonymous with symptoms or pathology. One of my father's many strengths was that he never rammed religion down my throat or those members of his actual, or potential, flock. Less is more.

I don't think Mike and I would disagree that strengthening the spirituality of both patients and staff, and meeting their needs for spiritual sustenance, would have a markedly favourable impact, one upon the other. Locally we are on the case with the development of a very promising draft spiritual and religious care strategy.

Salvation for in-patient units, and those who use them and work in them, may, as Mike suggests, lie among rectifying these spiritual issues and lead to a relighting of the candle within them. Ignoring them will leave us little option but to light a torch beneath them.

Thom Rudegair (Clinical Director)

The chaplain's essay is damning, challenging and potentially inspirational to all of us who work on 'in-patient' psychiatric units. The chaplain pulls no punches, opening with an announcement that the 'bright and articulate' service users with whom he worked were too intimidated to engage in a 'face to face' training workshop for staff members. This indictment made me cringe. Then the service users portrayed the staff as both inattentive and dismissive.

Again I cringe and, worse, I have no rebuttal. The perspective of these service users is all-too-common and the attentiveness of even the most dedicated staff members on many in-patient units is intermittent at best. If, as the chaplain suggests, we are focused on 'cure and control' then we will inevitably become bored and distracted once we've quelled all disruption as we wait for the medications to induce wellness. It is our philosophy, not our personal inadequacies that frustrate our best intentions.

The chaplain's proposed solution is wise. Although I am not a religious fellow, I think his concept of 'spiritual awareness' is right on the money. When curiosity about a person's 'inner self' is paramount in any relationship there is no boredom, no chasm between partners in the exploration, and no exploitation. The chaplain captures the essence, I think, when he encourages staff members to explore, 'what gives life some meaning and purpose' for the service users. I have come to understand that the 'art' of psychiatry (when it is there at all) resides in the search for 'meaning' in the acute moment for the distressed person whose life has been interrupted by hospitalisation. From this perspective, a 'symptom' becomes a manifestation, for example, of intimate turmoil, existential disruption, self-doubt, religious crisis, inter-personal betrayal . . . traumatisation of some description. It doesn't mean what *we* say it means. It means what the person experiencing the moment believes it means. I'm afraid we psychiatrists tend to impose meaning on the array of presented 'symptoms', based on our DSM-IV-skewed view of the world. From this perspective the events are indicative of medical syndromes rather than personal struggles. Service users are subjects rather than partners in a discourse and, as such, are 'subjected' to our prejudices and our reduc-tions. The chaplain is right; the process of 'walking alongside' a service user rather than 'observing' from a distance is not amenable to our traditional medicalised view of 'mental illness'.

It is easy to understand the seductiveness of the pharmacological perspec-tive on 'healing illness'. Many psychiatrists long to be respected as legitimate medical practitioners and that means we must examine, diagnose, and treat illness. This approach might be adequate for the management of diabetes (although an argument can be made about that as well) but it falls woefully short when we seek to understand the ailments of the mind. The brain is about neurons and neurotransmitters. The mind is about metaphors and meaning. If it is the practitioner's obligation or, rather, his or her opportunity to invite the service user to explore the meaning of the moment, then it is absurd to attempt to impose our own meanings, and equally absurd to judge a service user's faith-based understanding of his or her own struggle. If we can truly learn to walk alongside, then we will surely start to validate and not dismiss, enrich and not erode the metaphors by which another understands his or her personal journey.

I especially resonated with the chaplain's reference to 'the spiritual reality that underpins the dogma of the belief system in which one has grown up'.

Nobody escapes the imposition of a conceptual framework on life events. 'Dogma' emerges inevitably from the context in which we are raised, whether we assume the role of a priest or a parishioner, a psychiatrist or a service user. Some meanings remain malleable while others become crystallised as they hold sway in our world view for long enough. I think it is our obligation (that is, we who choose to serve those in mental anguish) to suspend our dogmatic formulations and invite others to explore theirs. If there is an acceptable dogmatic belief in psychiatry, it must be one that says 'meaning must be respected'.

It occurs to me that if we can practise by this dictum then service users are unlikely to feel intimidated by us and we are unlikely to become bored and seek distractions from our life's work. How could a companion on a personal journey be intimidating, and how could a magazine article possibly be as compelling as the stories of service users' lives, the meanings of their suffering and their quests for inspiration?

It may be disquieting for traditionally trained psychiatric practitioners to contemplate the formation of true partnerships with service users. Despite our most humane instincts, our training implies that our task is 'management' of a case, not intimate understanding of a fellow traveller. To the degree that a mentally unwell person is objectified, we will tend to experience them as 'other' and humans, being what they are, will encounter fear much sooner if they are confronted with someone who is 'other'. Fear is our mortal enemy, for it generates avoidance or, worse, self-defence. Very dedicated and highly principled people become aggressive in defence of themselves. We cannot embrace what we fear. We cannot be expected to explore a psyche that threatens us. So we must shift the traditionally held assumptions of our field. We must strive to support rather than control, to respect as equal rather than fear as different, and to open up to rather than defend against those in acute mental anguish. If we can do this not only will our service users feel respected, they will feel safe and they too will relinquish the need to defend against us.

If there is no fear and no defence then there will be little need for compulsion, coercion, or restraint.

The chaplain is a wise man.

Questions for your service

1 How does the staff team take into account their patients' faith systems?
2 What do staff do when patients try and convert others to their faith system or interpret everything through their religious beliefs?
3 Does the hospital chaplain have any role to play in helping the staff understand the patients' internal world?

Exercise

Role play: the chaplain informs the staff that a patient has told him in confidence that she can't trust her psychiatrist because he told her, when questioned, that he doesn't believe in God. Have a discussion between the chaplain, consultant and nurse to see how the team can respond to this dilemma.

Summary of the main issues in Section 4

All the staff who have reported in this section seem to be motivated by a genuine desire to help those in their charge. Despite this, much of what has been raised reflects the fact that more often than not, staff working in in-patient settings are beset by discomforting feelings. These feelings to an extent emanate from the distress communicated by their patients, which can sometimes reach intolerable levels. It is not surprising, therefore, that emotionally protective measures begin to be put in place in order to contain these feelings and make work more manageable. We hear of 'staff retreating into the office', ward rounds that are insensitive, rapid turnover of staff, rigid compliance with the 'medical model' of care, overarching concerns about risk assessments, too much paperwork (Menzies 1959).

The inevitable tension that develops when working with mentally unwell patients is partly related to the inherent desire, on the part of patients, to communicate their distress, and that communication carries with it all the feelings of fear, confusion, pain and anguish. The natural reaction from those around them is to build barriers against the intrusion of unwanted feelings. And yet, it is only when we are prepared to become 'fellow travellers' that we have a chance of establishing the bridges that are required to start genuinely therapeutic encounters. But in order to do this, mental health staff need adequate supporting structures, places and people where it is safe to think through and share the weight of projections, transferences and anxieties that they are asked to carry.

One of the themes that emerge is the difficulty experienced by those newly arriving on the scene. How does one successfully induct someone into such settings? Inevitably, many join the unit with a myriad of preconceptions, often based on popular myths and fictional accounts of what it is like to be in a 'loony bin'. Some staff come with their personal histories, perhaps attempting to heal internal wounds by their work with fractured souls. Others have already made up their minds to battle against 'the psychiatric system' from within. These internal 'agendas' have a strong influence on how the unit is viewed and on the initial felt experience. They also can contribute with their first impressions, offering a fresh and invaluable insight which sometimes can challenge institutionalised practices. Unfortunately, there is very little time and space given to new arrivals to share and discuss this. Some staff are fortunate, and align themselves to supportive mentors who guide them through the initial stages, or have adequate supervisory arrangements, but the truth of the matter is that most staff are left to manage with their own internal resources. In the same way that first admitted patients require guidance, information, and personal support at this stage, so do staff.

All units have rules. Yet it takes a considerable time for people who are admitted and staff who work in in-patient settings to discover exactly what they are. In fact, sometimes experienced staff do not realise a specific rule exists, until a question is raised by an observant newcomer which forces an answer so that it could be made explicit. Again, some of the rules might be so arcane that they require revision because they no longer suit the function or philosophy of the ward. Even if they make senior staff uncomfortable, there is much to be said for an atmosphere that invites such questions. Should patients stay in their rooms after breakfast? Can they stay in bed all day? When do I need a chaperone? What do I do when I am closely observing a patient? Can I relay to other staff something that the patient has told me in absolute confidence? How much of myself can I share with patients? It is impossible to cover all of the issues comprehensively, but some innovative units have started to collect these questions, and publish them to help future new staff.

A number of times contributors have criticised the 'medical model'. If by this they imply the hierarchical traditional nature of working in hospitals, with the medical consultant at the top of the pile, and nursing assistants and students at the bottom, one can understand how much will be invested in the power and discernment of the consultant, and how little in those staff who probably are in more direct contact with patients, and whose contribution to care will therefore feel relatively undermined. But there is more than that. The so-called 'medical model' also imposes a philosophy, one whereby a problem is assessed, categorised and treated, backed up by evidence using scientific methodologies, and these days, also liable to cost-effective analysis. Whilst this may bring security to staff and managers, and to a certain degree some patients, and whilst it does also allow a psycho-social perspective to be added to the identification of biological processes, the reality is that it has received a great deal of bad press because of its potential to objectify the patient. Without throwing the baby out with the bathwater, can a medical model become one where collaboration is established with the patient and their immediate carers and informed by multidisciplinary practice, and where communication and frank discussion can take place in a dialogical fashion? We see no contradiction in using medical terms and nosologies if this were to be the case, and according to surveys may well be what many patients desire from their admission to a mental health service.

We have also read about how multidisciplinary conflict can get in the way of establishing a consistent therapeutic environment in in-patient settings. Sometimes these conflicts are floating beneath the surface, and only emerge when particular patient issues bring them out to the fore. More often than not, clients are the ones to highlight them, and this may sometimes feed into their own psychopathology, and create even more splits between team members. We have heard that sometimes there exist traditional 'lines of demarcation' between professional groups, such as nurses and occupational therapists, or psychiatrists and psychologists, but that when actual practice is discussed openly, bearing in mind that there are common objectives that are shared between staff and between staff and patients, these differences appear much less important and in fact can be mutually inclusive.

This suggestion of a collaborative approach can be taken into formal ward reviews and care planning meetings. It is not necessarily 'what you do, but how you do it', as long as we bear in mind the issues we have identified above. For example, much has been said about the consultant psychiatrist taking on the final responsibility for decisions undertaken by the team, and this therefore underpins its power structures. With the suggestion of 'New Ways of Working' for consultants and teams, this power structure may be in the process of radical change (Department of Health 2005b). In this approach the consultant is not expected to take sole responsibility for care, and much of the decision making is devolved to other members of the team. There is no reason why, for example, a ward review could not be chaired and led by the senior nurse, and in fact, there is much to support that idea, considering the fact that nurses are generally the ones who carry out decisions made by the team. There is also no reason why a joint senior team, comprising senior nurse, consultant psychiatrist and senior occupational therapist or clinical psychologist, cannot together set the philosophical tone for the ward and take corporate responsibility and professional accountability for the service they offer. This of course has to be supported by senior management and Trust Board members, but a lot of good can potentially emanate from such arrangements. Within this setting, for example, the ward review or the care planning meeting can become an opportunity for clarification of responsibilities, discussion over prognosis, guidance on practical matters, dealing with criticisms and complaints, and this certainly does not have to be one-way traffic. Teams can and should also feel confident about being clear about what they do not feel they can or should do, and what should be returned to the patient and the family.

We have heard poignant and very helpful comments from staff who do not see themselves as fully involved in the daily life on the ward, and see themselves playing more marginal roles, introducing, for example, psychological, social, creative, practical and spiritual thinking to the holistic interpretation of events. The distinct contribution from these clinical and non-clinical staff (psychologists, social workers, art therapists, hotel assistants and chaplains) is rooted in the fact that not only do they bring an alternative dimension to bear, but they are also relatively unencumbered by the everyday pressures of those staff who have to keep their 'noses to the grindstone'. They also speak to patients from completely different perspectives, perhaps feeling freer to engage more directly as people, rather than from a patient/professional carer perspective. Rather than marginal, their contributions should form part of the everyday thinking on the ward, and that is no mean challenge. Whilst it is easy to see how often intertribal skirmishes develop between different professional groups, particularly in their entitlements to comment and have a say in the running of the ward, we can only see advantages to the inclusion of these voices, and perhaps one should discuss and seek more opportunities to join in discussions when specific problems or patients are being shared. With hindsight, we would have benefited from further contributions in this section, such as that from a psychotherapist who has experience of working with in-patient staff in support groups (Hinshelwood 2004). If these are operating successfully and feel safe, they can bring an invaluable source of help to staff, giving them an opportunity to share difficult feelings and thus prevent destructive acting-out behaviour or early disaffection and burnout. We also regret that we were not able to obtain the views of social workers assigned to help in-patients during their stay in hospital or more arts therapists broadening the range of expression for those requiring acute care, and consider this to be a partial failure on our part.

We have also heard how management can become once-removed from the life of the in-patient ward, and how much staff often feel un-held or unsupported by their seniors. If anything, one can understand why we see defensive practices in operation, because many on the coal-face have experienced criticism and possible job-threats from management when difficulties or crises have arisen. The only way this will change is if management becomes much more physically visible on the ward, and feels much more a part of what is going on. After all it is its staff who have been delegated to take on the objectives of the organisation for patients who require hospital care. And it is up to staff on the ward to ensure that management is kept on the loop, especially anticipating problems, and asking management to help work out possible realistic strategies and solutions, assessing benefits and risks and sharing responsibilities if things do not work out as expected. Management can be a lonely place, and often managers have invidious decisions to take, as they have to respond to other, non-clinical imperatives, but they can feel less alone and come to more in-tune decisions if they feel well placed to make them and have a more intimate knowledge of their implications. Here once again, management and staff must come to an agreement that they cannot be everything to all people, that they can only do what they can within the skills and resources available, that whilst there is still some room for improvement they can only be 'good enough'.

The atmosphere in an in-patient environment is constantly changing, often determined by the emotional and mental state of the patients. The ward can be quiet and tranquil one minute, and become a frightening, persecutory, noisy bedlam the next. Patients come and go often within days, and new arrivals or departures affect those patients who have longer in-patient stays, particularly if they have established trust or have bonded with others. Staff by contrast become the mainstay in giving the ward some degree of stability, but unfortunately this is also threatened by institutional practices (nursing shifts, doctors not available because of on-call commitments, doctors' training rotations, excessive use of a variety of agency nurses to plug shortfalls) which could contribute to patients feeling unsafe and to staff relating to the ward in a depersonalised manner, with clear implications for patient care. This problem is widespread, and very resistant to management intervention, because it also has to respond to the reality of staffing availability, training requirements and employment laws. Although some measures can be introduced to reduce staff movement to the minimum, the issue is how can we reduce the negative impact of change and take advantage of some of its benefits? Not all change is bad. One way of managing it is by making it more predictable. For example, very often neither patients nor staff know when staff will be on duty, even though rotas are prepared at least a week in advance. If, say, the named nurse of a patient is off for a few days, it would be helpful to let that patient know, so that arrangements can be made for another named staff to be available in their absence. Likewise, with doctors. It is often surprising how patients begin to develop their own resilience during these absences, begin to realise that in life many have to cope with change, and that one way of confronting it is by bringing it down to size by making it more manageable. In the same way, staff may benefit from knowing that during changes, for example whilst on night shifts, they might have more time to talk to patients with less pressure and distractions.

Admissions to hospital are very often arranged under compulsion. In fact, with increasing alternatives to care for patients in crises at home, the proportion of patients on the ward under sections of the Mental Health Act is increasing. This fact, plus the wide-ranging availability of illicit drugs, both off and on the units, has impacted seriously and played a major role in affecting the therapeutic climate on ward and the nature of relationships between staff and patients. It has also, undoubtedly, increased the chance that violent behaviour is becoming more common in in-patient settings. Very often staff are unnecessarily abused and maltreated in these circumstances. How do we respond to this in a way that does not seriously jeopardise the possibility of establishing therapeutic bonds with patients? Many of these patients require firm boundary setting, and this does not necessarily contradict the development of therapeutic bonds and opportunities to talk and clarify; on the contrary. Many patients are grateful, and to some extent seek this containment when they are feeling themselves out of control. It is perhaps understandable that staff will sometimes use measures of control as punitive responses to patients who have behaved in an abusive manner to other residents or staff. But the natural response to punish, understandable as it is, will obviously only escalate matters and impair the development of trust. Staff during these incidents need opportunities to discuss and reflect on what strategies to adopt because, and here we come back to where we have begun in this summary, it is at this time when they are likely to have uncomfortable and unpalatable thoughts or feelings which need not be suppressed. In fact, it is often experienced with some relief that others are feeling the same way. It is through this discussion and reflection that staff are more likely to adopt a response to this behaviour which will not only reduce the chance of someone being hurt, but can also give the opportunity for patients to feel that they can regain control over overwhelming feelings. If medication is then to be used as one of the answers, it can be placed in the context of a wider understanding of the patients' circumstances and distress. Even after giving medication under compulsion, staff can return at a calmer time to discuss with patients why it was considered necessary to do so, allowing the patient to express whatever feelings they may have about it.

Section 5

Afterword

Things you can do to make in-patient care a better experience

David Kennard, Leonard Fagin, Mark Hardcastle and Sheila Grandison

We have picked out a small number of themes that run through the accounts and commentaries in this book.

Be human, be yourself

Mental illness, in particular what is conveyed by a diagnosis of 'schizophrenia', touches us all to the core. To be told you have it, or that your son or daughter or partner has it, or that the person you are working with has it, creates a deep, personal impact. This impact may include a mixture of relief (that something frightening and incomprehensible has a name) and dread (that life has been forever lost and changed for the worse). What the person so labelled and his family often want above all is some recognition that they are still part of the human race. And this can be surprisingly difficult for hospital staff to provide. Hectic schedules, lack of continuity, emphasis on risk avoidance, administration and just plain fear of the unknown or of making things worse: all these work against staff offering the one thing that in some senses is what they have most of to give – themselves. Of course the legal, clinical and professional tasks have to get done, but doing them with a bit of ordinary humanity can make such a difference.

Tell people what's going on and why

Another theme is information – about different types of mental illness, the kinds of help that are available or the possible outcomes, couched in terms of the potential for recovery. People also need information about ward routines, rules and decision-making processes. By their nature wards are constantly absorbing new people – patients, relatives, staff, students. Once staff members have become familiar with the ward regime (even if they don't always understand its rationale) it is easy to forget how disorienting it is when you first arrive, especially if you are feeling angry or frightened because you have been brought in by the police, or your son or daughter has been behaving in bizarre and dangerous ways. The new arrival won't need huge amounts of information – and might not take it in anyway – but should be kept in the loop, to know what is going on and why. McGorry (2006) writes that, 'in our experience an open approach, guided by the curiosity of the patient and family, has worked well'. He also makes the point that all writers now make: that an optimistic attitude to treatment and recovery should be strongly communicated.

Involve patients and relatives in clinical care planning

The father of a patient tells us that the first time he was contacted by the ward was when his son was about to be discharged. A patient's mother says her interest in her daughter was treated with suspicion by ward staff. Patients who were put in seclusion, or chased and wrestled to the ground when they became violent or tried to escape, tell us that no one tried to explain what would happen or discussed with them ways of defusing or dealing with violent impulses. Yet it makes so much sense to involve both patients and relatives in the planning process, and not only to tick boxes on a checklist. Advance directives provide patients with some ownership of the treatment they will receive if they have another breakdown in the future and for those with a history of violence may help to avoid or reduce such episodes; and it is now well established that the family's relationship with the patient can have a major impact on outcome for better or worse.

Look after yourself: the value of communication, sharing and reflection between staff

All ward-based staff have difficult moments when they don't know what to do for the best. Those with greater clinical or management responsibility probably feel more anxious or impelled to act, while those with less probably feel more helpless, frustrated or disillusioned. We have given several examples: retreating to the office; interrupting a clinical interview to give medication; feeling warned off from talking to patients; feeling undervalued by management. The most powerful antidote to these negative experiences is to make time to talk about them, to reflect on them, if possible discuss them with colleagues who are experiencing the problem from a different angle. Regular staff support groups, supervision groups or reflective practice groups, if possible with an external facilitator, are the best way to do this, although carefully structured peer-led staff support groups can also work (Hawkins and Shohet 2006). If you are part of the ward leadership you will have an essential role to play in supporting staff at times when anxiety is at its highest, and need to make sure you have your own support available.

Staff need to recover too

A lot of emphasis is rightly placed on the importance of seeing mental illness as something the person can recover from. Recovery in this context is usually understood to mean reclaiming your life: that life can once more become meaningful and fulfilling. The accounts in this book suggest that the concept of recovery also applies to the professionals. Mental health professionals also need to maintain, and sometimes recover the sense of meaning and fulfilment in their work, and the humanity and compassion that first brought them into the field. The day-to-day work in settings that are pressured from many directions can lead to self-protective defences such as emotional detachment, reductive labelling, them-and-us blaming, retreat to the paperwork, etc. At such times it is just as important for staff to recover themselves and their human potential as it is for patients. Sharing with a trusted colleague what you are experiencing is sometimes the most important step to achieving this.

Carrying out meaningful practice audits

Finally, how do you know how well your ward is doing? Asking the simple question, 'How was it for you?' or 'How are you finding things? What would make things better here?' can often tell you a lot, if you want to listen. This is audit at its simplest, and is never time wasted. Larger audits take more time and organisation than ward staff may be able to give, and readers should know that the Royal College of Psychiatrists has taken the lead in setting up an Acute In-patient Mental Health Accreditation System (AIMS). This is focused on reviewing wards, using clinical, front-line, staff as well as users and carers, and some purpose-designed audit tools, so as to enable ward teams to assess how their facility is functioning. All aspects of the wards, such as design, staffing, activities, CPA planning, review arrangements, safety, etc. are included in the process, which then leads on to an inspection by another team(s) and agreement as to the accreditation level. This is an ongoing activity and very much staff/patient led, enabling them to work progressively at enhancing their wards to agreed quality standards, and ensuring that NHS Trusts prioritise acute wards in terms of funding and leadership. A similar service is offered through the Royal College of Psychiatrists CAMHS network called QNIC (Quality Network for In-Patient Care) and works very well as an independent peer-review quality audit cycle.

References

Acute In-patient Mental Health Accreditation System (AIMS) (2006) Royal College of Psychiatrists. www.rcpsych.ac.uk

Ainsworth, W.H. (1839) *Jack Sheppard*. London: Frederick Warne & Co., p.74.

Anthony, W. (1993) Recovery from mental illness: The guiding vision of the mental health system in the 1990s. *Psychosocial Rehabilitation Journal*, 16: 11–23.

Bateson, G. (ed.) (1974) *Perceval's narrative: A patient's account of his psychosis. 1830–1832*. New York: William Morrow & Co.

Berrios, G. and Freeman, H. (eds) (1991) *150 years of British psychiatry: 1841–1991*. London: Gaskell, Royal College of Psychiatrists.

Bhugra, D., La Grenade, J. and Dazzan, P. (2000) Psychiatric in-patients' satisfaction with services: A pilot study. *International Journal of Psychiatry in Clinical Practice*, 4: 327–32.

Bhui, K. (1977) London's ethnic minorities and the provision of mental health services. In Johnson, S., Ramsay, R. and Thornicroft, G. (eds) *London's mental health*. London: King's Fund, pp. 143–66.

Bion, W. R. (1957) Differentiation of the psychotic from the non-psychotic personalities. *International Journal of Psycho-analysis*, 38: 266–75.

Birchwood, M.J. and Tarrier, N. (eds) (1994) *Psychological management of schizophrenia*. Chichester: Wiley and Sons.

Bowers, L. (2002) *Dangerous and severe personality disorder: Response and role of the psychiatric team*. London: Routledge.

Bowers, L., Jarrett, M., Clark, N., Kiyimba, F. and McFarlane, L. (1999) 1. Absconding: Why patients leave. *Journal of Psychiatric and Mental Health Nursing*, 6(3): 199–206.

Bowers, L., Simpson, A., Alexander, J., Hackney, D., Nijman, H., Grange, A. and Warren, J. (2005) The nature and purpose of acute psychiatric wards: The Tompkins acute ward study. *Journal of Mental Health*, 14 (6): 625–35.

Brennan, G., Flood, C. and Bowers, L. (2006) Constraints and blocks to change and improvement on acute psychiatric wards – lessons from the City Nurses project. *Journal of Psychiatric and Mental Health Nursing* 13: 475–82.

Coate, M. (1964) *Beyond all reason*. London: Constable. Quoted in Porter, R. (ed.) (1991) *The Faber book of madness*. London: Faber & Faber.

Colom, F., Vieta, E., Martinez-Aran, A., Reinares, M., Goikolea, J.M., Benabarre, A., Torrent, C., Comes, M., Corbella, B., Parramon, G. and Corominas, J. (2003) A randomized trial on the efficacy of group psychoeducation in the prophylaxis of recurrences in bipolar patients whose disease is in remission. *Archives of General Psychiatry*, 60: 401–05.

Committee of Inquiry into Whittingham Hospital (1972) *Report*, cmnd 4681. London: HMSO.

Cooper, D. (1967) *Psychiatry and anti-psychiatry*. London: Tavistock Publications.

Cooper, J. and Sartorius, N. (1977) Cultural and temporal variations in schizophrenia: a speculation on the importance of industrialization. *British Journal of Psychiatry*, 130: 50.

Cowper, W. (1816) *Memoir of the early life of William Cowper, Esq*. 2nd edn, London: R. Edwards. Quoted in Porter, R. (ed.) (1991) *The Faber book of madness*. London: Faber & Faber. p. 213.

Department of Health and Social Security (1975) *Better services for the mentally ill*. London: HMSO.

Department of Health (1999a) *Mental health nursing: Addressing acute concerns*. Report by the Standing Nursing and Midwifery Advisory Committee (SNMAC). London: HMSO.

Department of Health (1999b) *The national framework for mental health: Modern standards and service models*. London: HMSO.

Department of Health (2000) *Framework for the assessment of children in need and their families*. London: Department of Health.

Department of Health (2001) *The mental health policy implementation guide*, London: Department of Health.

Department of Health (2002a) *National suicide prevention strategy for England*. London: Department of Health Publications.

Department of Health (2002b) *Mental health policy implementation guide: Adult acute inpatient care provision*. London: Department of Health.

Department of Health (2002c) *Developing services for carers and families of people with mental illness*. London: Department of Health.

Department of Health (2005a) *National service framework for long-term conditions*. http://www.dh.gov.uk/assetRoot/04/10/53/69/04105369.pdf

Department of Health (2005b) *New ways of working for psychiatrists: Enhancing effective, person-centered services through new ways of working in multidisciplinary and multiage contexts. Final report 'but not the end of the story'*. London: Department of Health.

Department of Health (2006) *From values to action: The Chief Nursing Officer's review of mental health nursing*, London: Department of Health.

Donnelly, M. (1986) *Managing the mind*. London: Tavistock.

Duffy, R. and Nolan, P. (2005) A survey of the work of occupational therapists in inpatient mental health services. *Mental Health Practice*, vol.8, No: 6, pp. 36–41.

Duncan, A. (1809) Observations on the structure of hospitals for the treatment of lunatics as a branch of medical police. Edinburgh, p.18. Quoted in Scull, A. (1979) *Museums of madness: The social organization of insanity in nineteenth-century England*. Penguin: Harmondsworth.

Dutton, N. (2004) On the role of the Occupational Therapist in the engagement of patients with acute psychotic conditions in an in-patient setting. *Mental Health Occupational Therapy*, 9(3): 85–7.

Fagin, L. (2001) Therapeutic and counter-therapeutic factors in acute ward settings. *Psychoanalytic Psychotherapy*, 15(2): 99–120.

Fagin, L. and Garelick, A. (2004) The doctor-nurse relationship. *Advances in Psychiatric Treatment*, 10(4): 277–86.

Fagiolini, A., Kupfer, D.J., Rucci, P., Scott, J.A., Novick, D.M. and Frank, E. (2004) Suicide attempts and ideation in patients with bipolar 1 disorder. *Journal of Clinical Psychiatry*, 65: 509–14.

Foucault, M. (1973) *Madness and civilization*. New York: Vintage Books.

Frank, E., Kupfer, D.J., Thase, M.E., Mallinger, A.G., Swartz, H.A., Fagiolini, A.M., Grochocinski, V., Houck, P., Scott, J., Thompson, W. and Monk, T. (2005) Two-year outcomes for interpersonal and social rhythm therapy in individuals with bipolar 1 disorder. *Archives of General Psychiatry*, 62: 996–1004.

Freeman, H. and Tantam, D. (1991) Samuel Gaskell. In Berrios, G. and Freeman, H. (eds) (1991) *150 years of British psychiatry: 1841–1991*. London: Athlone Press, pp. 445–51.

Garelick, A. and Fagin, L. (2004) Doctor to doctor: getting on with colleagues. *Advances in Psychiatric Treatment*, 10(3): 225–32.

Goffman, E. (1968) *Asylums: Essays on the social situation of mental patients and other inmates*. London: Penguin Books.

Green, H. (1964) *I never promised you a rose garden*. New York: Henry Holt & Co.

Hannigan, B., Edwards, D., Coyle, D. and Fothergill, A. (2000) Mental health nurses feel the strain. *Mental Health Nursing*, 20(3): 10–13.

Harrop, C. and Trower, P. (2003) *Why does schizophrenia develop at late adolescence? A cognitive-developmental approach to psychosis*. London: Wiley.

Hawkins, P. and Shohet, R. (2006) *Supervision in the helping profession*. 3rd edn Milton Keynes: Open University Press.

Healthcare Commission (2005) *A snapshot of hospital cleanliness in England. Findings from the Healthcare Commission's rapid inspection programme*. 2005 Commission for Healthcare Audit and Inspection.

Hinshelwood, R.D. (2004) *Suffering insanity: Psychoanalytic essays on psychosis*. Hove and New York: Brunner-Routledge.

Holloway, F. (2005) The forgotten need for rehabilitation in contemporary mental health services: a position statement from the Executive Committee of the Faculty of Rehabilitation and Social Psychiatry, Royal College of Psychiatrists. http://www.rcpsych.ac.uk/college/faculty/rehab/frankholloway_oct05.pdf

House of Commons Select Committee (1815) *Report (I) from the Committee on Madhouses in England*. London: House of Commons. pp. 93, 95, 98.

Joint Parliamentary Committee on Human Rights (2004) *Deaths in custody*: Third Report of Session 2004–05. 8 December. House of Lords and House of Commons. London: Stationery Office.

Jones, K. (1991) The culture of the mental hospital. In Berrios, G. and Freeman, H. (eds) (1991) *150 years of British psychiatry: 1841–1991*. London: Gaskell, Royal College of Psychiatrists, pp. 17–28.

Jones, K. (1996) Foreword. In Tuke, S. (1813) *Description of The Retreat. An institution near York for insane persons of the Society of Friends. Containing an account of its origin and progress, the modes of treatment and a statement of cases*. Rptd. London: Process Press.

Kennard, D. (1998) *An introduction to therapeutic communities*. London: Jessica Kingsley.

Kent Area Health Authority (1977) *Report of emergency panel on Warlingham Park Hospital, Maidstone*. Maidstone: Maidstone Health Authority.

Kielhofner, G., Butler, J. and Hubbel, W. (2002) *A model of human occupation: Theory and application*. London: Lippincott.

Killaspy, H., Harden, C., Holloway, F. and King, M. (2005) What do mental health rehabilitation services do and what are they for? A national survey in England. *Journal of Mental Health*, 14: 157–65.

Kingdom, D.G. and Turkington, D. (1995) *Cognitive-behavioural therapy of schizophrenia*. London: Guilford Press.

Laing, R.D. and Esterson, A. (1964) *Sanity, madness and the family. Volume 1. Families of schizophrenics*. London: Tavistock Publications.

Leibrich, J. (1999) *A gift of stories: Discovering how to deal with mental illness*. Dunedin: University of Otago Press.

Lindsey, C. and Griffiths, P. (2004) Developing a comprehensive CAMHS bed. *Young Minds*, 73.

London Development Centre (2006) *The acute care collaborative*. London: London Development Centre, NIMHE/CSIP.

McCann, E. and Bowers, L. (2005) Training in cognitive behavioural interventions on acute psychiatric inpatient wards. *Journal of Psychiatric and Mental Health Nursing*, 12: 215–22.

McGorry, P.D. (2006) The recognition and optimal management of early psychosis: Applying the concept of staging in the treatment of psychosis. In Johannessen, J.O., Martindale, B.V. and Cullberg, I. (eds) *Evolving psychosis: Different stages, different treatments*. London: Routledge.

McIntyre, K., Farrell, M. and David, A. (1989) What do psychiatric inpatients really want? *British Medical Journal*, 298: 159–60.

Main, T.F. (1957) The ailment. *British Journal of Medical Psychology*, 30: 129–45. Republished in Main, T.F. (1989) *The ailment and other pychoanalytic essays*. London: Free Association Books.

Mee, S. and Sumsion, T. (2001) Mental health clients confirm the motivating power of occupation. *British Journal of Occupational Therapy*, 64(3): 121–8.

Menzies, I. ([1959] 1988) The functioning of social systems as a defence against anxiety: A report on the nursing service of a general hospital. In Menzies Lyth, I. (1988) *Containing anxiety in institutions: Selected essays. Volume I*. London. Free Association Books. p. 3

Metcalf, U. (1818) The interior of Bethlehem Hospital. Quoted in Porter, R. (ed.) (1991) *The Faber book of madness*. London: Faber & Faber, p. 233.

Miklowitz, D.J., George, E.L., Richards, J.A., Simoneau, T.L. and Suddath, R.L. (2003) A randomized study of family-focused psychoeducation and pharmacotherapy in the out-patient management of bipolar disorder. *Archives of General Psychiatry*, 60: 904–12.

Mind (2000) *Environmentally friendly? Patients' views of conditions on psychiatric wards*. London: Mind Publications.

Muijen, M. (2002) Acute wards: Problems and solutions *Psychiatric Bulletin*, 26 (9): 342–3.

National Institute for Clinical Excellence (2002) *Schizophrenia: Core interventions in the treatment and management of schizophrenia in primary and secondary care, Clinical Guideline 1*. London: NICE.

National Institute for Clinical Excellence (2004) *Self-harm: Short-term physical and psychological management and secondary prevention of self-harm in primary and secondary care*. London: NICE.

National Institute for Clinical Excellence (2005) *Violence: The short term management of disturbed/violent behaviour in psychiatric in-patient settings and emergency departments*. London: NICE.

National Institute of Mental Health (NIMHE) (2005) *NIMHE: Guiding statement on recovery*. London: Department of Health.

NHS Executive (1996) *NHS psychotherapy services in England: Review of strategic policy*. London: Department of Health.

Parfitt, D. (1996) A mental hospital in 1929. In Freeman, H. and Berrios, G. (eds) (1996) *150 years of British psychiatry. Volume II. The aftermath*. London: Gaskell, Royal College of Psychiatrists.

Parkinson, S. (1999) Audit of a group programme for inpatients in an acute mental health setting. *British Journal of Occupational Therapy*, 62(6): 252–6.

Partners in Care Campaign (2005) *Working together to make a real difference*. London: The Royal College of Psychiatrists (Sedgefield Carers Centre personal communication).

Perrin, T. (2001) Don't despise the fluffy bunny: a reflection on practice. *British Journal of Occupational Therapy*, 64(3): 129–34.

Porter, R. (1996) *Foreword to D.H. Clark, The story of a mental hospital: Fulbourn 1858–1983*. London: Process Press.

Powell, E. (1961) *Opening speech at the annual conference*. London: National Association for Mental Health.

Quality Network for In-Patient Care (QNIC) (2006) Royal College of Psychiatrists. www.rcpsych.ak.uk

Quirk, A. and Lelliott, P. (2004) Users' experiences of in-patient services. In Campling, P., Davis, S. and Farquharson, G. (eds) *From toxic institutions to therapeutic environments*. London: Gaskell.

Royal College of Psychiatrists (1998) *Not just bricks and mortar: Report of the Royal College of Psychiatrists working party on the size, structure, siting, and security of new acute adult psychiatric in-patient units*. London: Royal College of Psychiatrists.

Royal College of Psychiatrists (2004) *Partners in care*. http://www.rcpsych.ac.uk/campaigns/pinc/index.htm

Royal College of Psychiatrists (2005) *Carers and confidentiality in mental health: issues involved in information sharing*. London: Royal College of Psychiatrists.

Sainsbury Centre for Mental Health (SCMH) (1998) *Acute problems: A survey of the quality of care in acute psychiatric wards*. London: SCMH Publications.

Sainsbury Centre for Mental Health (SCMH) (2004) *A national survey of acute psychiatric wards in England*. London: SCMH Publications.

Scott, J., Paykel, E.S., Morriss, R., Bentall, R., Kinderman, P., Johnson, T., Abbott, R. and Hayhurst, H. (2006). Cognitive behaviour therapy plus treatment as usual compared to treatment as usual alone for severe and recurrent bipolar disorders: a randomised controlled trial. *British Journal of Psychiatry*, 188: 313–20.

Scull, A. (1979) *Museums of madness: The social organization of insanity in nineteenth-century England*. Penguin: Harmondsworth.

Shiers, D. (2004) Editorial: Early intervention for first episode psychosis. *British Medical Journal*, 328: 1451–2.

Shiers, D. and Shiers, A. (1998) Personal views: Who cares. *British Medical Journal*, 316(7133): 785.

Short, N., Kitchiner, N. and Curran, J. (2004) Unreliable evidence, *Journal of Psychiatric and Mental Health Nursing*, 11(1): 117–19.

Simpson, A., Bowers, L., Alexander, J., Ridley, C. and Warren, J. (2005) Occupational therapy and multidisciplinary working on acute psychiatric wards: The Tompkins acute ward study. *British Journal of Occupational Therapy*, 68(12): 545–52.

Smith, J. and Birchwood, M. (1990) Relatives and patients as partners in the management of schizophrenia: The development of a service model. *British Journal of Psychiatry*, 156: 654–60.

Smith, L. (1996) 'A worthy feeling gentleman': Samuel Hitch at Gloucester Asylum, 1828–1847. In Freeman, H. and Berrios, G. (eds) *150 years of British psychiatry. Volume II. The aftermath.* London: Gaskell, Royal College of Psychiatrists, pp. 479–99.

Souter, A. and Kraemer, S. (2004) 'Given up hope of dying': A child protection approach to deliberate self-harm in adolescents admitted to a paediatric ward. *Child and Family Social Work*, 9(3): 259.

Sullivan, H. S. (1953) *The interpersonal theory of psychiatry*. New York: W. W. Norton.

Szasz, T. (1961) *The myth of mental illness: Foundations of a theory of personal conduct*. New York: Dell.

Tattan, T. and Tarrier, N. (2000) The expressed emotion of case managers of the seriously mentally ill: The influence of expressed emotion on clinical outcomes. *Psychological Medicine*, 30: 195–204.

Tooth, G.C. and Brooke, E.M. (1961) Trends in the mental hospital population and their effect on future planning. *Lancet*, I: 710–13.

Tucker, S. (ed.) (2000) *A therapeutic community approach to care in the community*. London: Jessica Kingsley.

Tuke, S. (1813) *Description of The Retreat: An institution near York for insane persons of the Society of Friends*. Rptd. London: Process Press (1996).

Warmark (1931) *'Guilty but insane': A Broadmoor autobiography*. London: Chapman & Hall. Quoted in Porter, R. (ed.) (1991) *The Faber Book of madness*. London: Faber & Faber. p. 221.

Winnicott, D. W. (1965) *The maturational processes and the facilitating environment*. London: Karnac. pp. 43–50.

Woodbridge, K. and Fulford, B. (2004) *A workbook of values-based practice*. London: Sainsbury Centre for Mental Health.

Yalom, I. (1983) *Inpatient group psychotherapy*. New York: Basic Books.

Index